TECHNICAL COMMUNICATION AFTER THE SOCIAL JUSTICE TURN

This is the first scholarly monograph marking the social justice turn in technical and professional communication (TPC). Social justice often draws attention to structural oppression, but to enact social justice as technical communicators, first, we must be able to trace daily practice to the oppressive structures it professionalizes, codifies, and normalizes. *Technical Communication After the Social Justice Turn* moves readers from conceptual explorations of oppression and justice to a theoretical framework that allows for the concepts to be applied and implemented in a variety of practical contexts. It historicizes the recent social justice turn in TPC scholarship, models a social justice approach to building theories and heuristics, and presents scenarios that illustrate how to develop sustainable practices of activism and social justice. Its commitment to coalition building, inclusivity, and socially just practices of citation and activism will support scholars, teachers, and practitioners not only in understanding how the work of technical communication is often complicit in oppression but also in recognizing, revealing, rejecting, and replacing oppressive practices.

Dr. Rebecca Walton is an associate professor of technical communication and rhetoric at Utah State University, USA, and the editor of *Technical Communication Quarterly*. Her co-authored work has won multiple national awards, including the 2018 CCCC Best Article on Philosophy or Theory of Technical or Scientific Communication, the 2016 and 2017 Nell Ann Pickett Award, and the 2017 STC Distinguished Article Award.

Dr. Kristen R. Moore is an associate professor of technical communication in the Departments of Engineering Education and English at the University at Buffalo, USA. Her scholarship has been published in a range of technical communication journals and has been awarded the CCCC Best Article on Philosophy or Theory of Technical or Scientific Communication in 2015 and 2018, the Nell Ann Pickett Award, and the Joenk Award.

Dr. Natasha N. Jones is an associate professor at Michigan State University, USA, and the Vice President for the Association of Teachers of Technical Writing (ATTW). She has published in several journals and been recognized for her scholarship, including with the Nell Ann Pickett Award and a CCCC Technical and Scientific Communication Best Article Award in 2014 and 2018.

ATTW Book Series in Technical and Professional Communication

Tharon Howard, Series Editor

For additional information on this series please visit www.routledge.com/ATTW-Series-in-Technical-and-Professional-Communication/book-series/ATTW, and for information on other Routledge titles visit www.routledge.com.

TECHNICAL COMMUNICATION AFTER THE SOCIAL JUSTICE TURN

Building Coalitions for Action

Rebecca Walton, Kristen R. Moore, and Natasha N. Jones

Routledge
Taylor & Francis Group

NEW YORK AND LONDON

First edition published 2019
by Routledge
52 Vanderbilt Avenue, New York, NY 10017

and by Routledge
2 Park Square, Milton Park, Abingdon, Oxon, OX14 4RN

Routledge is an imprint of the Taylor & Francis Group, an informa business

© 2019 Taylor & Francis

Library of Congress Cataloging-in-Publication Data
A catalog record has been requested for this book

ISBN: 978-0-367-18846-7 (hbk)
ISBN: 978-0-367-18847-4 (pbk)
ISBN: 978-0-429-19874-8 (ebk)

Typeset in Minion
by codeMantra

We dedicate this book to the intersectional coalitions working for justice each and every day—especially the coalitions filled with women of color, doing the often thankless work of setting forward paths of resistance, strength, and change. We see you, and we honor your work.

CONTENTS

FIGURES AND TABLES

Figure

Table

ACKNOWLEDGMENTS

This book would not have been possible without the support of so many colleagues whose work inspires us; whose feedback—in writing and in person—helped shape our thinking about intersectional, inclusive technical communication; and whose generosity models for us a coalitional approach to being scholars.

A big thank you to Miriam F. Williams and Angela M. Haas, whose support of this book early on gave us confidence to write and whose earlier scholarship serves as a foundation for the vision of the field we lay out here. We're indebted to J. Blake Scott for his careful read of the manuscript, his unwavering support of our work, and his helpful feedback. We are also thankful to Sean Zdenek, Amanda Booher, and Bailey Kirby, who spent time with chapters and helped us shape them to be more inclusive and more intersectional.

We've tried out pieces of this book's argument in various venues, and we're so thankful for the way our coalition has helped us along the way. Specifically, our Social Justice in UX panelists from SIGDOC 2018 solidified both the need for this book and our optimism for the future of the field: Emma Rose, Laura Gonzales, Genevieve Garcia de Mueller, Ann Shivers-McNair, Avery Edenfield, and Tetyana Zhvotovska—we want to be like you when we grow up!

A special thanks to Tony Walton for creating Figure 3.1 and to Kehinde Alonge for his supportive editorial work. Tharon Howard also helped to shepherd this book through the early stages, and for that, we're thankful.

So many other scholars have helped us develop this book through their mentorship and scholarship; we cite many of them here, but we are lucky to know many of them personally as well, and we acknowledge the impossibility of writing this book without Jerry Savage, Michelle Eble, Angela Haas, Michele

Simmons, J. Blake Scott, Pat Sullivan, Jeff Grabill, Sam Blackmon, Miriam F. Williams, GPat Patterson, and Huatong Sun, among others.

From Rebecca Walton

First and most of all, thank you to Tony Walton, whose unwavering support takes many forms. Thank you for encouraging me, for bringing me coffee, for taking on so much of the emotional and domestic labor of our family. I love and admire you for living out your values day by day, with consistency and without fanfare. What a delight it is to build a life with you!

I'm thankful as well for my family, who think I can do anything and do it well. Thank you for persistently asking about my work: What I'm doing, what it means, why it matters, and what kinds of legacies I'm trying to leave in the world. It is a blessing to love and be loved by you. Mama and Pop, you consistently ask for examples and seek to understand new ideas with an open mind and desire to understand. Thank you for inviting me to share my work with you. Heidi, you are my fiercest advocate. Thank you for being my hero and my best girl.

In addition, I'm so grateful to the Utah State University (USU) administration, my colleagues in the Technical Communication and Rhetoric program, and my current and former students. Without a year's sabbatical, I could not have done the slow, careful reading and thinking that this book required. Thank you for your supportive leadership, Department Head Jeannie Thomas and College of Humanities and Social Science Dean Joseph Ward. When I joined the Technical Communication and Rhetoric faculty at USU, I had no idea that in a few short years, we would work together to craft a program explicitly dedicated to social justice. That rare opportunity is possible thanks to my collaborative, mutually supportive, and hardworking colleagues, Jared Colton, Keith Grant-Davie, Ryan Moeller, and John McLaughlin, and our program has been greatly enriched by the contributions of newer members Avery Edenfield and Zarah Moeggenberg. I am grateful we are a team. Thank you to the current and former students who learn alongside me, who contribute valuable perspectives and questions, and who are patient with me as I grow into the role of mentor. Thank you, Breeanne Matheson, Chris Dayley, Beth Shirley, Cana Uluak Itchuaqiyaq, Emily Petersen, Sherena Huntsman, Jamal-Jared Alexander, Ryan Cheek, Andrew Hillen, Jennifer Scucchi, and Adam Bair.

Many thanks to my mentor, Mark Haselkorn, who believed in me and encouraged me, and provided priceless opportunities to learn what respectful, collaborative research can look like. Thank you as well to the brilliant, humble, and hardworking scholars with whom I've been so blessed to collaborate on various scholarship. Jerry Savage, what an honor it is to work with you; I am humbled. Godwin Agboka, Sarah Beth Hopton, and Emma Rose, I am a better scholar and a better person for our collaborations. Kristen and Natasha, what can I say but "thank you" and "I love you"? Your friendship and scholarship helped shape me into the scholar I am now and inspires whom I hope to become.

From Kristen R. Moore

Thanks to Red Button for your support, your listening ear, your commitment to justice and advocacy, and your love. You are the love of my life and the love of my every day.

I'm thankful to my families across the nation—both chosen and biological. It's a joy to be around so much love, especially the love that grows from being with my brother, Rob, and sisters, Angie, Steph, and Lauren. I'm particularly thankful for the ways y'all have loved me fiercely (even at my most unlovable moments) and modeled the kind of thinker and person I want to be. Mom, I'm thankful for you and your love—thanks for always picking up the phone. Dad, thanks for seeing my strengths and honoring them. And thanks to Jim (#bestjim) and Venus for loving and accepting me into the family.

I'm particularly thankful for my TTU family, whose love, friendship, guidance, and way of thinking/being have profoundly shifted how I think about the world and my responsibility in it. Thanks to Michael Faris, Erika Nuñez, Kendall Gerdes, D. Gilson, Joyce Locke Carter, and Becky Rickly. I'd be remiss not to acknowledge the ways my students have challenged me to think through the concepts in this book. Thanks to Erica Stone, Bailey Kirby, Rick Mangum, Maria Kingsbury, Ian Weaver, Tim Elliott, Angela McCauley, Sophie Frankel, and Kehinde Alonge: You are wonderful thinking partners.

I took one of my first classes with you, Michele Simmons, and am still in awe of how regularly I learn from you, want to be like you, and feel safe to be completely myself. Thank you for nurturing the unruly parts of myself that others might have stamped out. Perhaps you learned that from Pat, to whom I am also indebted. Pat, thank you for love, support, and intellectual guidance that endures and that shows up even years later: Sometimes in person and sometimes in the many lessons (both scholarly and personal) I've learned from you. I'm thankful to be part of your intellectual family. I wrote a good portion of this book while I watched Emma Rose take the helm of SIGDOC with grace; powerful empathy; and a clear-headed understanding of what it means to be inclusive, to be vulnerable, to listen, and to lead. Thank you, Emma, for helping me see in action the priorities and strategies we lay out in the book. I continue to be thankful for bearing witness to your leadership. Finally, to Jerry Savage. Perhaps you don't know, but I think you saved my career and my spirit when you came to TTU in 2013 and spoke about the role of social justice in TPC. In that visit, you saw the struggle I was having to find my place both at TTU and in the field, and you invited me into the coalition of scholars you'd been nurturing for years. I've always been so thankful for that kindness, that vision, and that openness to a lowly junior scholar. Thank you, a thousand times over.

I'm perhaps most thankful to my partners in crafting this book: Rebecca and Natasha. I'm humbled by your friendship and the loveliness of our collaboration, and I'm inspired by you both daily. Thank you for kind words; for space to breathe and be a whole person; for brilliant discussions about the world and our responsibilities in it; and for being the kinds of women, friends, sisters, scholars, advocates, teachers, and mentors I strive to be.

From Natasha N. Jones

First and foremost, I am thankful beyond words for my daughter, Ania Jones. You are my inspiration, my muse, my purpose, and my heart. You have been my number one cheerleader and supporter. Throughout graduate school, as a single mom, you have made my most important job (being your mom) so amazingly easy. You are the reason that I breathe. Ania, you make life so much fun! I hope you (always) dance!

I'd also like to thank my family for their support. My first best friend, Shalonda: You are the one that just "gets me." You've always been my defender (even though I'm YOUR big sister) and my touchstone. My sister Danielle: You are the quiet to my loud, and your easy-going nature is a true balance for me when I'm being "extra" (which is quite often). I'm immensely grateful to my parents, Freddie and Naomi (AKA the spirituals), for instilling in me a sense of justice and a passion for education. You know that I have a mind of my own (read: I'm so very stubborn), and you have worked hard to allow me my own space for expression and creativity. Thank you all for surrounding me with love and encouragement, and nurturing me in all of my wild and crazy ideas, and off-beat endeavors.

I'm also thankful to my friends who were always there to gas me up when I was unsure of myself: Crystal Williams (my bestie—Hey Crystallis!), Buffye Battle, Stephanie Wheeler, Esther Milu, and Chrissy Still. I could always pick up the phone or send a text, and you were there—for whatever it may have been that I needed. Thank you!

To my colleagues and the folks who surrounded me with love, support, and brilliance—there are too many to name, but here's a start: Tiffany Bourelle, Sonia Arellano, Genevieve Garcia de Mueller, Laura Gonzales, Dustin Edwards, Angela Rounsaville, Laurie Pinkert, Jamila Kareem, Stephanie LiVigni, Josie Walwema, Emma Rose, Han Yu, Temptaous Mckoy, Michelle Eble, Mark Hall, Elizabeth Wardle, Jackie McMurtrie, and Pat Sullivan. To my mentors, I stand on the shoulders of giants: Michele Simmons, Miriam Williams, Angela Haas, J. Blake Scott, Jan Spyridakis, Mark Zachry, Michelle Sidler, and Jerry Savage. Thank you for believing in me from the very beginning. Jerry, you sought me out and collaborated with me when I was still a PhD student, encouraging me to use my voice to try to make change in our field. Michelle, you shepherded me through my very first publication. I'm so very grateful that I was able to learn from you. Angela, I cannot imagine this field without your wisdom, your insight, and your advocacy. Jan, thank you for your candor and for always challenging me to make smart choices in academia and in my personal life. I never would have left the suburbs of Everett, WA, without you! A very special thanks to Miriam F. Williams. I look up to you, and I aspire to make as much of an impact on the field as you have. Can I be you when I grow up? Thank you for allowing me to see myself in you. Thank you for your compassion, your kindness, your intellect, and your guidance. Thank you for advising me, and thank you for supporting me.

To my co-authors, colleagues, friends—Kristen and Rebecca: What can I say other than thank you, thank you, thank you to my Nerd Squad! I love you both! You make me better!

Thank you to everyone that I wasn't able to name that helped me (in big and small ways) on this journey. Love to you all!

SERIES INTRODUCTION

I am excited and thrilled to include Rebecca Walton, Kristen Moore, and Natasha Jones's *Technical Communication After the Social Justice Turn: Building Coalitions for Action* in the ATTW Series in Technical and Professional Communication. Our field's interest in social justice and in creating technical communication projects which supplant oppressive and exclusionary practices has been steadily increasing over the past decade, making the subject of this book extremely timely. Our professional conferences and academic journals have offered some insights into the concept of social justice and even some practical approaches to incorporating social justice work in our classrooms and industry practices. However, until now, there hasn't been a scholarly monograph which provides readers with a history of the social justice turn, theories and heuristics of social justice from other disciplines, a three-part framework for applying social justice activism tailored to the technical and professional communication (TPC) curriculum, and a model for coalition building. *Technical Communication After the Social Justice Turn* therefore fills a gap in the TPC field.

I'm also thrilled to include this monograph in the ATTW Series in TPC because, from its beginning, through its middle, and until its end, this is the work of some of the most respected leaders on social justice scholarship in our field. The foreword is written by Dr. Miriam Williams, author of the only full-length monograph that specifically addresses race in TPC, winner of the 2016 CCCC Best Original Collection of Essays in Technical and Scientific Communication Award, and a Fellow of the ATTW. The afterword is written by Dr. Angela Haas, a leader in American Indian rhetorics, indigenous feminisms, and transnational cyberfeminist theory as well as president of the ATTW. And in the middle, of course, are the book's authors, who collectively received the CCCC Award for Best Article on Philosophy or Theory of Technical or Scientific

Communication in 2018 and who, in 2017, received the Nell Ann Pickett Award from the ATTW for their *Technical Communication Quarterly* article "Disrupting the Past to Disrupt the Future: An Antenarrative of Technical Communication." In short, you'd be hard pressed to find any authors who could speak more authoritatively and with greater ethos than those who produced this book.

Drawing extensively on the work of Patricia Hill Collins, bell hooks, and Iris Marion Young, the authors of this book provide both readers who are new to the social justice turn and those who have been following its development over the past decade with a fully synthesized and accessible way into the conversation. They use Marion Young's five faces of oppression, (1) marginalization, (2) cultural imperialism, (3) powerlessness, (4) violence, and (5) exploitation, as a heuristic for identifying instances of oppression tailored to TPC cases. They then provide analytic tools with what they call the 3Ps, (1) Positionality, (2) Privilege, and (3) Power, which readers can use as "praxis-oriented" approaches to identifying injustice and encouraging social justice in our technical communication practices. Last, since a sustainable approach to social justice requires communal engagement, they provide readers with specific steps for creating "coalitional action" that they call the 4Rs: (1) Recognize, (2) Reveal, (3) Reject, and (4) Replace. In this way, *Technical Communication After the Social Justice Turn* provides its readers with a timely, well-organized, and accessible introduction to social justice scholarship and practice in our field.

Again, I'm thrilled that this monograph is part of the ATTW Series in Technical and Professional Communication. The topic is totally consistent with and wholly appropriate for the ATTW Series and provides exactly the blend of solid scholarship and pedagogical application that we're seeking in the series.

Dr. Tharon W. Howard
Editor, ATTW Book Series in Technical and
Professional Communication
February 1, 2019

FOREWORD

Dr. Miriam F. Williams

In their award-winning article "Disrupting the Past to Disrupt the Future: An Antenarrative of Technical Communication" (recipient of the 2017 Nell Ann Pickett Award for Best Article in *Technical Communication Quarterly* and the 2018 CCCC Technical and Scientific Communication Award for Best Article on Philosophy or Theory), Natasha N. Jones, Kristen R. Moore, and Rebecca Walton, conclude:

> We suggest, but do not prescribe, social justice approaches—which need more definition, more methodological discussion, more clear articulations—as one way forward. Ultimately, we seek a field that is stalwart in its pursuit of social justice and inclusion.

In *Technical Communication After the Social Justice Turn*, Jones, Moore, and Walton continue this important conversation and provide us a framework for integrating principles of social justice in technical communication. The authors make the case for social justice as a core principle of our field, which accompanies our commitments to advocacy and ethics. If you are a technical communicator who advocates for your user, who considers your audience, and who values ethics in communication, it is also your responsibility to consider the oppressed. Some are resistant to the word "oppression" because, for them, it is an irksome word that rings of sensationalism or seems beyond the purview of our work. For many of us, though, oppression is an undeniable truth with historical evidence and real-life implications that few clear-minded researchers have found evidence to dispute. Regardless of where you stood when we first began this discussion of whether technical communicators should engage in social justice research, no matter your beliefs or political affiliation, we have now heard the daily news of aggressive bigotry, read the hate-filled language on social media, and witnessed oppression in real time and in color.

Whether academic or practitioner, faculty member or student, ally or reluctant bystander, technical communicators will find in this book the tools we need in an age where user profiles are far more complex than imagined. This work does not negate the need for us to study the uniqueness of user experiences with attention to their historical and cultural contexts, but the authors provide a framework that aids in the reliability and validity of our research, the precision of our practice, and content for our teaching.

The social justice perspective, as meticulously outlined in this book, fills a gaping hole that scholars in other disciplines found peculiar and serves as an admixture that helps the discipline advance and mature. Social justice research and practice in technical communication does not replace the work of other scholars, more rooted in areas of science, medicine, engineering, or technology, but it strengthens this work. This book allows us to join practitioners and scholars in these fields (e.g., computer scientists deleting racist algorithms, scientists identifying environmental injustices, medical professionals fighting health care disparities, and engineers designing assistive technologies) who are also coming to terms with deficits in their disciplines.

PROLOGUE

Reorienting toward coalition provides a different perspective on the present and the possibilities for a livable life that people are working to make a reality in the here and now…

Karma Chavez, Queer Migration Politics

The story of this book is the story of a coalition. As we know from so many scholars—especially multiply marginalized scholars in our field—stories are sites of knowledge making, theory building, and relational work. This prologue engages in storytelling as knowledge making, framing the book just as it is: A coalitional, intersectional activity and artifact. This coalition story is about how we collectively work and have worked, how we have "removed the veil," and how we continue to mindfully engage in coalitional approaches to technical communication scholarship that pursues social justice.

How did we become a coalition?

KRISTEN: When I met Natasha, she was wearing a bright purple dress and a big smile. We were at MLA (the Modern Language Association conference) in 2011, following each other in and out of interviews and struck up a friendly conversation while waiting for the 5th or 6th interview of the day. I was so relieved to find someone friendly, someone not completely anxiety-ridden [at least on the outside], someone who would share a coffee and conversation without worrying so much about the gravity of the immediate situation. Were we in competition? Maybe so. But it didn't feel like it then. And it didn't feel like it weeks later when we'd both gotten called for a campus visit at the same university. I emailed Natasha the DL on the campus visit after I'd completed mine and…well, we were both rejected from that job without so much as a kind word from the campus interviewers. Apparently, neither of us was fit for their job.

We decided to do some research together, to probe the social justice movement, and the lack of diversity and inclusion in the field. But Rebecca was really the one who gave the project momentum, right Natasha?

NATASHA: Absolutely right. We set out to identify the ways that scholars were contributing to ideas about social justice and inclusion. We had created a Google Sheet and attempted to trace and track which scholars were do-ing work that could be considered social justice oriented. The process was messy and tedious. As we worked, we realized that there was not a clear, direct line of research identifying the social justice work being done in technical and professional communication (TPC). The more we worked, the more we ended up lamenting the way that our field seemed to devalue social justice work or ignore social justice work altogether. We were emo-tionally drained, and we realized that we needed someone to help us fo-cus and re-energize us. We needed someone with a keen eye, someone to help keep us both measured and motivated. Rebecca, a friend of mine from graduate school, was also doing social justice work focused on intercultural and international technical communication. Having worked with Rebecca in grad school and beyond, I'd always valued her unique ability to be si-multaneously honest and compassionate. And, Rebecca has always had a kick-ass editorial eye! She can cut needless words and restructure sentences to improve conciseness and meet a word-count like nobody's business!

REBECCA: I remember when you two invited me to join the article you two had envisioned together and had been thinking through for so long. I was so honored and excited to join the coalition! Natasha I knew from grad school, where she won awards for both her teaching and her research but remained an approachable, awesome colleague. Kristen I knew first from her 2013 JTWC (*Journal of Technical Writing and Communication*) article. I loved that article, and when I learned from Natasha that the author, Kristen Moore(!), would be at an upcoming conference, I sought her out. This is a woman who thinks about research the same way I do.

NATASHA: After Kristen met Rebecca, I think that was it. We agreed that Rebecca would be just who we needed to push the project forward. It's one of the best decisions that we've made because Rebecca brought a fresh perspective to the work, and we became this small three-person coalition determined to bring social justice to the fore in our field and celebrate the minority and marginalized scholars who were doing that work.

KRISTEN: When we reflect on these moments, before we knew we would be a "we" and before we knew we needed each other to do certain parts of our work, we become aware of the ways our field had only just begun embracing coalitions as foundational to the scholarly and practical work of TPC. We were lucky, I think, to have Jerry Savage shepherd all three of us into the CPTSC Diversity Committee; he seemed to see the field's need for social justice collectives with such clarity—and he was committed to helping us find each other, I think. It was at that same conference, Rebecca, that I finally felt a part of a group dedicated to the project of shifting the field with you and Natasha but also with Jerry, Angela [Haas], Michelle [Eble], among others.

I guess I mean to say that we feel like a trio within a larger group of scholars who pursue the same vision of the field: a field that works for social justice and that cannot ignore the import of social justice. That's what we say in the introduction: it's "a fundamental and widespread shift in what the field is about, what it does, what it is for."

NATASHA: I just love that line.

KRISTEN: Me too. Rebecca—I think it was you who wrote that line, yes?

REBECCA: Probably.

KRISTEN: It sounds like you, and I think it helps to characterize how and why we became a team and how we think about coalitional work. We embrace difference—the three of us differ across racial, religious, and class lines (not to mention the way we write!)—but we know to gather and hold close others who share an understanding of what the field is for and who are interested in doing the hard work of making change.

When we three met, I think this was clear to us all: we had the same vision, and we could help one another achieve that reality. Now, I can't imagine working in the field without y'all.

What makes intersectionality such an important part of the thinking we're doing now?

REBECCA: Intersectionality is an important part of our thinking right now because it attunes us to the compounding nature of oppressions for people who are multiply marginalized. And it's a nuanced concept, a "both/and" concept, that allows for difference *and* for commonalities among coalition members. Just look at our own scholarly coalition in producing this book. We three represent difference across institutions, class background, race, geography, and religion. We also share commonalities of identity such as gender and profession and, importantly, commonalities in our values. I mean, this book was born of our shared commitment to social justice and deep desire to, well, to shift the core narrative of the field.

KRISTEN: Yep. But the term was missing from our article. And I think the book is working towards a more complete and full vision of what it looks like to build an inclusive approach to TPC.

REBECCA: Exactly! Keeping intersectionality at the forefront of our thinking reminds us that our own experiences and contributions are valid and may even be shared by some but are not universal. So it calls us to listen carefully to each other and to call each other into more respectful ways of being. Does that sound too esoteric?

KRISTEN: Not at all.

REBECCA: I'm thinking of an example just a few weeks ago when we were polishing this manuscript. Natasha asked Kristen and me if we had used the term "differently abled" anywhere in the manuscript because she'd learned that this term erases rather than respects. It was really important and helpful to me that she brought that up because I wasn't aware.

NATASHA: That example raises the point that, as a coalition, even as we shared commonalities and embraced our differences, we were very aware that we do not represent ALL of the difference in our field. We are missing A LOT. We are not an example of a perfect coalition. Each of us, because of our positionality, is attuned to varied concepts of difference and intersecting, interlocking marginalizations. We are aware that we are NOT fully representative: The three of us are all cisgendered, able-bodied, of Judeo-Christian religious backgrounds, college-educated, squarely middle-class, and on and on. We acknowledge our privilege, and we know that we have to think about coalitions more broadly (what coalitions am I a part of, what coalitions are Rebecca or Kristen a part of), so that our perspectives begin to expand. And so that we're better equipped for inclusive action.

KRISTEN: I think that's the real key to layering intersectional coalitions into the field: an intersectional coalition expects missteps and a limited view. GPat [Patterson] is so good at expressing this on social media, and they've been really good at reminding me that our most important role as an ally or coalition member is sometimes to listen and stand in the margins so that we can center other experiences.

Why this book? What does this book do that the article doesn't do?

NATASHA: After we completed the article "Disrupting the Past to Disrupt the Future: An Antenarrative of Technical Communication," we nearly immediately realized that we had more work to do. Our ideas about social justice work were evolving and changing. It's funny, because often as academics, it's frowned upon to say, "Yes, I think I have changed my mind a bit" or "Yes, I'm rethinking this thing that I wrote, researched, or said." But, that is what Rebecca, Kristen, and I were doing. We were rethinking, revisiting, and reenvisioning. We had a solid argument that we believed in, and we knew that the 3Ps section of the article needed further development. We toyed with the idea of writing another article, but we needed the space to fully work through our concepts: oppression, justice, positionality, privilege, and power. We wanted to interweave the theoretical and the pragmatic. We knew we needed to answer definitional and conceptual questions, but we also needed to think through what these concepts looked like in action. In other words, we were very clear that social justice in TPC absolutely cannot be purely theoretical. Social justice in TPC has to DO something.

REBECCA: Exactly! I remember that when we'd meet to talk through what we felt the field really needs to support social justice work, it just couldn't be done in an article. For one thing, the field needed an extended discussion of oppression that helps us to see how our own field is complicit, as well as an extended and wide-ranging discussion of justice. Reflecting deeply upon these core concepts equips us to take coalitional action. I mean, if we don't slow down and explicitly consider how we're conceptualizing justice, the strengths and shortcomings of that conceptualization, and what other ways of defining justice would allow us to see and do, then we're simply not well equipped to act. And this link between theory and action was another reason why we decided to draw so heavily upon Black feminist theory. Because that body of theory grows from lived experience.

KRISTEN: I'm glad you brought up Black feminist theory because I think another difference between the article and the book is the citation practices we engage in. Right? Because in addition to an extended discussion, we suspected that in order to really understand the way oppression works in TPC, we needed to delve deeply into scholars who have not traditionally been included in the TPC canon. We spent months reading and re-reading: Anzaldúa, hooks, Morrison.

REBECCA: Chavez, Combahee River Collective, Davis.

NATASHA: Crenshaw, Ahmed, Lorde, Noble. These are not names that are typically cited in TPC.

KRISTEN: So true. And I think we really wanted this book to build theory in a new way from new perspectives and positionalities. The book is a sort of love song or an ode to these scholars whose experiences and epistemological frames have opened up the field for us—and I think we hope that will happen for others as they read our book.

NATASHA: Right. We didn't put boundaries on what we read. Take Cooper's *Eloquent Rage*.

KRISTEN: YES!

NATASHA: I don't think that's a book we would have immediately thought of as "relevant" to TPC. But she shows up in a few places throughout, and I think was really influential in our thinking about the book.

KRISTEN: I think we took out the quote about how "[t]he idea that the path to freedom is found in better choices is bullshit," but yes. That's the point: our reading practices were really more like listening practices. We tried to block out some of the noise from the "go-to" theorists in the field and

INTRODUCTION

We write this book because technical and professional communication (TPC) has a problem. Well, many problems. But one problem is particularly concerning to us: Our sites of work, often mundane and driven by minutiae, remain sites of injustice. We choose to no longer remain silent and opt instead to speak real words. Because our work, our classrooms, and our conferences are indeed problematic sites of injustice, this book defines social justice and inclusion efforts in technical communication as problem-solving endeavors. This book articulates clearly the ways that the social justice turn presents and, in turn, responds to problems we face as a field, nation, and world. This approach is in keeping with popular texts in the field, like Selber and Johnson-Eilola's *Solving Problems in Technical Communication*, which offers a useful portrait of the kinds of problems technical communicators face in their daily work. Injustice IS a technical communication problem. In the structure of their chapters and topical choices, the Selber and Johnson-Eilola book provides strategies for navigating and (as the title suggests) solving problems. Yet as technical communicators dedicated to social justice in our roles as researchers, practitioners, and teachers, we face problems left largely unaddressed by our field. These social justice problems, too, need to be responded to, addressed, and solved.

We contend that problems of social injustice are more pernicious than other kinds of problems. Social injustices require coalitional action, collective thinking, and a commitment to understanding difference that is not necessarily demanded by other technical communication problems. As we note elsewhere (Jones, Moore, & Walton, 2016), problems of social injustice have been taken up by other threads of research in the past. The foundations of an inclusive technical communication have been laid by scholars who've integrated humanistic, social epistemic, and cultural studies frameworks into TPC. This book, building from and extending these frameworks, helps the field think about these problems in new ways by bringing in scholars and theories from outside the field, by developing a critical framework for understanding one's own complicity in injustice, and by providing a heuristic for action that can be applied in a range of technical communication contexts. By way of introduction to the text, we lay out in more detail the disciplinary problems this book (its theories, frameworks, and heuristics) aims to address, inviting the reader to identify herself in these difficult, uncomfortable problems. Our first claim is that we are all complicit in injustices and that our only recourse is to overtly, purposefully engage these injustices. This book seeks to aid in that work.

Problem 1: TPC remains white and patriarchal—as such, there is an inclusion and representation problem in TPC

Like many academic fields, technical communication is a predominately white, patriarchal field of study; in other words: we rely on white supremacist and patriarchal assumptions. As Bridgeford, Salvo, and Williamson noted in 2011, "we are an awfully white group" (p. 1). And, even though this assertion was made nearly a decade ago, it holds true. Even with our field's articulated goals of increasing diversity (Savage & Mattson, 2011; Savage & Matveeva, 2011; Jones, Savage, & Yu, 2014), minority populations are woefully underrepresented in our field. Specifically in regard to race and ethnicity, technical communication struggles to reflect national diversity in any meaningful way. In her 2012 keynote address for the annual conference for the Council for Programs in Scientific and Technical Communication (CPTSC), Williams, the field's first and only Black ATTW fellow, laments this continued lack of representation: "Yes, technical communication scholars have explored issues of diversity, but I found little that addressed the unique ways that historically marginalized racial and ethnic groups within the U.S. created or responded to technical communication" (p. 86). This homogeneity in the field is evident in technical communication scholarship, in our programs and classrooms, and in our academic and practitioner organizations.

In technical communication research and scholarship, lack of inclusivity and representation manifests not only in whom we read as foundational texts but also in whom we cite (see Chapter 7). Both our historical roots and our innovative developments remain alarmingly homogenous. Our field finds its foundations in rhetorical theory and practice that have long canonized the work of white men and Western thought. Indeed, much of the scholarship that is considered to be "seminal" works in TPC is written by white men. One needs only to view the tables of contents from edited collections in our field that are used to anchor our technical communication survey courses and introduction to technical communication theory courses. The lack of scholarly work by minority scholars points to a problem with how and whose knowledge we legitimize in the field. Whose voices do we consider to be most valuable?[1] Whose research is seen as most rigorous? Which, and what types, of research methodologies are considered acceptable? When we fail to ask ourselves whom we are leaving out, we continue to relegate the work of minority scholars to the margins of the field.

Moreover, the propensity to cite white, male scholars means that each generation of new technical communicators is reading the works of scholars from the same canon that fails to include work from minority scholars, sustaining and reinforcing the lack of inclusivity and representation. In other words, more of the status quo. This book resists this status quo and directly addresses the underexposure most members of our field have to scholars of color. We reject the idea that there simply aren't scholars of color doing work in TPC (see Chapter 7 for more details), and this book, particularly in its citation practices, commits to exposing the need and possibilities for including diverse perspectives in the field. As Hemmings (2011) argues, citation practices are political and create narratives about what the world should be like.

Not only does this overabundance of white, male, patriarchal voices impact the scholarship of our field—it also affects the trajectory of the field. If, as Blackmon (2004) notes, we want to develop truly diverse work forces, programs, and scholarly coalitions, we must commit to diverse and inclusive representation not only in our citation practices but also through representation in the classroom, in our programs, and in our leadership. Without this commitment, cycles of exclusion and white supremacy will continue as students and scholars of color decide (perhaps inevitably) to leave a field where their voices and experiences are dismissed, marginalized, and/or co-opted.

At present, TPC students who identify as minorities (racial, gender, sexuality, ability, etc.) are left to seek out other minority scholars on their own. As a doctoral student, for example, Natasha was dismayed that very few of the scholars she was reading in her courses and in preparation for her qualifying exams were people of color. She, almost by accident, stumbled upon the work of Miriam F. Williams and was elated to find that Williams is a Black woman scholar—and a full professor for that matter! Why had she not learned of Williams? It is imperative that, in our graduate programs, undergraduate programs, and introductory classrooms, we fully integrate the work of minority scholars. When our students perceive that they are not represented in any meaningful way in the scholarship of our field, it sends a message that minority scholars are not appreciated, not valued, and not viewed as important to the field at large.

If we are to be successful at the work we hope to do in projects on technological development and innovation, intercultural communication, medical and health communication, and other relevant topics, we must commit to diversifying our field in its foundational theories, its professoriate, its programs, and its citation patterns.

Problem 2: Social justice has been taken up by some scholars in technical communication as a "sexy" topic without a full commitment to redressing inequities and inclusivity

Technical communicators are constantly cross-training into new technologies, adopting new approaches, trying on different ways of thinking about the challenges of the field, and learning about innovative areas and concepts. In some ways, then, we can see why people may treat social justice in this way: As just another new tool for their TPC toolbelt, another theory for thinking about the field, or another framework that enables new work. However, we argue that social justice and inclusion are foundational to TPC and should imbue all topics and areas in the field. We see scholars across the field labeling their work "social justice" in service of one project or one class without fully committing to a vision of the field that is inclusive and just. When faculty engage, for example, in service learning as social justice, they may employ a charity model that fails to redress inequities in their communities and classrooms. This charity model can result in a white savior approach to community-based work that compounds the problems of injustice (see Cushman, 1996). Other times, the work is unsustainable or, as Simmons (2010) has noted, relies on a single course to make community change. This, too, introduces problems in the way social justice has been integrated into TPC and into communities. The coalitional, full-cloth approach we suggest in this book confronts short-sighted (if well-meaning) one-off projects. We propose that inclusive TPC should reframe the field and hold us accountable in expansive ways that shift how we think about the world, the field, and ourselves.

Scholars who want to contribute to the discussion of social justice and inclusion without sincerely investing in it create new problems for themselves and, more importantly, for others. Our most pressing concern is that folks picking up social justice because it's new or popular can compound the exploitation experienced by communities and multiply marginalized members of our field. For example, folks interested in a one-off approach to social justice may "weigh in" on the problems with exclusive spaces for women or scholars of color without thinking about the long-term implications of raising concerns about exclusive spaces.[2] The danger here is that as scholars and leaders make their one-off contributions to social justice efforts, members of our communities and coalitions are excluded, badly bruised, and tempted or prompted to leave the field. This danger is why we suggest an intersectional, coalitional approach (terms we unpack throughout the book) to inclusive forms of TPC. Further, just because scholars may be excited about social justice in the field doesn't mean they're well poised to do the work. We suggest that one of the only ways to become well poised is to invest in an intersectional understanding of oppression and to help build coalitions.

We hope that all members of our field will be willing to invest in social justice through a coalitional framework,[3] but the field has yet to establish what that work can or should look like. This book chips away at this problem, serving both as an invitation and as an informational guide to support others who see the social justice turn happening and want to contribute. Absent a guide like the one offered by this book, we suspect touch-and-go social justice scholars will do more to marginalize the already-marginalized groups negatively affected by TPC's complicity in oppression.

If we are to be effective proponents of a socially just and inclusive form of technical communication, we must engage fully in an intersectional, coalitional approach to our practices, programs, and research.

Problem 3: Once we understand the gravity of oppression in an intersectional way, scholars are often paralyzed at the thought of getting it wrong

On the other hand, the opposite problem also emerges: People want to engage in the work of social justice but are paralyzed by the fear of getting it wrong. If social justice takes action to affirm the humanity of oppressed people (and it does) and if social justice work is incredibly complex and particular to context (and it is), then entering into this work can be daunting. And perhaps it should be. Members of dominant groups often fail to recognize injustices they do not experience themselves, but even when those injustices are revealed to them, they still may not know what to do. Fear of taking the wrong action, saying the wrong thing, and doing more harm than good—these fears may prevent people from pursuing social justice, despite a sincere desire to do so. They recognize that social justice is not just another tool they can learn and add to their TPC tool chest, like data visualization or theories of posthumanism. But they don't know how to get started.

Of course, people in positions of privilege should not be the ones taking the lead in identifying and prioritizing interventions. But neither can they continue to remain inert and let those whose very survival depends on eradicating oppression do all the work. Recognizing these truths can render us afraid to act: Leaving it to others to do the work and worrying about making mistakes rather than engaging with injustices, revealing these injustices to others, and going about the work of addressing them. We propose that this problem, too, should be addressed through coalitional action, and this book is written to equip those daunted by the gravity and importance of social justice work. We offer terminology and language for social justice-minded scholars as well as strategies for thinking through our own margin of maneuverability as individual and collective technical communicators. Therefore, we lay out a theoretical framework for situating yourself: Reflecting upon your positionality within relevant contexts and your own positions of privilege to identify the power you have to take action. We also introduce an iterative series of coalitional actions: Recognizing oppression, revealing it to others, and rejecting and replacing unjust behaviors and practices.

We hope that readers see themselves in these problems—that readers will understand the kinds of paralysis caused by the daunting task of social justice work and that they will be able to admit when their commitments (like ours) have sometimes been less than steadfast in the pursuit of social justice. This book doesn't aim to let any of us off the hook; rather, it investigates how coalitions aid in sustainable efforts toward inclusive, activist, and socially just technical communication. Investing in coalitions allows for those with more power to pick up the slack as needed, with the important caveat that coalitions are built through listening and valuing difference. In this spirit, we think the book will require both being open to and valuing difference—being open to learning new terms and keywords, valuing texts that previously have not been centralized in the field, and engaging with both.

As a response to and in spite of the problems highlighted in this section, we know that scholars in TPC have already begun to do the hard and messy work needed to address and redress injustice in our field. Laura Gonzales, for example, is challenging user experience specialists to contend with issues of translation and to work in sites of translation. Angela Haas has long been working to decolonize programs and practices of technical communication. Miriam Williams has drawn attention to issues of race in regulatory writing practices. These efforts to problem solve make sense to us. TPC, as a discipline, has prided itself on practicality, on applicability, on being both an industry profession and an academic field of study. Indeed, this is what has drawn us to TPC: We, like Gonzales, Haas, Williams, and others invested in redressing injustices, are scholars and practitioners who prefer to get things done, to get to work, to engage with problems and solve them. Engaging these classic concerns of the field, the social justice turn extends core considerations of TPC, even as it shifts the field's identity. Tracing that turn helps us to reflect on our field's past in order to move forward.

What Is the Social Justice Turn in TPC?

A "scholarly turn" marks a shift in emphasis and perspective. A turn comprises not only a wave of scholarship engaging with a particular concept, theory, or topic but also a more substantial shift, a transformation in thinking and meaning making. Marking a scholarly turn, a growing body of scholarship represents a fundamental and widespread shift in what the field is about, what it does, what it is for. This is not to say that every member of the field embraces this new perspective but rather that an influential and recognizable body of scholarship introduces a new orientation, explores its implications, and changes the identity of the field such that future work can rarely proceed untouched by its effects. In tracing the social justice turn in TPC, we recognize momentum build from sparse-but-influential works of scholarship to a wave of award-winning pieces to collective, targeted scholarly conversations.

The precise beginning point of such a turn is debatable, of course, but we mark the beginning of the social justice turn in TPC with Rude's 2009 piece on mapping the field. She groups TPC scholarship into four threads of work—one of which is social action (2009). This highly influential article legitimized critical scholarship that not only analyzes but also acts—laying the groundwork for what became a powerful movement in TPC scholarship. Soon after Rude's foundational work, Savage and Mattson (2011) and Savage and Matveeva (2011) examined perceptions of diversity in TPC programs in the U.S. and Canada, and in TPC programs at historically Black colleges and universities, and tribal colleges and universities, respectively. The next major milestones we note occur in 2012. These include Miriam Williams's keynote address at the annual meeting of the Council for Programs in Technical and Scientific Communication, and the special issue of the *Journal of Business and Technical Communication* she co-edited with Octavio Pimentel. These groundbreaking contributions drew attention to the relevance of race and ethnicity to TPC. Williams's keynote address, subtitled "Debunking the Fallacy of Colorblind Technical Communication," identified five broad areas of study in which new TPC scholars were engaging in research that centralized considerations of race and ethnicity. The next milestone we mark in the social justice turn is Godwin Agboka's 2013 article in the special issue of *Technical Communication Quarterly* on intercultural technical communication. This article centralized the term "social justice," including it in the subtitle and citing a definition by communication studies scholars.

In the years that followed, social justice scholarship was recognized as the best scholarship of the field:

- 2014 CCCC Outstanding Dissertation Award in Technical Communication for Natasha N. Jones's ethnographic study of how an activist organization reconciled disparate individual goals while pursuing shared socially motivated goals
- 2015 CCCC Outstanding Dissertation Award in Technical Communication for Erin Frost's work which investigated the potentials of feminisms to support social justice agendas in technical communication
- 2016 CCCC Technical and Scientific Communication Award for Best Edited Collection awarded to Miriam Williams and Octavio Pimentel for *Communicating Race, Ethnicity, and Identity in Technical Communication*
- 2017 Nell Ann Pickett award for best *Technical Communication Quarterly* article for a disruptive history of the field that traces the precedents for social justice work (an article that is the precursor to this book)

Social justice scholarship was also foregrounded in a number of journal special issues and national conference themes (e.g., the 2015 journal special issue of *Rhetoric, Professional Communication, & Globalization* on human rights; *connexions International Professional Communication Journal* 2016 special issue on professional communication, social justice, and the Global South; and the 2016 ATTW national conference theme of Citizenship and Advocacy in Technical Communication and 2018 theme of Precarity and Possibility: Engaging Technical Communication's Politics). Most recently, an edited collection grounded in social justice was published with Angela M. Haas and Michelle Eble at the helm as editors and a range of up-and-coming scholars articulating social justice-driven approaches to teaching technical communication. Over the past decade, momentum has built from groundbreaking individual works of scholarship to texts recognized as the best of the field to dedicated spaces for scholarly conversations about social justice. This is the social justice turn: A growing, influential collection of work that underscores an unignorable shift in the field.

And why is the social justice turn necessary? We assert, simply, "because our field is complicit in injustice." To explain and own up to this complicity, we explore key concepts and perspectives of oppression (in Chapter 1) and justice (in Chapter 2), drawing from scholars and activists from political theory, philosophy, education, and other fields. As Black feminist scholar Patricia Hill Collins (2000) asserts, a shared language is vital to effective coalition building: "Social justice projects need a common, functional vocabulary that furthers their understanding of the politics of empowerment" (p. 275). We embark upon this exploration not to coin a new overarching theory of justice but rather to clarify relevant concepts and issues, address complex social relations, and articulate principles at the heart of socially just TPC work (see Young, 1990, p. 5).

Some considerations of justice in our field draw upon notions of diversity and inclusion (see Shivers-McNair, 2017). We see diversity as a precursor to inclusion: Necessary but insufficient. Diversity brings a wide range of people to the table. But all too often, organizations and institutions remain unchanged by the addition of seats. Consider professional workspaces: Hiring a wider diversity of people into organizations will not automagically result in socially just policies, procedures, and professional cultures. Meetings continue to be scheduled when children need to be picked up from school, for example, and physical presence in the office continues to be conflated with productivity. The dominant narrative (which so often excludes and/or further marginalizes those already at the margins of our cultural narratives) can scarcely be countered through mere diversity, which often does little more than invite multiply marginalized populations into spaces where they will continue to be marginalized and excluded from decision making and positions of power. Diversity efforts often serve to quell liberal guilt about white supremacist culture and other times fill quotas, leaving nonwhite/male/het-cis/able-bodied colleagues to serve as token members of a marginalized group. Yes, diversity can offer potential for change and progress—but additional work must be done to reach inclusion and pursue justice. This work begins by centralizing the systematically oppressed in our consideration of justice and in the formation of society (and its norms): The mere presence afforded by diversity is woefully insufficient.[4] After all, dominant groups have already established the rules of play and the criteria by which outcomes are measured (Young, 1990, p. 164). All too often, mere presence preserves marginalization, exploitation, and powerlessness—the very faces of oppression itself. Feminist social activist bell hooks (2013) describes diversity's shortcomings this way:

> Many people of color begin to see the evocation of diversity as a smoke-screen obscuring the reality that those in mainstream power do not intend to change structures in even small ways so that there can be a genuine shift in thought and practice that will transform the worlds we inhabit day to day. Diversity could not and cannot have meaningful transformative significance in any world where white supremacy remains the underlying foundation of thought and practice. A huge majority of unenlightened white folks believe that the mere presence of "difference" will change the tenor of institutions. And while no one can deny the positive power of diverse representation, representation alone is simply not enough to create a climate supportive of sustained diversity.
>
> *(p. 27)*

Scholars in our own field and adjacent fields make the same point. In her keynote address at the 2003 CPTSC conference, Samantha Blackmon identified specific institutional practices that contribute to the isolation of minority scholars and weaken their ability to replace oppressive structural norms: Practices such as sole diversity hires rather than cluster hires, which are better suited to community and coalition building. Indeed, "hiring one minority faculty member is not sufficient, especially if by the time you hire another the first has moved on because of conditions that have grown to be unbearable" (2004).[5]

Presence, that is, diversity alone, is insufficient to engender cultural and institutional change. Extending past the mere presence of diversity, inclusion exists where everyone's contributions are sought and valued, and where difference is preserved, not assimilated. In describing the goal of what feminist critical theorist Nancy Fraser (2009) calls the politics of recognition, Fraser captures this core value of inclusion:

> Here the goal, in its most plausible form, is a difference-friendly world, where assimilation to majority or dominant cultural norms is no longer the price of equal respect. Examples include claims for the recognition of the distinctive perspectives of ethnic, 'racial,' and sexual minorities, as well as of gender difference.
>
> *(p. 72)*

Recognizing and valuing marginalized perspectives makes space for people to move toward the center, allowing them to shape, re-imagine, and re-envision the institutions and organizations forming the context for much of TPC.

This re-envisioning is just beginning in TPC as the field dedicates itself to re-dressing inequities, pursuing justice, and demanding inclusion. But we need common language and a shared understanding of coalition building in order to effectively engage in this work. This book is intended to help us, and others in the field, do the work that needs to be done.

How Is This Book Organized?

Technical Communication After the Social Justice Turn is organized into three parts: I. Laying the Groundwork; II. Strategically Contemplating the 3Ps; and III. Building Coalitions. The book moves readers from conceptual explorations of oppression and justice (in Section I) to a theoretical framework of social justice (in Section II) that then allows for the concepts to be applied and implemented in a variety of contexts, including academic programs, community organizations, and industry (in Section III).

Section I: Laying the Groundwork

Section I introduces meaningful terms, contexts, and disciplinary histories for the social justice work we have seen and hope to inspire through this book. Chapter 1 answers one central question: Why is oppression a technical communication problem? Chapter 1 defines oppression, asserting that it is necessary for us to understand because of our field's complicity in oppression and injustice. Like political philosopher Iris Marion Young (1990), we believe that "a conception of justice should begin with the concepts of domination and oppression" (p. 3). We think these atrocities should motivate, inspire, and inform social justice work. Therefore, the chapter explicates the five faces of oppression, drawing upon the work of critical race theorists, political philosophers, and other activists and scholars. Reflecting upon oppression—its various forms, its devastating effects, its insidious nature—raises urgent questions: "How can we recognize, reveal, reject, and replace oppression? What is the ideal we seek in its place?" This is where justice comes in. Chapter 2 addresses the question "What does justice look like, and how is it enacted?" This chapter presents several conceptions of justice, including distributive, procedural, and retributive justice, among others. Each is defined and described according to who or what is centralized as well as its strengths and weaknesses. Chapter 2 closes with a discussion of social justice that hones in on two core characteristics: Collective and action oriented.

Section II: Strategically Contemplating the 3Ps

In our 2016 article "Disrupting the Past to Disrupt the Future," we develop a framework for enacting inclusivity and social justice in the field of technical communication. This framework focuses on macro-level concepts that can ground the enactment of socially just technical communication:

> Our focus on the goal of inclusion allows scholars to examine macro-level concepts that can impact social capital and agency. We term these macro-level concepts the 3Ps: positionality, privilege, and power. The 3Ps inarguably affect and co-construct the ways in which people engage with identity markers such as race, ethnicity, gender, sexuality, ableness, religion, and class. [...] This heuristic scaffolds researchers in (1) thinking more critically about how certain groups are marginalized and disempowered and in (2) recognizing specific ways that our research can either reinscribe marginalization and disempowerment or promote agency and advocacy.
>
> *(p. 220)*

This section of the book offers each macro-level concept its own chapter, examples, and—borrowing from Royster and Kirsch (2012)—space as the focus of strategic contemplation. Chapter 3 explores the concept of positionality, illustrating through extended examples how positionality informs complex perspectives of identity that are essential for coalitional work. Chapter 4 confronts the undertheorization of privilege, advocating for an epistemological shift in the way that privilege is framed and arguing that privilege operates along five interrelated and overlapping ontological paradigms. Chapter 5 defines and operationalizes power through the lens of oppression and domination using Patricia Hill Collins's Black feminist theory of power so as to prepare technical communicators for action-oriented coalition building. In these chapters, we build on social justice icons whose scholarship is seldom taken seriously as theoretical storehouses of knowledge. For example, Anzaldúa offers a meaningful theory of positionality in her articulation of the borderland, but her work has not been used as a foundation for TPC practices.[6] Chapters 3–5 model social justice forms of TPC theory by taking seriously the praxis embedded in the work of social justice-minded scholars and foregrounding the voices of marginalized and minority scholars who are often overlooked or dismissed by TPC as a discipline.

Section III: Building Coalitions

Finally, Section III explicitly equips scholars, teachers, practitioners, and community members for action. Addressing sites of TPC, Chapter 6

- Articulates the need for social justice in these sites: The risks, problems, and potential complicity in injustices that can occur in TPC
- Acknowledges that readers have varying levels of power and privilege, given their positions as technical communicators, and, based upon this acknowledgment, makes recommendations for how to recognize (oneself),

reveal (to others), reject oppressive structures, and replace injustices, enacting social justice within sample contexts
- Provides sample case studies for readers to engage with as practice for their work in the world

The final chapter, Chapter 7, anticipates and responds to critiques waged against the social justice turn in TPC. Modeling our chapter on Delgado and Stefancic (2012), we acknowledge the limits of the social justice turn and the kinds of work that we engage. We do so in an effort to be transparent about the constraints and tension inherent in social justice work, and to acknowledge, reveal, and reflect on our own positions as authors, researchers, and women. This chapter is structured in a Q&A format, with potential critiques followed by responses, serving as a reference to which we refer throughout the book in other chapters. Chapter 7 equips technical communicators to dismantle some barriers to coalition building, setting the stage for action.

The primary argument we forward in this book is that technical communication after the social justice turn must adopt an intersectional, coalitional approach to problem solving. Intersectionality, which we discuss throughout the book, is an approach to understanding oppression that sees oppressive structures as intersecting, interlocking, and inseparable. That is, if we are to understand the ways that oppression functions in the life of, say, a Black woman, we must consider the various oppressive structures that she lives with; the same is true for a transgender man with a low socioeconomic status. We cannot analyze race, gender, or class separately as independent categories, identity markers, or oppressive structures (Collins & Bilge 2016; Crenshaw, 1990; Hancock, 2016). An intersectional understanding of oppression requires a coalitional approach to change—and we suggest coalitions can help reshape the field to be more socially just. Early coalitional work, like intersectionality, is well illustrated by Black women and Black feminists, whose understandings of justice, resistance, and empowerment are fundamental to this book. As Taylor's 2017 collection of interviews demonstrates, coalitions in Black feminism commit to justice for all, accept difference as a positive feature, and prioritize the experiences of those who live at the margins. When we take seriously the coalitional approach to making decisions, we accept our own shortcomings; rely openly on others' perspectives and experiences; and remain alert for justice that extends beyond the boundaries of our own disciplinary, personal, or institutional positionality.

Notes

1 Here, we suspect some readers might be saying, "There simply are not enough scholars of color from whom to draw." We address this point in Chapter 7, and we agree that the field is underrepresented in many marginalized groups. But, as Haas (2012) helpfully models in her article "Race, Rhetoric, and Technology," the move is not to simply throw up one's hands and, for lack of a better strategy, to populate all of our

syllabi with straight, white, male authors. Rather, she demonstrates (and we follow her example) how sincere pursuit of inclusive citation and reading practices can help diversify our syllabi.

2 See Chapter 1 for a fuller discussion of why we see a need for focusing on marginalized groups and Chapter 7 for a more complete discussion of why marginalized groups often require (and should have) sacred spaces without the intrusion of members from dominant groups.

3 Here, we are reminded of Ruth Bader Ginsberg's famous quote, "When I'm sometimes asked when will there be enough [women on the supreme court] and I say when there are nine, people are shocked. But there'd been nine men, and nobody's ever raised a question about that." That is how we feel about the social justice turn. When will there be enough people invested in social justice? When all of us are invested.

4 The claim that mere diversity potentially harms efforts toward inclusion and justice is hardly new and need not be rehashed exhaustively here. For a more complete discussion, see *Presumed Incompetent* by Gutierrez et al. and *On Being Included* by Ahmed; within TPC, see Savage and Mattson (2011), Jones et al. (2014, 2016), Blackmon (2004).

5 We might think of Blackmon's Keynote as demonstrating this point in the most ironic way possible: Her 2003 keynote was (as best we can tell) all but ignored by the field. Nearly a decade later, when Williams made similar points alongside important work by Savage, Matveeva, Mattson, and others, her keynote suddenly (or not so suddenly) had traction.

6 However, Leon and Pigg (2016) notably and usefully explicate Anzaldúa's concept of *conocimiento* for the related field of rhetorical theory.

References

Agboka, G. Y. (2013). Participatory localization: A social justice approach to navigating unenfranchised/disenfranchised cultural sites. *Technical Communication Quarterly, 22*(1), 28–49.

Blackmon, S. (2004). *Which came first?: On minority recruitment and retention in the academy.* West Lafayette, IN: CPTSC Proceedings.

Collins, P. H. (2002). *Black feminist thought: Knowledge, consciousness, and the politics of empowerment.* New York, NY: Routledge.

Collins, P. H., & Bilge S. (2016). *Intersectionality.* Malden, MA: Polity Press.

Crenshaw, K. (1990). Mapping the margins: Intersectionality, identity politics, and violence against women of color. *Stanford Law Review, 43*, 1241–1300.

Cushman, E. (1996). The rhetorician as an agent of social change. *College Composition and Communication, 47*(1), 7–28.

Delgado, R., & Stefancic, J. (2012). *Critical race theory: An introduction.* New York, NY: New York University Press.

Fraser, N. (2009). Social justice in the age of identity politics: Redistribution, recognition, and participation. In G. Henderson & M. Waterstone (Eds.), *Geographic thought: A praxis perspective* (pp. 72–89). Albany, NY: State University of Albany Press.

Haas, A. M. (2012). Race, rhetoric, and technology: A case study of decolonial technical communication theory, methodology, and pedagogy. *Journal of Business and Technical Communication, 26*(3), 277–310.

Hancock, A. M. (2016). *Intersectionality: An intellectual history.* Oxford: Oxford University Press.

Hemmings, C. (2011). *Why stories matter: The political grammar of feminist theory.* Durham, NC: Duke University Press.

hooks, b. (2013). *Writing beyond race: Living theory and practice*. New York, NY: Routledge.

Johnson-Eilola, J., & Selber, S. A. (Eds.). (2012). *Solving problems in technical communication*. Chicago, IL: University of Chicago Press.

Jones, N. N., Moore, K. R., & Walton, R. (2016). Disrupting the past to disrupt the future: An antenarrative of technical communication. *Technical Communication Quarterly, 25*(4), 211–229.

Jones, N. N., Savage, G., & Yu, H. (2014). Tracking our progress: Diversity in technical and professional communication programs. *Programmatic Perspectives, 6*(1), 132–152.

Leon, K. & Pigg, S. (2016). Conocimiento as a path to ethos. In K. Ryan, N. Myers, and R. Jones (Eds.), *Rethinking ethos: A feminist ecological approach to rhetoric*, (pp. 257–280). Carbondale, IL: Southern Illinois University Press.

Royster, J. J., & Kirsch, G. E. (2012). *Feminist rhetorical practices: New horizons for rhetoric, composition, and literacy studies*. Carbondale, IL: Southern Illinois University Press.

Rude, C. D. (2009). Mapping the research questions in technical communication. *Journal of Business and Technical Communication, 23*(2), 174–215.

Savage, G., & Mattson, K. (2011). Perceptions of racial and ethnic diversity in technical communication programs. *Programmatic Perspectives, 3*(1), 5–57.

Savage, G., & Matveeva, N. (2011). Toward racial and ethnic diversity in technical communication programs. *Programmatic Perspectives, 3*(1), 58–85.

Shivers-McNair, A. (2017). Localizing communities, goals, communication, and inclusion: A collaborative approach. *Technical Communication, 64*(2), 97–112.

Simmons, M. (2010). Encouraging civic engagement through extended community writing projects: Rewriting the curriculum. *Writing Instructor*.

Young, I. M. (1990). *Justice and the politics of difference*. Princeton, NJ: Princeton University Press.

SECTION I
Laying the Conceptual Groundwork

1

OPPRESSION

According to feminist scholar Sara Ahmed, the work of accounting for racism (or any other form of oppression, we would add) allows a path forward toward transformation and requires a new understanding and account of the world. This, we think, is emerging from the social justice turn in technical communication: A new way forward, a transformation, a new understanding of the field. And yet, we find the social justice turn ill-defined, only loosely articulated, and at risk for remaining at the margins if definitions and articulations remain abstract and ephemeral. As scholars in technical and professional communication (TPC) who are committed to doing this work, we argue that the social justice turn needs some definition—and a linguistic corpus—if it is to function as the foundation of an intersectional, coalitional approach to technical communication. Therefore, this chapter introduces key terms for social justice work in technical communication, answering one central question: Why is oppression a technical communication problem? Oppression makes social justice necessary. And so to do the work of social justice, we must understand oppression and how it operates, particularly within the context of our own field.

Why Is Oppression a Technical Communication Problem?

Like Young (1990), we believe that to consider justice, we must start with oppression. Traditionally, theories of justice extend from positions of power or from theoretical ruminations on ethics—and these theories seem to evade engagement with the kinds of atrocities (from physical violence to microaggressions to the suppression of thoughts, ideas, and lived realities) that occur within systems of domination and oppression. Yet these atrocities should motivate, inspire, and inform social justice work. Because technical communication often appears to be removed (sometimes twice removed) from the atrocities of domination, the field can maintain (and has maintained) its distance from the violence, oppression, and injustices it perpetuates. After all, if the oppressive effects of products and services themselves can be easily ignored and dismissed by designers (products being once removed from the oppressive outcomes they perpetuate), how much more can the oppressive effects of documentation for those products be overlooked and ignored (documentation being once removed from products which are once removed from their oppressive outcomes)? But, of course, when technical communicators choose to look carefully and steadily at oppressive and dominating systems in their work, the mundane injustices we engage with in our practices are more easily visible.

As we articulate in "Disrupting the Past to Disrupt the Future," a wealth of TPC scholarship refutes any feeble claims of neutrality our field may unwisely try to make (Jones, Moore, & Walton, 2016). Examples abound of TPC that legitimize and naturalize oppression—in some cases not just contributing to injustice but legally establishing injustice as official procedure. One historical example is the *requerimiento*, a formal statement read aloud to Indigenous peoples in a language they did not understand by Spanish terrorists (also known as "explorers" or "conquerors" in many mainstream history books) (Mills, 1997 citing Carey-Webb, 1992). The *requerimiento* stated that Native lands now belonged to the Spanish king and that Indigenous peoples must immediately swear him fealty. Failure to do so upon the reading of this technical documentation justified their enslavement and dispossession of land. Political philosopher Charles Mills (1997) concludes, "While appearing to respect the 'rights' the requerimiento, in fact, takes them away" (p. 22).

Unfortunately, this example is not an isolated, ancient exception but rather the norm. Contemporarily, TPC scholar Williams (2010) examines the ways business regulatory codes such as Texas Black Codes of 1866 disenfranchised Blacks and impeded economic advancement. Though these codes, which she calls tacit laws, were not overtly racially discriminatory, the ways they were enforced and implemented rendered the laws complicit in the oppression of Black business owners (p. 57). Her analysis traces the legacy of these policies to today: For example, Black business owners in the Austin area distrusting current government laws and regulations due to their continued role in instantiating marginalization. As this research reveals, in an unjust society, the professional and technical communication that documents policies, procedures, regulations, and institutional norms not only reflects but also codifies oppression.

Given these examples, we reject any suggestion of blamelessness or neutrality of technical communication. We admit that—despite the recent social justice turn—the field of technical communication historically has done little to articulate oppression as a central concern and still less to define oppression and its systems of domination. Because oppression varies by type, target, and expression, it can be challenging to define this concept in a way that includes all oppressed groups and precludes claims of oppression by dominant groups (e.g., "reverse racism"). To address this challenge, Young (1990) developed categories for the various forms and conditions, which she called the five faces of oppression: Marginalization, cultural imperialism, powerlessness, violence, and exploitation. These faces of oppression overlap in social institutions and structures, affecting the lives of oppressed people in myriad ways. But breaking them apart in this framework can be useful for recognizing and revealing oppression, particularly forms that are often invisible to dominant groups, such as marginalization and cultural imperialism. To summarize, in order for technical communicators (as practitioners, educators, and community-based advocates) to understand our role in systems of domination and injustice, we must first understand the various manifestations of oppression, recognize the ways they have worked, and develop sensitivities to them. Therefore, we discuss each of the five faces of oppression, articulating how they contribute to systems of oppression, as well as how technical communication may contribute to each.

Marginalization

Throughout this text, we refer to "multiply marginalized" and "marginalized" groups to signal that particular collectives, populations, and individuals experience oppression through their positions at the edges of societal and organizational decisions, cultural representation, and legitimated experience and expertise. Arguably the most dangerous of oppressions, marginalization excludes particular groups from meaningful participation in society, relegating shamefully large numbers of people to the societal margins (Young, 1990, p. 53). Of course, the term marginalization implies that some groups are at the center, and in order for technical communicators to understand oppression, we should also note the centralization of particular experiences and individuals. Think, for example, of the ways our universities tend to be designed for particular groups of students—especially historically. As Kristen has experienced recently, the lack of women's restrooms in engineering buildings serves as a constant reminder that the building she's in is not designed for her. So, too, are the accessible bathrooms relegated to every other floor, a reminder that ableism is built into our universities as well. Even more, on many campuses (and in many places), there are no gender-neutral restrooms at all! These instantiations of marginalization can help us to recognize who is at the center: In this case, cisgender able-bodied people. For feminist civil rights activist Audre Lorde, this centralization can be understood as the "mythical norm," in which the experiences of white, straight, male, middle class, and Christian are the assumed, the de facto, and the "right." This mythical norm, with the addition of able-bodied and cisgender characterizes the center in broad strokes, challenging those who do not adhere to these norms (or even those who do not appear to adhere to these norms) to have a say, to have a space, to occupy a meaningful position in contemporary society. That is marginalization.

Marginalization manifests in many ways, but one example is marking people as unemployable: Designating their labor as unneeded or unwanted; devaluing their contributions and potential contributions; and creating targeted, severe material deprivation. We may notice this deprivation concentrated within social groups such as older people, who often have difficulty re-entering the workforce after losing a position, and young people of color, who are often blocked from entering the workforce in the first place (Young, 1990, p. 53). Informal structures such as social norms function as gatekeepers to societal contributions like employment (e.g., social norms such as exclusionary notions of what it means to "look professional"[1]), thus instantiating marginalization. But marginalization is also instantiated in formal structures such as legal systems that govern societal contributions. In the U.S., when people are convicted of a felony, they often lose the legal right to vote for government representation (e.g., permanently revoking voting rights of people convicted of a felony and invalidating the heart of the 1965 Voting Rights Act[2]). Technical communicators like Miriam Williams and Sam Dragga (among others) attune practitioners and scholars alike to policy-based exclusionary practices, revealing the ways technical communication genres like regulations and policies instantiate marginalization.

It would be a mistake, though, to think marginalization manifests only in formal structures or by dominant groups. Unfortunately, marginalization manifests even within oppressed social groups. Touching on activist work that is relevant to our own field (the work of crafting shared meaning to lay the groundwork for action), hooks (2000) explains that shared definitions lay a necessary "foundation on which to construct theory or engage in overall meaningful praxis" (p. 18). The lack of a shared definition of feminism, she argues, contributes to marginalization within an oppressed social group. Many feminist efforts are led by white, bourgeois women who "maintain their dominance over the leadership of the movement and its direction" (p. 27) while at the same time relegating women of color, women with disabilities, women in poverty, and other women whose identities occupy multiple positions of disadvantage to the outskirts of the movement, if not pushing them outside the movement altogether. A contemporary example of this is the #metoo movement, which aims to call attention to sexual harassment, assault, and rape. This movement, though started by a Black woman, Tarana Burke, was quickly co-opted by white women celebrities who did not acknowledge Burke's work. Within the #metoo movement, women of color are often pushed aside. To centralize voices of marginalized women, struggles against sexist oppression must not only be individual but also collective, with feminism defined not just to include but to "call attention to the diversity of women's social and political reality" (hooks, 2000, p. 27). Thus, we see here the insidious nature of marginalization, pushing people to the outskirts of society at large and even excluding and silencing within oppressed groups. This ubiquity makes clear the importance of coalition building: Taking collective action against oppression in ways that preserve and account for difference while consciously, intentionally centralizing marginalized perspectives.

One explanation for the persistence with which marginalization maintains its stronghold is interest convergence theory. Introduced by critical race theorist Derrick Bell, interest convergence theory posits that progress against marginalization occurs when such progress serves dominant interests (Delgado & Stefancic, 2012, pp. 22–24). Initial research by Bell and later archival work by Mary Dudziak supported this theory by investigating the national and international contexts surrounding the landmark ruling on the U.S. court case Brown v. Board of Education (Delgado & Stefancic, 2012). After years of blocked progress toward racial justice, the U.S. Supreme Court suddenly overturned the "separate but equal" legal justification for racial segregation and discrimination. Bell's and Dudziak's respective work uncovered the self-interest of dominant groups motivating this reversal:

> When the Justice Department intervened on the side of the NAACP for the first time in a major school-segregation case, it was responding to a flood of secret cables and memos outlining the United States' interest in improving its image in the eyes of the Third World.
>
> *(Delgado & Stefancic, 2012, pp. 23–24)*

The U.S. was competing to win the loyalties of these nations as a Cold War strategy to prevent the spread of communism, and international news stories of racial violence and discrimination in the U.S. did not serve its interests in winning over nations comprised largely of people of color. The U.S. needed a highly visible move to reduce race-based marginalization: "The interests of white and blacks, for a brief moment, converged" (p. 23). Many activists agree that this convergence is essential for major progress toward justice. As author and activist Ta-Nehisi Coates asserts, "Human communities rarely cede privileges out of simple altruism" (Morrison, 2017, p. xvi). For people who enjoy the privileges of centrality and dominance to cede space requires that "privileges become a luxury they can ill afford" (Morrison, 2017, p. xvi).

Cultural Imperialism

As a form of oppression, cultural imperialism reflects the colonial values that undergird contemporary American culture. Cultural imperialism makes invisible the perspectives of oppressed groups, even while stereotyping them and rendering them Other (Young, 1990, pp. 58–59). This form of oppression is often manifested through erasure, which critical race theorists Delgado and Stefancic (2012) define as the "practice of collective indifference to the identity, history, stories, and culture of a group, rendering them invisible" (p. 173). Although "indifference" may sound inert or non-threatening, cultural imperialism is far from benign (See Chapter 7). Cultural imperialism sets up the dominant culture as a norm by which other cultures are judged—and always found lacking. In so doing, it often functions as a "gateway oppression," serving as an excuse and paving the way for other forms of oppression such as marginalization, exploitation, and violence.

Mills (1997) argues that, since the birth of colonialism, society has operated and continues to operate according to two sets of rules that establish perspectives of justice and the law, notions of who can and cannot serve as a contributing member of society, expectations regarding who is civilized and fully human: One set applying to white people and one set applying to everyone else. The specific designations regarding who "counts" as white has shifted somewhat throughout history: For example, the categorization of Irish people and of Jewish people has varied. Whiteness shifts in order to maintain dominance over the Other; it is far more costly to lose dominance altogether than to decrease the exclusivity of privilege by shifting the "who" of categorical whiteness. Those two basic categories—"white" and "Other"—established in the context of colonialism create a premise that denies the full humanity of the majority of humans on the planet.

This premise (that full humanity accrues only to whites) is often justified and euphemized by cultural imperialism, specifically Eurocentrism ("tendency to interpret the world in terms of European values and perspectives and the belief that they are superior," per Delgado & Stefancic, 2012, p. 174) coupled with exceptionalism (the "belief that a particular group's history justifies treating it as unique and special" p. 174). Indeed, a common explanation for the economic and technological rise of Europe is that Europeans must be particularly creative, intelligent, and capable: "Europe made it on its own, it is said, because of the peculiar characteristics of Europe and Europeans" (Mills, 1997, p. 33). The truth, however, is that a number of places in Asia, Africa, and Europe all showed similar levels of development before Europe pillaged and pilfered Africa and Asia and forced them into colonial networks (read: slavery) that exploited their labor and extracted their resources to fuel Europe's ascent (Mills, 1997, p. 35). Colonialism is not only the conquering of lands; conquering lands also means conquering bodies. Justifying this violent and exploitative oppression was cultural imperialism. Cultural imperialism downplayed the brutality and injustice of colonialism by allowing dominant groups to deny the humanity of those they enslaved, slaughtered, and exploited. Driven by patriarchal dominance, colonizers claimed the right to name and erase the Other at will. In summary, it is insulting and dehumanizing for dominant groups to erase the value, history, and significance of nondominant cultures and perspectives, but the damage wrought by cultural imperialism does not stop there. Its harm is compounded by its role in paving the way for other forms of oppression while justifying oppressions as the destiny and birthright of dominant groups.

In the field of technical communication, cultural imperialism has been addressed by the decolonial methodologies and pedagogies offered by Haas (2012) and Agboka (2013), among others. Haas (2012), for example, suggests that a decolonial approach to teaching TPC should include texts and theories that move outside of the traditional technical communication canon. Agboka (2013) moves decolonizing approaches into the field and across the globe, arguing that technical communicators ought to address cultural imperialism by developing research practices that honor local communities and build knowledge with them. More decolonial approaches are needed if technical communicators are to resist and change oppressive structures to which the field has contributed.

Powerlessness

People experience powerlessness when they lack autonomy and authority, the ability to engage in creativity or decision making in their work, and a status that commands respect (Young, 1990, pp. 56–57). It is true that most people within capitalist societies such as the U.S. are affected by many decisions to which they are not a party. For example, few workplaces are democratically organized, policies are rarely affected by public engagement, and those policies tend to be hierarchically implemented (Young, 1990, p. 56). But Young (1990) argues that members of society who lack professional status in their employment tend to experience much more significant powerlessness, to the point of oppression.

She identifies three ways this oppression manifests through lack. First, powerless people lack opportunities to garner professional recognition and to increase their professional development (p. 57). Second, they lack autonomy in their own day-to-day work tasks, as well as in their roles as consumers: For example, few lending options, limited housing, little-to-no choice of transportation. Third, powerless people lack respect in their lives beyond the workplace in ways associated with ethos: People's willingness "to listen to what they have to say or to do what they request because they have some authority, expertise, or influence" (p. 57). Within the field of technical communication, scholars are beginning to push back against exclusionary, narrow views of professionalism which reinforce the oppression of powerlessness. For example, in her study of mom bloggers, Petersen (2014) explicitly calls for the recognition and respect of women who work extra-institutionally as professional communicators, flatly stating, "Their lack of legitimacy as professionals is a problem" (p. 278). Walton (2016a) similarly notes that within TPC scholarship the over-representation of white collar workplaces in the Global North reinscribes oppressively narrow views of expertise and professional legitimacy: "The relation of this narrow scope to issues of social justice becomes clear when we note that many of the people whose work experiences and practices are underrepresented and whose expertise is underrecognized occupy positions of lesser privilege" (p. 159). Recognizing powerlessness as oppression, then, requires attention to not only dominant power structures but also to the mundane: Who speaks, how one's day unfolds, who garners attention and—as Freire reminds us—who garners respect.

Educator and philosopher Paulo Freire (2015) rejects notions that only dominant perspectives of knowledge have authority, urging people not to despair under the oppression of powerlessness:

> To the extent that we accept that the economy, or technology, or science, it doesn't matter what, exerts inescapable power over us, there is nothing left for us to do other than renounce our ability to think, to conjecture, to compare, to choose, to decide, to project, to dream.
>
> *(p. 33)*

He instead calls people to be consistent in all of their roles—for example, parent, friend, teacher—to demonstrate respect for others' humanity. He asserts that fundamental to the demonstration of respect for others' rights and humanity is a belief that things can change, a refusal to perpetrate, accept, or submit to powerlessness. This is not to imply that powerlessness can be easily thrown off; we do not ascribe to harmful and false ideals of escaping powerlessness by pulling yourself up by your bootstraps. Indeed, a maddening and dangerous characteristic of powerlessness is its invisibility to many of those it does not shackle. People who occupy positions of privilege are often oblivious to the advantages of automatically commanding respect in their knowledge, authority, and perspectives. Intersectional feminism and critical race theory remind us that people who occupy multiple positions of disadvantage—such as a lesbian with a low socioeconomic status or a Black man with disabilities—experience compounded powerlessness. (See Chapter 5 for a more cohesive, though not comprehensive, theory of power.) Powerlessness, vis a vis Young and Freire, reminds us that oppression is experienced and embodied; it renders individuals helpless. As such, as we move forward to understand oppression and our own field's complicity in it, powerlessness reminds us to center the individual and her experiences, quibbling less over definitions of power and rather committing to active listening and understanding.

Violence

Violent oppression includes attacks and threats of attacks, physical and psychological violence, harm to people's bodies and harm to their possessions (Young, 1990, p. 61) and in many cases the re-living and witnessing of violence and violent acts (e.g., the viral videos of police brutality victims that are often played on repeat across mass and social media platforms). Violence contributes to systems of oppression in explicit, perhaps obvious, ways: Rape, genocide, enslavement are all examples of violence that seem to be personal, individually experienced forms of violence. But in pursuing social justice, we are concerned particularly with systems and networks of violence that aim to degrade, humiliate, or destroy. For example, it is not merely that Michael Brown[3] was violently killed and left to roast in the sun; rather, violent systems of power and oppression enabled that one violent act. And the system not only functioned to destroy his body but also to humiliate him as a synecdoche for the entirety of young Black men. This example reflects, too, the violence of linguistic systems, which Morrison (1993) explains are not merely metaphorical; language threatens, enables, and enacts violence:

> Oppressive language does more than represent violence; it is violence; does more than represent the limits of knowledge; it limits knowledge. Whether it is obscuring state language or the faux-language of mindless media; whether it is the proud but calcified language of the academy or the commodity driven language of science; whether it is the malign language of law-without-ethics, or language designed for the estrangement of minorities, hiding its racist plunder in its literary cheek - it must be rejected, altered and exposed.
>
> *(para. 13)*

For example, Officer Darren Wilson's description of Brown as demonic renders Brown and his societal counterparts a clear and present danger, a rendering that violently erases their humanity and justifies—even demands—their destruction (Sorkin, 2014).

An often-overlooked form of violent oppression is microaggressions (see Chapter 6), which are often conceived in terms of racial attacks but apply across many oppressed groups. Sue et al. (2007) define racial microaggressions as "brief and commonplace daily verbal, behavioral, and environmental indignities, whether intentional or unintentional, that communicate hostile, derogatory, or negative racial slights and insults to the target person or group" (p. 273). This definition conveys the insidious, subtle, continual, varied nature of this psychological violence, a nature that makes instances of microaggression at once hard to pin down yet also widely resonating. Indeed, Women's Studies scholar Katie King (2016) notes that microaggressions are somewhat oxymoronic: "massively distributed yet also micro somehow in relation to persons, indeed crowd-sensible among personal storifyings" (p. 279). Microaggressions range from, for example, touching a Black woman's hair without permission to using the wrong pronouns to address a colleague to parking in an accessible parking space when you are able-bodied.

Although many microaggressions are unintentional, some are intentionally hurtful, and sometimes microaggressors seek to absolve themselves of wrongdoing by gaslighting or excusing their attacks. And, it must be said, intention does not matter. Intention does not erase harm. Poet and activist Maya Angelou

(1993) vividly describes those who throw sheep's clothing over wolfish comments by first announcing that they are brutally honest and that no harm is intended: "I recognize the timid sadist who would like to throw a stone and hide her hand or, better, who would like not only to wound but to be forgiven by the soon-to-be-injured even before the injury" (p. 117). She warns off these oppressors:

> I advise the speaker that it would be better to remain silent than to try to collect the speaker's bruised feelings, which I intend to leave in pieces scattered on the floor. I am never proud to participate in violence, yet I know that each of us must care enough for ourselves to be ready and able to come to our own self-defense.
>
> *(p. 118)*

Violence may appear obvious, but oppressive institutions have strategies for veiling violence's visibility. For example, hooks (1981) hones in on a common strategy of injustice: Blaming oppressed people for their own oppression, such as the myth of Black women as sexually loose and therefore to blame for sexual violence they experience (pp. 54–56). This strategy allows oppressors to change the subject away from "distasteful" details of violent oppression while also eluding guilt through blame shifting. This strategy underlies respectability politics (see Chapter 7), in which victims of oppression are blamed for injustice (read: violence) they experience because they did not closely enough follow the rules of the unjust society in which they live. This strategy is used to shut down conversations about violent oppression by police who are not held accountable by the U.S. justice system for killings of unarmed civilians, many of them people of color. Efforts to raise awareness of this widespread violent oppression by government-sanctioned authorities are gummed up, derailed, and shut down by shifting the focus onto the "worthiness" of victims to experience just treatment. This face of oppression, too, is relevant to our field, though little scholarship directly addresses it. Moore, Jones, Cundiff, and Heilig (2018) is a notable recent exception: Examining the ways in which Eric Garner, a Black man killed by police in New York in 2014, was dehumanized before, during, and after his murder. Violent oppression, then, includes both acts of violence and the systems that perpetuate it.

Exploitation

Thanks in part to Marxism and activist movements such as Occupy Wall Street, exploitation is one of the more visible and widely recognized oppressions. People are exploited when they do not benefit fairly from their own work, which, instead, maintains the authority and wealth of those in power (Young, 1990, p. 49). This face of oppression is widely associated with people in poverty, who are disproportionately people of color. Both Mills (1997) and Delgado and Stefancic

(2012) expose a causal relationship between exploitation and racism: History shows that when one group of people is able to take advantage of another and exploit them, "conquering nations universally demonize their subjects to feel better about exploiting them" (Delgado & Stefancic, 2012, p. 21). In other words, oppressors deny the humanity of the oppressed to justify exploiting their labor. This relationship between dehumanizing oppressed people and robbing them of the advantages of their labor is so strong that some activists argue justice should start with a focus on material conditions: Arguing that improving the material conditions of exploited people, especially people of color, will lead to a reduction in systems of oppression such as racism and sexism. Delgado and Stefancic (2012) refer to this as the materialist camp of critical race theorists; materialists posit that to reduce racism we must first change the material circumstances of people of color. For materialists, distributive approaches to justice (see Chapter 2) play a central role in the pursuit of racial justice.

In the university, the material circumstances of graduate student and adjunct labor present perhaps the most apparent form of exploitation that technical communication scholars encounter on a daily basis. Because of graduate students' positionality in programs as both subservient to their graduate advisors and desperately in need of approval in order to secure jobs after their graduate work, graduate students are easily exploited for their labor. Except where students are unionized, graduate students' hours are seldom documented, and expectations for work can easily fall into the "as much as necessary" category. Graduate students work for free, doing service to their departments and, especially in the sciences, conducting research for faculty, without pay and often without acknowledgment, all in the hopes that they may attain a dreamy position on the tenure track after graduation. Marc Bousquet (2008) describes graduate students as the literal excrement of the university, pointing out that the university extracts labor from graduate students, only to eject them with little to no opportunity for sustainable employment. Even with this graphic description, it can be easy, perhaps, to downplay the exploitation of graduate students: After all, factoring in their tuition waivers, graduate students are compensated much more than just through stipends. It is less simple to ignore the exploitation of non-tenure track and adjunct faculty, who, as Meloncon and England (2011) report, make up the bulk of the instructors in the field of technical communication. Many adjunct instructors develop new courses with no compensation; they participate in our programs with little to no acknowledgment or respect, and they receive alarmingly low compensation for their classroom labor. These forms of exploitation can be brushed away as "the way it is" or as "the way it has always been done," but they demonstrate one way in which exploitation functions at a structural level: Indeed, if adjunct faculty and graduate students refused to work, our programs and universities would cease to function. In other words, we rely on their oppression and exploitation in order to do scholarship, teach, and proceed through our daily lives as scholars in the academy.

Intersectional Oppressions

If Young's five faces of oppression allow us to understand more fully the way oppression shows up in the world, they also require us to understand oppression through a layered, intersectional theoretical lens. An intersectional approach to understanding oppression insists we acknowledge that systems of oppression are interlocking, overlapping, and experienced all at once by those who are multiply marginalized. Kimberlé Crenshaw, a legal scholar and Black feminist theorist, coined the term intersectionality in the 1980s as she explicated the ways discourses surrounding rape and battery failed to account for the intersections of race and gender experienced by Black women. Intersectional approaches to thinking about feminist, anti-racist, and social justice discourses honor difference among and within groups and—perhaps more importantly—theorize oppression in a new way: Not singularly, but pluralistically; not as if one identity category (say, race or sexuality) can be addressed and then once that has been handled, we can move on to another identity category. In other words, intersectionality acknowledges the problems of focusing on one form of oppression while excluding another. Scholars who embrace intersectional approaches to technical communication may look to Black feminist thought and queer theory. For example, in discussing his approach to teaching queer rhetorics in technical communication, Cox (2018) reminds us that queer theory accounts for intersections in that it "is not only concerned with whatever is non-normative but also seeks to constantly disrupt the normative as well" (p. 291). As he asserts, intersectional approaches to TPC require that we "move beyond oversimplified ideas of 'diversity' and monolithic categories that do not allow for multiplicity and complexity" (p. 289). This accounting for complexity and multiplicity is why the concept of intersectionality emerged from Black feminisms and womanisms in part because both the feminist and the Black power movements isolated efforts to redress sexism and racism (respectively), completely missing the compounded impact of these oppressive systems on Black women.

In the decades since the term was coined, intersectionality has developed more fully into both a theoretical and an analytical framework used by a range of disciplines, including rhetoric, law, nursing, social work, and education, among others. Both Collins and Bilge's (2016) introduction to intersectionality and Hancock's (2016) recent history of the term clarify that the history and use across these disciplines are varied and heterogeneous. These recent treatises remind us that intersectionality is both a theory and a practice, a way of understanding the world and a way of doing work in the world. This plurality becomes important for technical and professional communicators because, as we articulate later in Chapters 3–5, intersectionality has meaningful implications for understanding how power works in the construction of social inequality and, therefore, how it can work in the construction of social justice.

We close this chapter with an explanation of intersectionality to suggest that social justice scholarship needs both to recognize the ways the faces of oppression are layered throughout our work and to understand that systems of oppression cannot be disentangled and handled piecemeal. That is, technical communicators invested in social justice must begin to recognize the ways their work may be rooted in the oppressive practices of cultural imperialism and exploitation, to understand the violence that language can do, and to confront the ways our programs, practices, and organizations render particular social groups powerless and keep them at the margins. And, as we argue throughout this book, we must strategize ways to redress the interrelated, intersectional oppressions that technical communication explicitly or implicitly endorses.

As Walton (2016b) discusses, each face of oppression is explicitly relevant to the field of TPC. For example, labor norms are reflected in and shaped by workplace communication, including public and private policies, written by TPC practitioners and studied by TPC scholars. Noting that exploitation, powerlessness, and marginalization address the social division of labor (Young, 1990, p. 58), Walton asserts that "TPC is well positioned to combat forms of oppression that are expressed through inequitable structural and social constraints on division of labor because TPC is involved in crafting the communications that perpetuate or chip away at these constraints" (p. 412). Exploring the faces of oppression, then, is not a merely intellectual exercise in which we can be disinterested scholars. After all, "if the society is divided by oppressions, [we] either reinforce or struggle against them" (Young, 1990, p. 6). We could not be neutral even if we wanted to be; there is no neutral.

This discussion of oppression surfaces the difficulty of recognizing oppressive structures and the faces of oppression that reveal them. Without crippling the field by engaging in a constant hermeneutics of suspicion, we find the five faces of oppression startlingly difficult to identify in our daily work, especially when we are involved in the system of oppression that needs to be recognized or revealed. That is, we know that most of us (including you, reader) are committed to ethical daily practices of technical communication. But the limits of our own perspectives (our privilege and positionality) necessarily challenge us to really understand and address our own practices and our complicity. And given the complexities of most technical communication work, where ethical obligations to clients, supervisors and, community members (among others) converge, the difficulty of finding a socially just path forward is difficult, especially if we aren't vigilant about noticing how systems of oppression infiltrate our work. By highlighting the way oppression manifests (through marginalization, cultural imperialism, powerlessness, violence, and exploitation), we offer a foundational sketch of oppressive systems, bringing oppression into the view of technical communication.

This work—the work of addressing injustice and oppression—is difficult-but-necessary work. This chapter provides a beginning place for understanding the ways our practices render us complicit in the oppression of others.

The next chapter invites us to move toward justice purposefully, with a shared vocabulary, and it challenges us to be precise in our articulations of justice. This shared language allows us to move, then, toward theories and practices that can support and sustain social justice-minded and coalitional forms of TPC.

Notes

1 In her ATTW 2018 presentation, "Headwraps & Hoops in TPC: Decolonizing Professionalism through Dress & Work Practices," Constance Haywood articulates the ways professional dress implicates the dresser in colonizing practices; DressProfesh founder, Kate Manthey also critiques and calls attention to the ways sartorial expectations function to marginalize those whose cultural or bodily manifestations of "professional" do not adhere to dominant culture. Linguistic and societal normalizing serve as additional examples of the way that professionalization functions to marginalize non-dominant groups: As Presumed Incompetent (and, we might add, contemporary discussions on the WPA listserv) demonstrates, the choice to adopt language outside of American Standard English (ASE) often invites critique of those speakers as "unprofessional," a thinly veiled attempt to marginalize those whose professional personas resist colonial, patriarchal expectations.

2 In 2013, the Supreme Court ruled in a 5-4 vote to strike down Section 4 of the 1965 Voting Rights Act, a decision which also rendered Section 5 unenforceable. These sections required prior federal approval of voting-relevant changes in locations historically rife with racial discrimination in voting. Shortly after the Supreme Court decision, Texas passed a voter identification law which previously had been blocked because of racial discrimination. Subsequently, additional states passed voter identification laws, redrew voting districts, and restricted voting eligibility.

3 Michael Brown was an 18-year-old unarmed Black man who was shot and killed by a Darren Wilson, a white police officer, in Ferguson, Missouri, in August 2014. His death sparked protests and demonstrations for more than a week, and police enforced a nightly curfew. In November 2014, a grand jury refused to indict the officer, and in March 2015 the Department of Justice cleared the officer of any civil rights violations. Yet upon investigation of the Ferguson Police Department at large, the Justice Department found a pattern of civil rights violations in police and court practices, driven by racial bias and the prioritization of revenue over public safety.

References

Agboka, G. Y. (2013). Participatory localization: A social justice approach to navigating unenfranchised/disenfranchised cultural sites. *Technical Communication Quarterly, 22*(1), 28–49.

Ahmed, S. (2012). *On being included: Racism and diversity in institutional life*. Durham, NC: Duke University Press.

Angelou, M. (1993). *Wouldn't take nothing for my journey now*. New York, NY: Random House.

Bousquet, M. (2008). *How the university works: Higher education and the low-wage nation*. New York, NY: New York University Press.

Carey-Webb, A. (1992). Other-fashioning: The discourse of empire and nation in *Lope de Vega's El Nuevo mundo descubierto por Cristobal Colon*. In R. Jara & N. Spadaccini (Eds.), *Amerindian images and the legacy of Columbus* (pp. 433–434). Minneapolis, MN: University of Minnesota Press.

Collins, P. H., & Bilge, S. (2016). *Intersectionality.* Malden, MA: Polity Press.

Cox, M. (2018). Shifting grounds as the new status quo: Examining theoretical approaches to diversity and taxonomy in the technical communication classroom. In A. M. Haas & M. F. Eble (Eds.), *Key theoretical frameworks for teaching technical communication in the 21st Century* (pp. 287–303). Logan, UT: Utah State University Press.

Delgado, R., & Stefancic, J. (2012). *Critical race theory: An introduction.* New York, NY: New York University Press.

Freire, P. (2015). *Pedagogy of indignation.* New York, NY: Routledge.

Haas, A. M. (2012). Race, rhetoric, and technology: A case study of decolonial technical communication theory, methodology, and pedagogy. *Journal of Business and Technical Communication, 26*(3), 277–310.

Hancock, A. M. (2016). *Intersectionality: An intellectual history.* Oxford: Oxford University Press.

hooks, b. (1981). *Ain't I a woman.* Boston, MA: South End Press.

hooks, b. (2000). *Feminist theory: From margin to center* (2nd ed.). Cambridge, MA: South End Press.

Jones, N. N., Moore, K. R., & Walton, R. (2016). Disrupting the past to disrupt the future: An antenarrative of technical communication. *Technical Communication Quarterly, 25*(4), 211–229.

King, K. (2016). Microaggressions as boundary objects. *Australian Feminist Studies, 31*(89), 276–282.

Meloncon, L., & England, P. (2011). The current status of contingent faculty in technical and professional communication. *College English, 73*(4), 396–408.

Mills, C. (1997). *The racial contract.* Ithaca, NY: Cornell University Press.

Moore, K. R., Jones, N., Cundiff, B. S., & Heilig, L. (2018). Contested sites of health risks: Using wearable technologies to intervene in racial oppression. *Communication Design Quarterly, 5*(4), 52–60.

Morrison, T. (1993). *Nobel lecture.* Retrieved from https://www.nobelprize.org/nobel_prizes/literature/laureates/1993/morrison-lecture.html

Morrison, T. (2017). *The origin of others.* Cambridge, MA: Harvard University Press.

Petersen, E. J. (2014). Redefining the workplace: The professionalization of motherhood through blogging. *Journal of Technical Writing and Communication, 44*(3), 277–296.

Sorkin, A. D. (2014, November 26). Darren Wilson's demon. *The New Yorker.* Retrieved from https://www.newyorker.com/news/amy-davidson/demon-ferguson-darren-wilson-fear-black-man

Sue, D. W., Capodilupo, C. M., Torino, G. C., Bucceri, J. M., Holder, A., Nadal, K. L., & Esquilin, M. (2007). Racial microaggressions in everyday life: Implications for clinical practice. *American Psychologist, 62*(4), 271.

Walton, R. (2016a). Making expertise visible: A disruptive workplace study with a social justice goal. *Connexions: An International Professional Communication Journal, 4*(1), 159–186. doi:10.21310/cnx.4.1.16wal

Walton, R. (2016b). Supporting human dignity and human rights: A call to adopt the first principle of human-centered design. *Journal of Technical Writing and Communication, 46*(4), 402–426.

Williams, M. F. (2010). *From black codes to recodification: Removing the veil from regulatory writing.* Amityville, NY: Baywood.

Young, I. M. (1990). *Justice and the politics of difference.* Princeton, NJ: Princeton University Press.

2

JUSTICE

What Does Justice Look Like, and How Is It Enacted?

Reflecting upon oppression—its various forms, its devastating effects, its insidious nature—raises urgent questions: "How can we recognize, reveal, reject, and replace oppression and oppressive practices? What is the ideal we seek in its place?" Neutrality will not suffice if we hope to rid the world of oppression. Indeed, we will miss opportunities to resist oppressive structures if we are not constantly attuned to injustice. This is particularly true in technical and professional communication (TPC), where the work of injustice and oppression is often concealed. Across the field, the social justice turn has taken up the project of redressing inequities, but as we explained in the introduction, the field's approaches to addressing injustices have not always had a shared language or conceptual frame. This chapter continues our articulation of foundational terms, acknowledging that, of course, there are many ways of conceiving justice and that having a strong understanding of the range of frames for justice can aid in the project of building a more inclusive field.

What is the purpose of justice? Does it enact or administer fairness? Uphold the law? Ensure that people get what they are due? That depends on how you conceive of justice. The United Nations definition of justice, for example, incorporates each of these notions:

> For the United Nations, justice is an ideal of accountability and fairness in the protection and vindication of rights and the prevention and punishment of wrongs. [...] It is a concept rooted in all national cultures and traditions and, while its administration usually implies formal judicial mechanisms, traditional dispute resolution mechanisms are equally relevant.
>
> *(UN, 2004, p. 4)*

Other common understandings of justice are informed by philosophers or political authors who attempt to universalize theories of justice and arm themselves and others with a unified and comprehensive approach to what should be and has been.[1] But common understandings of justice like these are ill-suited to coalition building for social justice work because they are too abstract to be actionable (i.e., too broad) and, at the same time, often fail to question social structures and institutions, thus reinforcing top-down power dynamics (i.e., too narrow).

Considering roles for technical communicators in the work of social justice, we align with scholars and activists who caution that justice should not be framed as universal and abstract because it loses value for actually, practically doing things in the world, and abstract notions of justice can actually reinscribe oppressive norms. Young (1990) explicitly rejected the goal of forming a new theory of justice for these reasons:

> If the theory is truly universal and independent, presupposing no particular social situations, institutions, or practices, then it is simply too abstract to be useful in evaluating actual institutions and practices. In order to be a useful measure of actual justice and injustice, it must contain some substantive premises about social life, which are usually derived, explicitly or implicitly, from the actual social context in which the theorizing takes place.
>
> *(p. 4)*

In other words, evaluating the social institutions which affect our lives and the organizations of which we are a part requires that we consider their particular social, historical, physical, and cultural contexts. To date, technical communicators have not carefully considered theories of justice: Which definitions they're operationalizing and which they are rejecting (see Colton & Holmes, 2016). How we conceive of justice matters because our understanding of what justice is informs what actions we take (and do not take) to pursue justice in the world, in our local communities, in our relationships.

Of course, no conception of justice is perfect; especially dangerous is a one-size-fits-all, always-right position on what justice is and how to enact it. Rigid conceptions of justice are dangerous because some important and necessary ways of enacting justice are insufficient alone and, especially troubling, can be twisted into maintaining oppressive status quos. Thus, we—we technical communicators, we scholars, we humans committed to social justice—must remain vigilant. We find, even in our own work, that we move from one approach of justice (well, everyone got the same thing) to another (well, the process was fair!) without realizing that we've reconceived of justice, perhaps to quell our own fears about being unfair or unjust. We should consciously and intentionally interrogate our own conceptions of justice in collaboration with others to avoid all-too-easy complicity in oppression of various types. Thus, we must be equipped with various conceptions of justice, understanding their promise for revealing and rejecting oppression as well as their blind spots, common misusages, and shortcomings. In reflecting upon the various paradigms of justice, it can be useful to consider them in terms of what they centralize.

Scholars invested in the social justice turn must recognize how forms of justice imbue our thinking about what can and should happen, and in this chapter, we offer an overview of frameworks for understanding and conceiving of justice. This overview is a broad strokes survey of various conceptions of justice, meant to provide a shared language for discussing justice in the field of TPC. Though not a comprehensive list, this overview addresses distributive justice, procedural justice, and three forms of legal justice (retributive, restorative, transitional) before landing on social justice.

Distributive Justice

Distributive paradigms place "stuff"—material goods, resources, benefits—at the center of justice considerations. This form of justice is concerned with people getting their fair share. Young (1990) defines distributive justice as "the morally proper distribution of social benefits and burdens among society's members" (p. 16). Also called economic justice or redistributive justice, this perspective was historically widespread among social justice advocates. In fact, Fraser (2009) asserted that the basis of most social justice claims up until the late 1990s were redistributive claims: "Egalitarian redistributive claims have supplied the paradigm case for most theorizing about social justice for the past 150 years" (p. 72). We can see this historical trend reflected in critical race theory, in which most early theorists were members of what Delgado and Stefancic (2012) call the "realist" camp. Realists defined racism as "a means by which society allocates privilege and status" (p. 21), a definition that places distribution of benefits at the center of racial justice considerations.

One strength of a distributive perspective of justice is its ability to reveal economic effects of oppressive systems such as racism. And these effects are mind boggling. In revealing the racially exploitative foundation of the U.S. economy, Mills (1997) presents findings by the National Economic Association in 1983 regarding the economic effects of slavery and subsequent racial discrimination. These findings conclude,

> An estimate for the total of 'diverted income' from slavery, 1790–1860, compounded and translated into 1983 dollars, would yield the sum of $2.1 trillion to $4.7 trillion. And if one were to try to work out the cumulative value, with compound interest, of unpaid slave labor before 1863, underpayment since 1863, and denial of opportunity to acquire land and natural resources available to white settlers, then the total amount required to compensate blacks 'could take more than the entire wealth of the United States'.
>
> (p. 39)

Distributive justice is violated primarily through exploitation, as well as economic expressions and consequences of marginalization and powerlessness. Those who ascribe to this view of justice, then, see economic structures at the root of injustice and may believe that social and cultural injustices emerge as a result of or justification for economic injustice (Delgado & Stefancic, 2012; Fraser, 2009). Based upon this view of injustice, distributive justice calls for strategies of economic restructuring such as "redistributing income, reorganizing the division of labor, or transforming other basic economic structures" (Fraser, 2009, p. 73). Other strategies focus on the vicious cycle of poverty reinforced by an unjust judicial system: For example, fining the poor for minor infractions like parking violations, garnering their wages for payment, charging high interest and penalties for late payment, and jailing people when they are unable to pay, thus causing them to lose their jobs.[2] The Southern Poverty Law Center's (n.d.) three-pronged economic justice agenda specifically addresses this concern, in addition to protecting the poor from predatory lending services, such as payday loans, and ensuring healthcare coverage and other safety nets for people in poverty. Advocates of economic justice emphasize the importance of reforming material, concrete economic conditions, rather than solely focusing on social issues like media representation of marginalized groups for example. New materialists Coole and Frost (2010) put it this way:

> ...it is ideological naivete to believe that significant social change can be engendered solely by reconstructing subjectivities, discourses, ethics, and identities—that is, without also altering their socioeconomic conditions or tracing crucial aspects of their reproduction to the economic interests they unwittingly serve.
>
> *(p. 25)*

However, no single conception of justice can address every instantiation of injustice. A major problem with a (solely) distributive view of justice is that it frames people as consumers and therefore cannot address injustices that have nothing to do with the material or are not solely material. Young (1990, p. 23) identifies three arenas that distributive justice paradigms are unsuited to address: Decision-making procedures, division of labor, and culture. Thinking in terms of oppression, these unaddressed injustices may include powerlessness (e.g., being cut out of decision making on issues that directly affect one's life) and cultural imperialism (e.g., being represented in negative, Othered ways).

Another common problem with distributive perspectives is conflating charity with justice. Charity occurs when people in a position of greater privilege give to those in positions of lesser privilege: A redistribution from haves to have-nots. Charity typically meets immediate or short-term needs, and it is true that a just society would not ignore the basic needs of people unable to meet those needs themselves: "The immediate provision of basic material goods for people now suffering severe deprivation must be a first priority for any program that seeks to make the world more just. Such a call obviously entails considerations of distribution and redistribution" (Young, 1990, p. 19).

But charity differs from justice in important ways—chief among them that charity does not threaten systemic injustice and problematic hierarchies. For example, consider the societal problem of homelessness among domestic abuse victims. Charity may take the form of a women's shelter, meeting immediate needs of women who need a safe place to stay. But charity would not address the rights of cities to pass nuisance ordinances that have been shown to trigger evictions of domestic violence victims, contributing to homelessness through unjust policies[3] (see Miller & Park, 2011). In other words, merely redistributing goods preserves the problematic institutional and social context that perpetuates systems of domination and oppression. A purely charitable redistributive view is also problematic because it frames people primarily as consumers and uses a deficit model to account for inequality: In other words, people are individual consumers who fall short in their ability to meet their own needs, and therefore others in society charitably make up the difference. This view elides consideration of social groups, of institutional context, structural inequality, and any kind of value that is not economic.

When charitable redistribution is private (i.e., directly between individuals or mediated by a charitable organization), it preserves an unbalanced power dynamic. The charitable giver generally has full control over the terms of redistribution, may feel justified in expecting gratitude and humility from recipients, and can decide whether and when to engage in any future charity. When charitable redistribution is public (i.e., facilitated by the government), it both preserves and veils the unjust policies and systemic inequalities contributing to a need for charity in the first place. Further, calling charitable redistribution "justice" is not only inaccurate but also divisive and dangerous. For example, see conservative think tank the Heritage Foundation's online "report" on the meaning and implications of social justice (Novak, 2009). This piece intentionally preserves the ignorance of privilege: Concealing injustice and redirecting attention by sowing fear that social justice threatens people's ability to "live free of state control" by redistributing rightfully earned goods and materials away from those who proportionally contribute more to society, presumably giving those goods to people whose contributions are worth less (Novak, 2009). It is a slippery slope, the organization warns, from state-mandated redistribution to state-mandated uniformity, controlling the minutiae of citizens' lives down to the clothes they are allowed to wear and the times they are allowed to have sex. (The report says this; we are not kidding.) By conflating social justice with state-mandated charitable redistribution, the organization not only misrepresents justice but also breeds resentment among the privileged while stiffening resistance to anything purporting to support "social justice." This example showcases a danger of distributive justice: Its reliance on economic frames makes it susceptible to those whose neoliberal concerns remain purely about the distribution, not the justice.

Another shortcoming of distributive justice is that many versions (such as Rawls's) are framed at the individual level, so the big-picture, complex outcomes that result from myriad individual and group actions and decisions cannot be understood (Young, 1990). And at the same time, distributive justice may take institutional context, social relations, and class relations as givens. Thus, the injustice that is structured into society is rendered invisible: For example, assuming that two-adult, heteronormative family units are the units by which distribution occurs in society with each family represented by a wage-earning male head of household (Young, 1990, p. 21). Another example is when considering the just distribution of jobs and offices among individuals, common perspectives on distributive justice assume that some of these positions will offer significant autonomy, decision-making authority, and income, whereas other positions will lack those things (Young, 1990, p. 22). Considerations of distributive justice ask if the distribution of these jobs is fair across social groups but rarely question whether it is just for some jobs to lack autonomy, to pay less than a living wage, or to be considered menial (p. 22). Young (1990) concludes, "Distributive injustices may contribute to or result from these forms of oppression, but none is reducible to distribution and all involve social structures and relations beyond distribution" (p. 9). In other words, distributive justice can be productive in addressing some instantiations of oppression such as exploitation, but it falls far short of fully redressing all injustice.

Procedural Justice

Whereas distributive justice is concerned with fair share, procedural justice focuses on fair play. Central to perspectives of procedural justice are policies and process: Are the policies and processes by which outcomes are determined fair? Procedural justice can be considered a precondition for other types of justice in the sense that respectful, participatory processes can clear paths for pursuit of outcomes that multiple stakeholders find to be just (see, e.g., Simmons & Grabill, 2007). Two TPC contexts for procedural justice considerations are community-police relations and workplace policies. Briefly examining procedural justice in each of these contexts can clarify major considerations, strengths, and shortcomings of procedural justice.

The U.S. Department of Justice's fact sheet on procedural justice in community-police contexts defines it as "fairness in the processes that resolve disputes and allocate resources" (n.d.). In these contexts, procedural justice includes four pillars: Police demonstration of (1) neutrality in their decision making, (2) respect for the dignity of community members, (3) trustworthy motives, and (4) encouragement of community participation (Mazerolle, Bennett, Davis, Sargeant, & Manning, 2013). Proponents of procedural justice point to benefits such as increased public safety and decreased crime (Hough, Jackson, Bradford, Myhill, & Quentin, 2010). Research shows that when police engage with local communities in ways that demonstrate any of the four pillars of procedural justice, those encounters increase the public's sense of police legitimacy (Bennett et al., 2013). Indeed, Hinds and Murphy (2007) claim that "the most important factor in public assessments of police legitimacy is procedural justice" (p. 27). The sense that the authority of police is legitimate is a factor shown to affect community trust and willingness to cooperate with the police, and mutually supportive relationships between communities and police are key to effective policing (Hinds & Murphy, 2007). As the National Initiative for Building Community Trust and Justice (n.d.) points out, it makes sense that procedural justice can play a key role in improving community perceptions of law enforcement:

> This makes intuitive sense—people welcome being treated as equals with a stake in keeping their communities safe, as opposed to being treated as subjects of a capricious justice system enforced by police who punish them for ambiguous, if not arbitrary, reasons.

Key to procedural justice is an authority figure's perceived fairness, in the sense of treating people in ways that are not discriminatory. But one concern with procedural justice is that it is prone to slippage: People can mask discrimination by claiming a version of procedural justice. For example, police officers can claim neutrality in decision making by meticulously following official procedures during an individual encounter with a motorist but can use discriminatory judgment in selecting which motorists to pull over. Numerous research studies have documented patterns of such discrimination (e.g., Harris, 1999, 2003; Welch 2007). For example, investigations into allegations of racial profiling in New Jersey in the 1990s revealed that

> only 15 percent of all drivers on the New Jersey Turnpike were racial minorities, yet 42 percent of all stops and 73 percent of all arrests were of Black motorists—despite the fact that Blacks and whites violated traffic laws at almost exactly the same rates.
>
> *(Alexander, 2012, p. 133)*

Similar studies in Maryland revealed the same pattern but with greater discrepancies: Racial minorities comprised only 21% of all motorists but 80% of motorists pulled over by police. And both studies found that white motorists were more likely to be carrying illegal drugs or contraband (p. 133). In other words, not only is this discriminatory practice able to masquerade as procedurally just (i.e., following official procedures; going by the book) while violating the rights of people of color and remaining litigically unassailable:[4] It is also ineffective in crime detection.

Are these examples of police stops procedurally just? Perhaps. But they would not be considered fair, in part because the procedure enables discrimination. Delgado and Stefancic (2012) define discrimination as the "practice of treating similarly situated individuals differently because of race, gender, sexual orientation, appearance, or national origin" (p. 172). As Alexander's (2012) examples illustrate, procedural justice does not (necessarily) equate with fairness in policing (or other contexts); and yet Bradford (2014) identifies fairness as the most important factor affecting people's opinions and ideas about police: "Fairness promotes a sense of inclusion and value, while unfairness communicates denigration and exclusion" (p. 22). Procedural justice can lose sight of its core values (equity and fair play) because it binds itself to laws rather than to principles; it relies on the standardization of processes without necessarily considering the ways those processes can be imbued with discrimination, effectively stripping some stakeholders of their rights. Officially, according to the law, U.S. citizens have the same rights. As Young (1990) defined rights, this would mean that the rules governing the social actions people can and cannot engage in apply equally to all: "Rights are relationships, not things; they are institutionally defined rules specifying what people can do in relation to one another" (p. 25). However, the application of institutionally defined rules in relation to oppressed groups differs significantly from the application of rules to dominant groups. Anthropologist Clifford Geertz may explain this disparity by claiming that the law is aspirational: It conveys how we want the world to be. But Mills (1997) would dispute this claim, arguing that discriminatory application of law is exactly how those in power want the world to be. Fairness requires recognition of another's humanity, a recognition long denied to people of color, especially by the U.S. law enforcement and judicial system (Mills, 1997).

Another concern with procedural justice is when programs reflect a heavier emphasis on authoritarian control and lighter emphasis on true participatory contributions by communities. For example, the National Initiative for Building Community Trust and Justice notes that procedural justice is linked to increased "belief that authorities have the right to dictate proper behavior" among the public—authoritarian language we find concerning especially in light of widespread, documented violence and other forms of oppression in what some authorities deem proper behavior. Research on efficacy of procedural justice notes that if people believe police authority is legitimate, they are more likely to allow "intrusive police tactics" (Sunshine & Tyler, 2003, p. 519), more likely to accept punitive outcomes (Tyler & Wakslak, 2004), and less likely to suspect they were racially profiled (Mazerolle et al., 2013). Again, in light of rampant injustice, these outcomes are not necessarily positive. In fact, they may contribute to systemic oppression through the marginalization of any citizen who resists authority, permission to enact violence on resistors, and complete absolution of authority figures who strip citizens of power or rights. Reflecting this prioritization of authority figures over citizens, the U.S. Department of Justice's (n.d.) fact sheet frames procedural justice as "ultimately" about officer safety rather than participatory relationships, despite listing three pillars of community policing (problem solving, partnership building, and organizational transformation), each of which has participatory implications. And nowhere on the factsheet does it advocate—nor even mention—community authority, knowledge, and priorities. As demonstrated in these examples, procedural justice in the context of community-police relations may appear to centralize participation and mutual respect (ostensibly fair play), but the motivation and intention of many procedural justice efforts appear to focus on shoring up authoritarian control.

Community-police relations may seem an easy target for such critiques of procedural justice. But not all contexts of procedural justice are as politically charged or obvious: Organizations and workplaces often rely on procedural justice, too. In corporate contexts, procedural justice is concerned with the fairness of an organization's decision-making procedures demonstrated through, for example, consistency, accuracy, correctability, ethicality, bias suppression, and representativeness (Leventhal, Karuza, & Fry, 1980). Proponents of procedural justice in workplace contexts point to effects such as improving employee morale in terms of attitudes about the overall company and its leadership (McFarlin & Sweeney, 1992) and reducing turnover (Greenberg, 1990) and employee retaliation (Skarlicki & Folger, 1997). In organizational literature, sometimes procedural justice (the fairness of organizational policies and procedures) is broken out from interactional justice (fair and respectful treatment of employees during the implementation of said procedures), and sometimes the two are combined under the umbrella of procedural justice (Barling & Phillips, 1993). For TPC scholars, both policing and organizational policy should be considered relevant sites of technical communication, where policy, instructions, and risk communication often intersect.

Relevant to fairness in organizational decision-making procedures are considerations of equality and equity. All but two of the values in Leventhal et al.'s (1980) framework of fairness directly relate to these considerations: Consistency, ethicality, bias suppression, and representativeness. Equality upholds the principle of sameness: In distributive perspectives, equality dictates that everyone gets the same thing/amount; in procedural perspectives, equality dictates that the same procedures and measures apply to everyone. It ties into myths of a level playing field, which resonate with dominant U.S. culture and laws such as Title VII of the Civil Rights Act of 1964, which prohibits employers from hiring discrimination based on certain identity markers and other factors. Compared to the more complex "equity" (discussed below), equality tends to be easier, simpler, and less expensive to enact because it does not account for context, history, need, or other factors. Unfortunately, this lack of context can conceal privilege and lay the groundwork for tools of oppression, like colorblindness (refusal to recognize the realities of racial injustice), deficit models (blaming oppressed people for their own oppression), and bootstrapping[5] (urging oppressed people to work harder to improve their own circumstances within existing systems of oppression). Equality is enacted through impartiality: The same treatment for everyone. Young (1990) identifies two problems with impartiality: (1) It lets dominant views and perspectives masquerade as universal (i.e., it feeds oppression in the form of cultural imperialism), and (2) it reinforces authoritarian hierarchies (i.e., it preserves marginalization and devalues other ways of knowing). Bottom line, the sameness required by equality-based perspectives of fairness may sometimes support justice, but in a society whose members have different amounts and types of privilege (see Chapter 4) and where oppression is hardwired into social structures, equality often cannot help but preserve the status quo, operating as a tool of oppression. Procedures founded upon the principle of equality, then, instantiate oppression while masquerading as just.

The related principle of equity offers a more flexible tool for constructing procedurally just organizations. Equality assumes that sameness and fairness are synonymous; equity allows for that to be true but does not assume so. Equality is absolute, whereas equity is relative. Factors such as relative need, relative contribution, and relative levels of oppression may be taken into consideration by equitable procedures and equitable distributions. Linking conceptions of equity and inclusion, Young (1990) argues against "the assimilationist ideal" of equality that is enacted by "treating everyone according to the same principles, rules, and standards" (p. 158). Emphasizing the importance of active participation by all social groups, she argues that fairness "sometimes requires different treatment for oppressed or disadvantaged groups" (p. 158). Through this lens, procedural justice centers equity rather than equality. Equitable procedural justice allows for difference of outcome even within fair procedures; that is, it relies on the sameness of procedures (e.g., everyone gets a reward for good work) not the sameness of goods (e.g., everyone's reward for good work is $100). In the context of workplace procedures, an equitable perspective of fairness would allow for organizational decision making to vary, provided that the variation is transparent and that the variation is perceived as equitable (not necessarily equal) by workers. Compared to equality, then, equity has a greater margin of maneuverability; it can be envisioned and enacted in different ways in support of different values. Of course, this means it can be wielded in support of oppression. But as a more flexible tool, it also offers promise for interventions in support of justice, particularly in sites of slippage (see Chapter 6). When procedures are just, they pave the way for further conditions of justice by offering fair mechanisms by which to evaluate conditions, determine value, and set goals.

Legal Perspectives of Justice

TPC has a history of borrowing terms, research methods, and theories from other fields for use in our own scholarship and practice, so it is not anomalous to look outside our own field for productive lenses through which technical communicators can view justice. Distributive justice and procedural justice are transdisciplinary concepts and therefore may be familiar to some TPC scholars.

These concepts are relatively clear cut in scope: Distributive paradigms addressing the "what" of justice and procedural addressing the "how." As such, they can be useful for envisioning justice but are not well suited to redressing injustice. In other words, neither equips actors to expiate harm done. These concepts alone, therefore, are too limited to inform technical communication after the social justice turn. Technical communicators committed to projects of justice must be alert for opportunities to intervene in the wake of injustice to set things right. Thus, we draw from the sister fields of legal studies and criminal justice because "the study of social justice is intimately connected with the study of causes of harm (including officially defined crime)" (Capeheart & Milovanovic, 2007, p. 4). Indeed, the institutional and legal structures that purport to enact justice in society often create the very contexts and conditions for crime (p. 4). Engaging with these complexities, we introduce three terms from legal studies and criminal justice, terms which pose approaches to redressing harm: Retributive justice, restorative justice, and transitional justice.

Retributive Justice

Retributive justice pursues fair punishment for wrongdoing, placing offenders and offense at the center of justice concerns. The U.S. criminal justice system relies on an approach to justice that is primarily retributive: Focused on the punitive, with justifications of punishment including deterrence, social defense, and retribution (Capeheart & Milovanovic, 2007). Rejecting a systemic view of oppression in favor of an individualized perspective of wrongdoing, the criminal justice system implies that the solution to injustice is to punish wrongdoers and that doing so resolves injustice. In other words, a foundational assumption of a retributive criminal justice system is that the confines of justice are clearly demarcated through the judicial system, avoiding issues of social justice while nodding in its direction and maintaining a disinterested relationship with the systemic oppressions that enable injustices to occur. A retributive perspective of justice considers the punishment of guilty parties to be both a moral duty and a justifying ideal, though critics question the value of an ideal that lacks clear guidance for law enforcement practice (Cahill, 2007). For example, in the context of limited financial and human resources, retributive justice does not help police and prosecutors to make difficult choices regarding which crimes to investigate and prosecute, how to prioritize law enforcement, and when, if ever, to compromise (Cahill, 2007). Sometimes called the "just desserts" perspective, retributive justice requires that wrongdoers experience punishment commensurate with their offense. A key consideration, then, is how desserts are determined to be just: What factors affect how people gauge fair punishment?

Proponents of retributive justice may answer by pointing to legal standards such as the U.S. Federal Sentencing Guidelines, which set forth policies for sentencing those convicted of felonies and serious misdemeanors. But legal guidelines are not the only factors guiding the determination of fair punishment. Human emotion plays a key role as well, particularly the moral outrage (i.e., levels of disgust, anger, and contempt) triggered by the offense. For example, if someone does harm to others through carelessness, societies are more likely to call for restitution; whereas if someone inflicts harm intentionally, social reactions primarily include moral outrage, prompting a desire for punishment (Darley & Pittman, 2003). Child molestation prompts higher levels of moral outrage than violent crimes, which prompt higher levels of moral outrage than white-collar crimes (Bastian, Denson, & Halmas, 2013). Punishing offenders justifies societal rules, reinforcing the legitimacy of group values, norms, and laws among non-offenders (Vidmar, 2002). After presenting several case studies of community reactions to crime, Vidmar concludes, "These case studies strongly suggest that the more criminal events threaten group or community values, the stronger will be the punitive reactions and attempts to achieve consensus to rearm those values" (2002, p. 298).

Moral outrage matters in considerations of retributive justice because it affects people's perceptions of what constitutes fair and appropriate punishment (i.e., legal judgments): High levels of moral outrage correlate positively with longer sentences and negatively with perceived suitability for rehabilitation (Bastian et al., 2013, p. 5). When moral outrage is high and desire for social cohesion is great, righteous ends can be used to justify unjust means. For example, a random survey of adults in Northern California revealed that the best predictor of highly punitive views of justice[6] was concern regarding lack of moral cohesion in society (Tyler & Boeckmann, 1997). In light of this finding, Vidmar (2002) concludes that "persons holding strong concerns about moral cohesion were willing to abandon procedural protections for persons charged with criminal offenses" (p. 298). This conclusion raises a chilling question: If, in their zeal to preserve cohesion regarding social values, people are willing to sacrifice the rights of those *accused* of crimes, how much less would they protect people who have been *convicted?*

A related factor shown to have even stronger effects on people's perceptions of fair punishment is dehumanization of the offender. For example, Myers, Godwin, Latter, and Winstanley (2004) found that cases involving victim impact statements with dehumanizing language were associated with harsher jury-recommended sentences. Similarly, a series of studies found that dehumanizing sex offenders by comparing them with animals correlated with more punitive attitudes: For example, less support for rehabilitation; calls for harsher punishment; and support for excluding them from society and even violent treatment, such as castration (Viki, Fullerton, Ragett, Tait, & Wiltshire, 2012). A series of three studies investigating the effects of moral outrage and dehumanization on views of retributive justice concluded that both factors were influential in triggering more punitive perspectives, but only dehumanization predicted harsher punishment severity "and did so irrespective of crime type and any effects associated with moral outrage" (Bastian et al., 2013, p. 6). Further, dehumanization of offenders correlated positively with longer recommended sentences and negatively with perceived suitability for rehabilitation (p. 5).

Considering these findings alongside the dehumanizing effects of oppression (e.g., see Violence and Cultural Imperialism in Chapter 1) sheds some light on patterns of discrimination by the U.S. criminal justice system, such as increased rates of arrests and incarceration among people of color. In doing so, it reveals the complicity of the criminal justice system in forms of oppression, especially forms of oppression that are invisible to (or easily denied by) those in power (unless and until it is in their interest to change them, per interest convergence theory). At the same time, it also reveals some sites of slippage for technical communicators invested in justice. When we understand how dehumanizing language, for example, shapes people's perceptions of what constitutes fair punishment, we recognize roles for communicators to intervene: To reveal myths of neutrality in sentencing, to reject narratives calling for moral cohesion at the cost of just procedures, and to replace dehumanizing lenses with contextualized understandings of institutionalized oppression.

Restorative Justice

Whereas distributive justice puts material goods at the center of justice concerns, procedural justice centralizes process, and retributive justice centralizes punishment, restorative justice puts social harmony at the center of justice concerns. One of the most influential early voices in restorative justice, criminologist Howard Zehr, originally framed it as an alternative system that is principally opposed to the basic premises and objectives of retributive justice, though he later amended that position somewhat, clarifying that both theories of justice seek vindication for wrongdoing but that they differ in what is considered necessary and beneficial to set matters right (2015, p. 75). Retributive perspectives are authoritarian, seeing the aim of the criminal justice system as punitive and setting aside as irrelevant future concerns such as rehabilitation (Bastian et al., 2013). In contrast, restorative perspectives are participatory, seeing the aim of the criminal justice system as healing: Helping communities to live more harmoniously and restoring peace in the lives of victims. Restorative justice seeks to do the following: (1) Meet victims' needs, with needs conceived broadly to include financial, emotional, material, and social; (2) reintegrate offenders into the community, thereby reducing the likelihood of reoffense; (3) enable offenders to actively take responsibility; (4) support communities in rehabilitating offenders and victims and in actively preventing crime; and (5) avoid the escalation of legal justice, with its costs and delays (Marshall, 1999, p. 6).

Many cultures have both retributive and restorative traditions of justice, though peace activist and sociology scholar John Braithwaite points out that restorative was the dominant perspective of justice worldwide for a long time:

"Restorative justice has been the dominant model of criminal justice throughout most of human history for all the world's peoples" (Braithwaite, 1999, p. 2). But in the later Middle Ages in Europe, notions of restorative justice—wherein offenses are conceptualized primarily as between victims and offenders—were replaced by conceptions of crime as an offense against the state (specifically, the king) to strengthen the dominance of the state over its people. Retributive justice is by far the more dominant perspective undergirding the U.S. criminal justice system, but in the 1970s, restorative justice emerged again with the founding of victim-offender reconciliation programs, which innovate solutions because of their participatory nature. Many of these programs draw upon restorative justice traditions of Indigenous cultures, such as Navajo Justice and Healing Ceremonies, the New Zealand tradition of family group conferences, and Canadian native peoples' practice of healing circles and sentencing circles (Braithwaite, 1999). Indeed, in societies where Western legal traditions have suppressed and replaced Indigenous justice perspectives and procedures, restorative justice offers a mechanism to push back against institutionalized cultural imperialism in the criminal justice system (Zehr, 2015, pp. 18–19).

Restorative justice is often defined by contrasting it with other views of justice, but a descriptive (rather than contrastive) definition that is relatively widely embraced was coined by Tony Marshall: "Restorative justice is a process whereby all the parties with a stake in a particular offense come together to resolve collectively how to deal with the aftermath of the offense and its implications for the future" (e-mail, Marshall to McCold, 1997; quoted in Braithwaite, 1999, p. 5). The parties with a stake in a particular offense typically include victims, offenders, and affected communities, such as the families of victims and offenders. These parties together determine what restoration looks like, what is to be restored, and how. Thus, restorative justice is not a specific practice but rather an approach to redressing injustice that is guided by a set of principles: (1) Prioritizing the involvement of victims, offenders, and their families or communities; (2) placing crime within its social context; (3) taking a preventative view to problem solving; and (4) valuing creativity and flexibility in the practice of restoration (Marshall, 1999, p. 5). Guided by these principles, restorative justice upholds values such as "healing rather than hurting, moral learning, community participation and community caring, respectful dialogue, forgiveness, responsibility, apology, and making amends" (Braithwaite, 1999, p. 6). In the U.S., juvenile crime has become the most common site of restorative justice approaches. In this arena in particular, restorative justice offers a range of strengths, such as offering opportunities for citizens to democratically and directly engage with questions of justice that are important to them:

> Restorative justice gives adult citizens a genuine say in something they deeply care about – what the state is to do about their children when those children suffer some abuse, or perpetrate some abuse, that gets them into serious trouble with the state.
>
> (Braithwaite, 2016, p. 9)

A preponderance of evidence also suggests that victims of crime benefit more from restorative justice approaches than from the traditional retributive approach of the U.S. judicial system, with benefits including reduced fear, helplessness, and vengefulness, as well as an increased sense that justice has been done (Braithwaite, 2016).

There is, of course, no perfect conception of justice. Much like the inadequacies of distributive justice and slippages of procedural justice, restorative justice has its weaknesses. As described by Zehr (2015), the restorative justice movement has at times lost its way (p. 8) due to factors such as the rapid proliferation of restorative justice programs (presumably outstripping the availability of training, funding, and other support), pressures and constraints of real-world contexts, and conflicting stakeholder priorities. Critics question, for example, whether restorative justice programs are actually prioritizing the restoration of peace in victims' lives as opposed to focusing primarily on offenders or, alternatively, whether restorative programs offer sufficient support to offenders in reintegrating back into their communities. In response, Zehr (2015) calls proponents of restorative justice to return to its principles, explicitly drawing upon them to craft ways forward and using them to evaluate programs and outcomes (pp. 9–10).

Braithwaite (2016) identifies another concern with restorative justice: Studies have shown that the actions agreed upon in restorative justice processes are more likely to be carried out than actions ruled by a judge. For productive actions (e.g., attending an effective drug treatment program), this is a strength. But if stakeholders agree upon a counterproductive strategy (e.g., standing outside a store holding a sign reading, "I am a thief"), it may be more damaging than if such a decision were ruled by a judge because the counterproductive strategy is likely to be carried out[7] (Braithwaite, 2016). As with retributive justice, then, restorative justice offers opportunities for technical communicators to intervene. Such interventions can draw upon classic, core strengths of our field: Drawing out the goals of users (goals which vary and even conflict across user groups) and sharing information that supports users in pursuing their goals. Instantiations of this work in restorative justice contexts could include educating stakeholders regarding principles of restorative justice and facilitating stakeholders in identifying strategies likely to be productive in terms of their own desired outcomes: For example, restoring peace to victims and restoring a place for offenders within their communities.

Transitional Justice

Unlike the other conceptions of justice discussed thus far, transitional justice typically operates at the nation-state level. Positioning rule of law at the center of justice considerations, transitional justice plays a role in political change, using legal mechanisms to address atrocities of outgoing regimes and help countries peacefully transition to a stable government (Teitel, 2003, p. 69). According to the International Center for Transitional Justice (n.d.),

> Transitional justice refers to the ways countries emerging from periods of conflict and repression address large scale or systematic human rights violations so numerous and so serious that the normal justice system will not be able to provide an adequate response.

Transitional justice emerged in the mid-1940s with the international cooperation, sanctions, and war trials which marked the way forward after World War II (WWII) (Teitel, 2003, p. 70). Although transitional justice mechanisms have changed since then, the basis for contemporary human rights laws today was formed by the post-WWII trials, which "criminalized state wrongdoing as part of a universal rights scheme" (Teitel, 2003, p. 70). As noted in a United Nations Security Council report (2004), transitional justice is typically enacted through official judicial mechanisms, with international agencies coming into post-conflict societies to temporarily restore rule of law "in order to ensure accountability, serve justice and achieve reconciliation" (p. 4). Transitional justice can include a range of actions, such as prosecuting individual offenders who violated human rights in the previous regime, making reparations for injustice and atrocities, or vetting and dismissing people who are serving in positions of authority (UN, 2004).

Reestablishing peace—both immediately post-conflict and in the long term—requires that people can settle disputes, feeling "confident that redress for grievances can be obtained through legitimate structures" (UN, 2004, p. 3). An important question in the context of transitional justice, then, is what constitutes "legitimate structures." One concern with transitional justice is its tendency to be top down and exclusively directed by professionals, that is, owned by lawyers, policy makers, and governing bodies (international and national) instead of by long-oppressed communities themselves (McEnvoy, 2007, pp. 413–414). This emphasis on official, governmental transitional justice mechanisms may well be rooted in concern for oppressed parties: For example, the UN (2004) urges that "the heightened vulnerability of minorities, women, children, prisoners and detainees, displaced persons, refugees and others, which is evident in all conflict and post-conflict situations, brings an element of urgency to the imperative of restoration of the rule of law" (p. 4). And it should be acknowledged that the absence or perversion of a rule of law is often what defined the previous authority structures in societies pursuing transitional justice mechanisms (McEnvoy, 2007, p. 417).

But dangers lurk in a rule of law envisioned and enforced solely or primarily by professional legal parties. McEnvoy (2007) summarizes many of these problems, but arguably the most insidious are those flying the banner of human rights. For example, widespread and unquestioning support for "human rights" can create an environment in which simplistic, top-down visions of justice are pursued, legalized, and praised by international bodies, who claim the right to speak for local communities. But local communities are left to wrestle with social and historical complexities of injustice and reconciliation. Human rights protections can also be twisted into tools of hegemony. As Ding and Pitts (2013) point out, what some purport to be universal human rights, others have argued are Western cultural values. And ironically, the values that Western-led transitional justice efforts seek to enforce have been long violated in the Global South by the West itself.[8] Equally infuriating are oppressive governments' use of fallacious syllogism to veil human rights violations: For example, our laws condemn torture, and our nation has signed onto the Convention against Torture; therefore, our law enforcement's questioning techniques obviously cannot be considered torture (McEnvoy, 2007, p. 419). To return, then, to the UN's urgent imperative that post-conflict societies restore the rule of law, we caution against uncritically equating restoration of the rule of law with protection of marginalized people. All too often, the opposite is true, with state institutions enforcing rule of law unequally and oppressively—and not only in conflict-ridden or recently post-conflict states (see discussion of retributive justice).

Because U.S.-based technical communication, legal scholarship, and other areas of study concerned with justice remain primarily focused on the domestic challenges of justice (e.g., environmental justice, participatory frames for public engagement, discrimination in schools)—if it is concerned with justice at all—many members of our field lack familiarity with global forms of justice that have emerged in the past century to redress inequities that are blackboxed by the U.S. criminal justice system. In global contexts, additional frames for justice have expanded in ways that expose the limits of the U.S. criminal justice system. In reflecting upon the relevance of transitional justice to TPC, we assert that it is shortsighted to overlook theories of justice because they may not be relevant to our immediate local context, and it is colonizing to fail to consider justice mechanisms because they are rarely employed within Western contexts. As Capeheart and Milovanovic (2007) assert, "Multiculturalism and globalism are realities of our current society. Whether one is actively engaged in these processes or not they affect our social world and therefore our understandings of justice and social justice" (p. 77). Further, international and intercultural professional communication is a growing, influential subset of our field (Ding & Savage, 2013), and those of us engaged in global TPC work, especially, must be familiar with transitional justice. As TPC expands its vision of justice and the field to global contexts (see the works of Agboka, Walton, and Dura, among others), we can augment our theories, practices, and frameworks both by engaging with and studying lesser known (but no less important) theories of justice.

Further, these legal perspectives of justice, new to many technical communicators, equip us for coalition building. If technical communicators want to contribute meaningfully to justice work, we need to identify contexts for the various conceptions of justice: Is it legal? Is it social? Is it political? Our field is not asking these questions, and this gap is limiting our ability to innovate and to productively contribute to coalitions, particularly those involved in creating legislation, protecting communities, and redressing criminal offenses. And yet, we would argue that many members of our field, particularly those in the U.S., have internalized perspectives of justice drawn from the U.S. criminal justice system. One need not be a lawyer or legal studies scholar to be impacted by the effects, limits, and influences of the criminal justice system's version of justice. Thus, it is important to name and define these perspectives so that we can intentionally consider when, whether, and how they offer productive lenses on justice for our own lives and our own work.

As we move forward toward articulating an approach to technical communication that is socially just, all of these conceptions of justice are relevant—but not all are applicable in each case. Technical communicators may miss opportunities for redressing injustices if we settle on one approach to justice—particularly if we haven't surveyed various conceptions of justice. For example, we can be swayed to believe that equal distribution of money is the most fair and just way to dole out scholarships. Yet we know that not all students begin from the same starting point and that, in fact, an equal distribution does not redress inequities experienced by underrepresented minorities. This is not to say that an equality-based approach is unjustified, of course. But *justifiable* is not necessarily *just*. So, too, with procedural conceptions of justice. Pursuing fair and equitable procedures has been germane to the work of many technical communicators in design, user experience, and public forms of technical communication. But as many scholars have demonstrated (Johnson, 1998; Rose, 2016; Simmons & Zoetewey, 2012), sometimes the devil is in the details. The implementation of procedures can complicate claims about procedural justice, revealing that procedural justice is not enough to address social inequities. Social justice-oriented scholars, like Rose and Walton (2018), help demonstrate ways that the procedures of transportation, for example, are embedded with other forms of structural and social injustices. In these ways, TPC research can reveal hidden, embedded oppressions and identify alternative procedures to replace them, drawing upon various frameworks of justice.

Like an ethical and just methodology, thinking through justice needs a contextualized, coalition-driven approach to decision making, and we offer these frameworks for understanding justice to augment the justice-oriented arguments of our field, which can be oversimplified by adopting just one frame. We also offer these frameworks to differentiate them from what we mean when we say social justice.

Social Justice

Despite a growing body of social justice scholarship in technical communication, the term itself is rarely defined and described effectively in our work. Given that a shared vocabulary is essential for activism (Collins, 2002, p. 275), scholarly and otherwise, this gap is concerning. One notable exception is Jones and Walton's (2018) proposed definition for the field:

> Social justice research in technical communication investigates how communication broadly defined can amplify the agency of oppressed people—those who are materially, socially, politically, and/or economically under-resourced. Key to this definition is a collaborative, respectful approach that moves past description and exploration of social justice issues to taking action to redress inequities.
>
> *(p. 242)*

Apparent in this definition are two core characteristics of social justice, which are, at best, indirectly implied and, at worst, missing altogether from much social justice literature in TPC: Social justice is collective and active. To engage in and with the concept at the heart of the social justice turn, we must work collectively and consider collective forces and effects of oppression, and we must be ready not only to recognize oppression but also to reveal, reject, and replace it: To take action.

Collective

The work of social justice cannot be limited to individual actions or perspectives because the oppressions it targets are structural: Historical-but-dynamic and built into the fabric of societies. Black feminist scholars including bell hooks (2000) and Patricia Hill Collins emphasize that although social justice does require internal, individual change in terms of self-determination and self-definition, radical changes to social structures and institutions are absolutely necessary: "Empowerment also requires transforming unjust social institutions that African-Americans [and other disadvantaged social groups] encounter from one generation to the next" (Collins, 2002, p. 273). Pursuing social justice, then, requires a willingness to scrutinize and to change the organizations of which we are a part, the practices in which we engage, and the norms that shape our perceptions and expectations. No sphere is sacrosanct. As Young (1990) explains, "social justice means the elimination of institutionalized domination and oppression. Any aspect of social organization and practice relevant to domination and oppression is in principle subject to evaluation by ideals of justice" (p. 15). In fact, political philosopher Brian Barry (2005) explains that historical notions of justice operated primarily at the individual level, and when the concept of social justice emerged, what made it so revolutionary "was that the justice of a society's institutions could be challenged not merely at the margins but at the core" (p. 5). For example, one could question not only the justice of a particular employer's policies that maximize profit by curtailing employee autonomy but—fundamentally—the legitimacy of capitalist extremes which value profit over people.

Oppressive structures work in concert, producing what Collins (2002) calls a "matrix of domination" (p. 276). For social justice work to be effective, we must take a complex, collective view of oppressions. Otherwise, we risk wasted action: Rejecting or replacing one instantiation of oppression, the effects of which are overdetermined[9] and therefore continue to exist due to other oppressive factors. Failure to understand how oppressive structures work together can keep us from seeing what it is that restricts people's capacities. As Young (2000) explains,

> An account of someone's life circumstances contains many strands of difficulty or difference from others that, taken one by one, can appear to be the result of decision, preferences, or accidents. When considered together, however, and when compared with the life story of others, they reveal a net of restricting and reinforcing relationships.
>
> *(p. 93)*

Philosopher and feminist theorist Marilyn Frye (1983) uses the analogy of a wire birdcage (pp. 2–7). When you examine a single wire, you cannot understand how it could entrap a bird, which should be able to merely fly around this small impediment. Of course, pulling back one's view and looking at the wires collectively makes all the difference in understanding entrapment: The network of impediments work together, connecting and supporting one another to imprison the bird.

> One can study the elements of an oppressive structure with great care and some good will without seeing the structure as a whole, and hence without seeing or being able to understand that one is looking at a cage and that there are people there who are caged, whose motion and mobility are restricted, whose lives are shaped and reduced.
>
> *(Frye, 1983, p. 5)*

In responding to interconnected structures of oppression, social justice calls for collective action, which offers promise for informing agendas that are beneficial to heterogeneous groups: "Social justice is concerned not in the narrow focus of what is just for the individual alone, but what is just for the social whole. [...] It requires the consideration of and sensitivity to all voices and all concerns" (Capeheart & Milovanovic, 2007, p. 2). This is not to say that it is impossible for an individual's actions to support empowerment. Distinguished University Professor of sociology and Black feminist scholar Collins (2002) provides a powerful example:

> When my mother taught me to read, took me to the public library when I was five, and told me that if I learned to read, I could experience a form of freedom, neither she nor I saw the magnitude of that one action in my life and the lives that my work has subsequently touched.
>
> *(p. 275)*

Relatedly, Colton and Holmes (2016) introduce a theoretical model of active equality to support technical communicators in enacting social justice independent of institutional mechanisms. This model offers a useful tool for individuals to maneuver around institutional constraints they lack the power to change. Thus, we acknowledge that the effects of an individual's ideas and actions can ripple outward, affecting her own position in relation to various kinds of oppression as well as some of the people she comes into contact with. But, in the context of social justice work, we believe individualism can be dangerous (it easily lends itself to oppressive misuse by those in positions of power; e.g., see the discussion of charity versus social justice) and simply is not ideally suited to social justice work. Collective opposition to oppressive power better allows for complexity: For example, acknowledging that various oppressed groups may find themselves on opposing sides of issues and that the roles of oppressors and victims, dominant and marginalized, will shift, depending on the issue under consideration and aspect of identity that is at the forefront (Collins, 2002, p. 274). In light of this complexity, inclusivity is all-the-more important in not only the *goals* of social justice but also the *processes* by which goals are set and pursued. Socially just processes require that everyone involved can, in principle, consider and agree without coercion (Young, 1990, p. 34). Indeed, Young (1990) claims that "democratic decision making procedures [are required] as an element and condition of social justice" (p. 23).

For people in positions of privilege, inclusivity requires a willingness to decenter oneself, to relinquish the ease that comes with privilege, and to recognize the legitimacy of many ways of knowing, accepting that some people's knowledge will call into question one's own long-held truths. What might this look like in practice? Let's say that an academic program in TPC aims to support social justice. Like many programs, it seeks to increase the diversity of its students, but program stakeholders recognize the inadequacy of diversity alone to support marginalized and underrepresented groups. Efforts toward inclusion, then, would catch within their scope not only the program curriculum but also the sources of information guiding curricular revision. For example, many academic programs in TPC seek input from businesses to improve the relevance of their curriculum and prepare their students for the job market. A move toward inclusion could involve intentionally seeking perspectives relevant to the employment of marginalized groups: For example, a person of color who started her own business to avoid discrimination, a person with a chronic illness who freelances for the flexible schedule, a nonprofit organization with atypical processes and genres of professional communication. The guidance from these sources may call into question curricular goals (e.g., teaching students to write and edit for "neutrality"), genres considered central to professional communication (e.g., instruction sets and manuals), and myths (e.g., hiring discrimination is illegal in the U.S.). But if an academic program were committed to social justice, it would pursue not just diversity but inclusion: For example, it would aim to recruit students from a variety of backgrounds and also invite guiding expertise from marginalized groups whose perspectives should shape curriculum to reflect goals, challenges, and experiences of a wider variety of students.

Active

Another key characteristic of social justice is that it is active—which is not to say that theories and ideas are irrelevant. As Collins (2002) says, "Ideas matter, but doing 'plenty of work' may matter even more" (p. 273). As we develop an approach to social justice in TPC, then, theory's role in social justice must be to inform action.[10] Critical theory is particularly useful for informing notions of justice that are rooted in real, particular contexts and can therefore inform action. That is, in part, because critical theory contextualizes claims of what should be (i.e., the normative) within a current reality (i.e., the descriptive):

> critical theory is a normative reflection that is historically and socially contextualized. [...] Normative reflection must begin from historically specific circumstances because there is nothing but what is, the given, the situated interest in justice, from which to start. Reflecting from within a particular social context, good normative theorizing cannot avoid social and political description and explanation.
>
> *(Young, 1990, p. 5)*

In contrast to situated approaches, theories of justice that claim to be universal lack the specificity to not only identify and describe particular instantiations of injustice but also—even more importantly—to account for what causes them. Mills (1997) makes similar critiques of classic political theory, contrasting with his own critical theory introducing the notion of the Racial Contract, which offers practical application and value:

> As I have emphasized, the 'Racial Contract' seeks to account for the way things are and how they came to be that way—the descriptive—as well as the way they should be—the normative—since indeed one of its complaints about white political philosophy is precisely its otherworldliness, its ignoring of basic political realities.
>
> *(p. 11)*

Ignoring basic realities of power and oppression allows classic social contract theories of justice to skirt the very questions that should inform the pursuit of justice: "Without such a critical stance, many questions about what occurs in society and why, who benefits and who is harmed, will not be asked, and social theory is liable to reaffirm and reify the given social reality" (Young, 1990, p. 5). In other words, critical theory reflects upon what is—the social and historical context—to inform what should be. Otherwise, any "should" is too abstract to be useful and too obtuse to ask pointed questions that aid in recognizing and revealing injustice.

A socially just society enables and supports a variety of actions by all members: For example,

> learning and using satisfying and expansive skills in socially recognized settings; participating in forming and running institutions, and receiving recognition for such participation; playing and communicating with others, and expressing our experience, feelings, and perspective on social life in contexts where others can listen.
>
> (*Young, 1990, p. 37*)

We recognize in these example actions a quality that Women's Studies scholar Elizabeth Grosz characterizes as freedom (2010). Extending the work of Bergson, Grosz (2010) poses a theory of freedom that is relevant to social justice, particularly to coalition building. In laying out her position, Grosz first refutes two perspectives of possibility: Determinism (which claims that the selection of a particular action from among possible choices is inevitable and predictable, given sufficient information) and free will (which claims that the selection of a particular action from among possible choices is unpredictable). Instead, she points out that we can only know that a particular action was possible in retrospect—that is, we know it must have been possible because it happened. Thus, what is possible is not dependent upon preconfigured and pre-existing choices, which are available to us or not, depending upon how free we are. Rather, it is *actions* that can be characterized according to their degree of freedom, with free acts being those in which we express the whole of ourselves and simultaneously are transformed, incorporating that free act into our history, our identity. This conception of freedom can be productive in the work of coalitions, particularly when envisioning a coalition's goals and identities, because it allows for the rejection of preconceived identities and possibilities granted (or withheld) by those in positions of power. Political activist and scholar Angela Davis (1998) asserts

> It is important to recognize the various forms of agency with which identities can be and are constructed, in order not to get stuck in them, in order not to assume that racialized identities have always been there. [...] That is what much of this forum [on coalition building] is about: How can

we construct political projects that rethink identities in dynamic ways and lead to transformative strategies and radical social change?

(p. 300)

We see in Grosz's theory of freedom a key role for informing action: Posing perspectives that can expand coalition members' vision of identities and possibilities.

Because social justice is primarily collective, much of its action is driven by coalitions.[11] Coalition building is not familiar work for many technical communicators—at least not coalition building explicitly framed as such. Chapter 6 equips technical communicators for coalition building in contexts relevant to many of us, such as academic programs and community organizations. Important to the work of coalition building is the recognition that coalition members do not necessarily need to share a common worldview. American Chicana feminist and activist Elizabeth "Betita" Martinez (Davis, 1998) explains,

> One handy distinction is to think of coalitions being built around issues, and ideology being a worldview. An ideology is a set of ideas that explains what makes society tick and what its values are. You don't have to agree on that with other people in order to fight for health care, housing, affirmative action, or whatever.

(p. 301)

In other words, a shared viewpoint of the world is not a prerequisite for temporarily joining together to take action on an issue of mutual importance, as long as coalition members can agree on principles and actions relevant to that issue. Rhetorical critic and Latinx Studies scholar Karma Chavez (2013) draws upon Lugones to use the analogy of a horizon to explain coalitions. The horizon is a place where formerly distinct entities merge and coalesce while at the same time retaining their difference (Chavez, 2013, p. 8). This coalescence may be fleeting or may endure for some time, but it requires dedicated work to maintain (2013).

Another common misconception relevant to coalitions is that people who share particular identity markers (such as shared race or gender) constitute a more homogenous group than people without shared identity markers who may hold certain perspectives or values in common. That inaccurate assumption can be problematic for identifying and drawing together people willing to take collaborative action on shared issues. Davis (1998) advises,

> I think we need to be more reflective, more critical and more explicit about our concepts of community. [...] An African-American woman might find it much easier to work together with a Chicana than with another Black woman whose politics of race, class, gender, and sexuality would place her in an entirely different community.

(p. 299)

The key consideration is whether potential coalition members—each of whom may draw upon different values, perspectives, identity markers, and worldviews—can come together to take action on issues of mutual interest.

Technical communicators (and others) drawn to the work of social justice and eager to take collective action against oppression also may be scared of taking risks and intimidated by the limits of their own knowledge. Take heart. People rarely join coalitions as "theoretically informed activists from the outset, in possession of a full-blown political consciousness, as well as having the capacity to organize for social change" (Davis, 1998, p. 302). Rather, research on social movements has shown that it is *by engaging* in activist work that people form sophisticated, complex understandings of social structure and social justice (Capeheart & Milovanovic, 2007). For example, studying women activists in the movement to obtain benefits and healthcare for people experiencing Gulf War syndrome, researchers found that many of the women joined the movement because of direct family ties to an affected veteran (Shriver, Miller, & Cable, 2003). It was through the work of activism that they developed broader understandings of inequalities surrounding healthcare access and related issues, expanding and spinning off activist movements addressing some of these injustices (Shriver et al., 2003). Summarizing this study and others like it, Capeheart and Milovanovic (2007) conclude, "as activists engage in the process of demanding justice, they are also developing their own understandings of justice and building their own processes for expression of justice" (p. 160). In other words, you do not have to be an expert on activism, political philosophy, or social justice as a prerequisite for joining coalitions that fight oppression. At the same time, let us be clear that inexperience is no excuse for people in positions of privilege to jump into leadership, drowning out the voices and dismissing the priorities of the most oppressed members (see white feminism). To guard against perpetuating oppressive norms, activists invested in social justice should be guided by its key characteristics: Collective and active. We authors are committed to social justice as scholars and as humans. We write this book as a way to explore these characteristics ourselves and invite readers to join us in exploration. These characteristics structure the book: The next three chapters delve deeply into what we call the 3Ps (positionality, privilege, and power) to provide a framework for collectively considering social justice and for recognizing the oppressions it works against, and the final two chapters equip technical communicators for coalitional action to recognize, reveal, reject, and replace oppression.

Notes

1 See, for example, Thomas Hobbes, John Locke, and John Rawls, who formed theories of justice based upon the notion of an unwritten agreement between individuals and their society (called a social contract) that forms the rules of human societies and explains the motivations for individual members to follow those rules. These philosophers made general claims about the nature of human beings, society, and

reason to construct theories of justice purported to be applicable across societies regardless of particular societal configurations.

2 For an extensive discussion of these problematic policies, consult *Evicted* (Desmond, 2016).

3 For example, Milwaukee, WI, passed an ordinance that fined landlords when police were called out to a property three times or more within a 30-day period. Landlords responded by evicting "disruptive" tenants, including those who were the victims of crimes who called the police for protection from abusers.

4 See Alexander (2012, pp. 137–139).

5 It is no coincidence, we suggest, that many tools of oppression—for example, "color-blindness" and "bootstrapping"—are problematic for the ableist undertones of their terminology, as well as for their function in society.

6 The study investigated bases for support of a California law that mandated life imprisonment for anyone convicted of three felonies. The survey assessed respondents' crime-related concerns, concerns about social conditions, and social values.

7 Shaming is a strategy considered rarely appropriate at best: Insufficiently punitive for retributive perspectives (Rosen, 1993) and rarely useful for community reintegration valued by restorative perspectives (Marshall, 1999), though it is advocated by Braithwaite in specific circumstances and contexts.

8 For example, see Mills's brief overview of colonialism, focusing on European legal and philosophical justifications for enslavement, exploitation, and other atrocities enacted against people of color around the world (1997, pp. 19–31).

9 Overdetermination occurs when there are more factors contributing to an outcome than are necessary to cause it. Thus, eliminating one of these factors would not change the outcome because enough other causes exist for it to occur anyway. For example, if a young man of color with a criminal record is unable to earn a living wage near his home in a poor rural area, expunging his criminal record is unlikely to be sufficient to change his circumstances. Lack of jobs, racial discrimination, and other factors may be sufficient to ensure that he continues to lack employment.

10 We reject the inaccurate and unproductive dichotomy of theory *versus* practice or thinking *versus* acting, instead prioritizing theory *as* action and theory *as* experience.

11 Although the terms "network," "alliance," and "coalition" are sometimes used interchangeably, they do represent somewhat different types of groups: whereas networks are ongoing, more permanent relationships, and alliances focus on shared interests, coalitions are temporary formations of alignment focused on taking action.

References

Alexander, M. (2012). *The new Jim Crow: Mass incarceration in the age of colorblindness.* New York, NY: The New Press.

Barling, J., & Phillips, M. (1993). Interactional, formal, and distributive justice in the workplace: An exploratory study. *Journal of Psychology, 127*(6), 649–656.

Barry, B. (2005). *Why social justice matters.* Cambridge: Polity Press.

Bastian, B., Denson, T. F., & Haslam, N. (2013). The roles of dehumanization and moral outrage in retributive justice. *PLoS ONE, 8*(4): e61842. doi:10.1371/journal.pone.0061842

Bradford, B. (2014). Policing and social identity: Procedural justice, inclusion and cooperation between police and public. *Policing and Society, 24*(1), 22–43.

Braithwaite, J. (1999). Restorative justice: Assessing optimistic and pessimistic accounts. *Crime and Justice, 25,* 1–127.

Braithwaite, J. (2016). *Restorative justice and responsive regulation: The question of evidence.* RegNet Working Paper No. 51, School of Regulation and Global Governance (RegNet).

Cahill, M. T. (2007). Retributive justice in the real world. *Wash. U. L. Rev., 85,* 815. Retrieved from http://openscholarship.wustl.edu/law_lawreview/vol85/iss4/3

Capeheart, L., & Milovanovic, D. (2007). *Social justice: Theories, issues, and movements.* New Brunswick, NJ: Rutgers University Press.

Chavez, K. R. (2013). *Queer migration politics: Activist rhetoric and coalition possibilities.* Urbana, IL: University of Illinois Press.

Collins, P. H. (2002). *Black feminist thought: Knowledge, consciousness, and the politics of empowerment.* New York, NY: Routledge.

Colton, J. S., & Holmes, S. (2016). A social justice theory of active equality for technical communication. *Journal of Technical Writing and Communication.* doi/10.1177/0047281616647803.

Coole, D., & Frost, S. (2010). Introducing the new materialisms. In D. Coole & S. Frost (Eds.), *New materialisms: Ontology, agency, and politics* (pp. 1–46). Durham, NC: Duke University Press.

Darley, J. M., & Pittman, T. S. (2003). The psychology of compensatory and retributive justice. *Personality and Social Psychology Review, 7*(4), 324–336.

Davis, A. (1998). Coalition building among people of color: A conversation with Angela Davis and Elizabeth Martinez. In J. James (Ed.), *The Angela Y. Davis reader* (pp. 297–306). Malden, MA: Blackwell.

Delgado, R., & Stefancic, J. (2012). *Critical race theory: An introduction.* New York, NY: New York University Press.

Desmond, M. (2016). *Evicted: Poverty and profit in the American city.* New York, NY: Broadway Books.

Ding, H., & Pitts, E. (2013). Singapore's quarantine rhetoric and human rights in emergency health risks. *Rhetoric, Professional Communication, and Globalization, 4*(1), 55–77.

Ding, H., & Savage, G. (2013). Guest editors' introduction: New directions in intercultural professional communication. *Technical Communication Quarterly, 22*(1), 1–9.

Fraser, N. (2009). Social justice in the age of identity politics: Redistribution, recognition, and participation. In G. Henderson & M. Waterstone (Eds.), *Geographic thought: A praxis perspective* (pp. 72–89). Albany, NY: State University of Albany Press.

Frye, M. (1983). *The politics of reality: Essays in feminist theory.* Freedom, CA: Crossing Press.

Greenberg, J. (1990). Employee theft as a reaction to underpayment inequity: The hidden cost of pay cuts. *Journal of Applied Psychology, 72*(5), 55–61.

Grosz, E. (2010). Feminism, materialism, and freedom. In D. Coole & S. Frost (Eds.), *New materialisms: Ontology, agency, and politics* (pp. 139–157). Durham, NC: Duke University Press.

Hinds, L., & Murphy, K. (2007). Public satisfaction with police: Using procedural justice to improve police legitimacy. *The Australian and New Zealand Journal of Criminology, 40*(1), 27–42.

hooks, b. (2000). *Feminist theory: From margin to center* (2nd ed.). Cambridge, MA: South End Press.

Hough, M., Jackson, J., Bradford, B., Myhill, A., & Quinton, P. (2010). Procedural justice, trust, and institutional legitimacy. *Policing, 4*(3), 203–210.

Johnson, R. R. (1998). *User-centered technology: A rhetorical theory for computers and other mundane artifacts.* Albany, NY: SUNY Press.

Jones, N. N., & Walton, R. (2018). Using narratives to foster critical thinking about diversity and social justice. In M. Eble & A. Haas (Eds.), *Key theoretical frameworks for teaching technical communication in the 21st century* (pp. 241–267). Logan, UT: Utah State University Press.

Leventhal, G. S., Karuza, J., & Fry, W. R. (1980). Beyond fairness: A theory of allocation preferences. In G. Mikula (Ed.), *Justice and social interaction* (pp. 167–218). New York, NY: Springer-Verlag.

Marshall, T. F. (1999). *Restorative justice: An overview.* London: Home Office, Information & Publications Group, Research Development and Statistics Directorate. Retrieved from http://webarchive.nationalarchives.gov.uk/20110218143308/http://rds.homeoffice.gov.uk/rds/pdfs/occ-resjus.pdf

Mazerolle, L., Bennett, S., Davis, J., Sargeant, E., & Manning, M. (2013). Procedural justice and police legitimacy: A systematic review of the research evidence. *Journal of Experimental Criminology, 9*(3), 245–274.

McEnvoy, K. (2007). Beyond legalism: Towards a thicker understanding of transitional justice. *Journal of Law and Society, 34*(4), 411–440.

McFarlin, D. B., & Sweeney, P. D. (1992). Distributive and procedural justice as predictors of satisfaction with personal and organizational outcomes. *Academy of Management Journal, 35*(3), 626–637.

Miller, K., & Park, S. (2011). *Calling the police can get you evicted.* ACLU. Retrieved from https://www.aclu.org/blog/calling-police-can-get-you-evicted

Mills, C. (1997). *The racial contract.* Ithaca, NY: Cornell University Press.

Myers, B., Godwin, D., Latter, R., & Winstanley, S. (2004). Victim impact statements and mock juror sentencing: The impact of dehumanizing language on a death qualified sample. *American Journal of Forensic Psychology 22*, 39–55.

National Initiative for Building Community Trust and Justice. (n.d.). *Procedural justice.* Retrieved from https://trustandjustice.org/resources/intervention/procedural-justice

Novak, M. (2009, December). *Social justice: Not what you think it is. Heritage Foundation.* Retrieved from http://www.heritage.org/poverty-and-inequality/report/social-justice-not-what-you-think-it

Rose, E. J. (2016). Design as advocacy: Using a human-centered approach to investigate the needs of vulnerable populations. *Journal of Technical Writing and Communication, 46*(4), 427–445.

Rose, E., & Walton, R. (2018). From factors to actors: Implications of posthumanism for social justice work. In K. R. Moore & D. Richards (Eds.), *Posthuman praxis in technical communication* (pp. 93–119). New York, NY: Routledge.

Rosen, R. (1993). Shaming penalties and social forgiveness deficit. In F. Van Loon & K. Van Aeken (Eds.), *Sociology of law, social problems and legal policy* (pp. 185–191). Amsterdam: Acco Leuven.

Shriver, T. E., Miller, A. C., & Cable, S. (2003). Women's work: Women's involvement in the Gulf War illness movement. *The Sociological Quarterly, 44*(4), 639–658.

Simmons, W. M., & Grabill, J. T. (2007). Toward a civic rhetoric for technologically and scientifically complex places: Invention, performance, and participation. *College Composition and Communication,* 419–448.

Simmons, W. M., & Zoetewey, M. W. (2012). Productive usability: Fostering civic engagement and creating more useful online spaces for public deliberation. *Technical Communication Quarterly, 21*(3), 251–276.

Skarlicki, D. P., & Folger, R. (1997). Retaliation in the workplace: The roles of distributive, procedural, and interactional justice. *Journal of Applied Psychology, 82*(3), 434.

Southern Poverty Law Center. (n.d.). *Economic justice*. Retrieved from https://www.splcenter.org/issues/economic-justice

Sunshine, J., & Tyler, T. R. (2003). The role of procedural justice for legitimacy in shaping public support for policing. *Law and Society Review, 37*(3), 513–548.

Teitel, R. G. (2003). Transitional justice genealogy. *Harvard Human Rights Journal, 16*, 69–94.

Tyler, T. R., & Boeckmann, R. J. (1997). The three strikes and you are out, but why: The psychology of public support for punishing rule breakers. *Law & Society Review, 31*, 237.

Tyler, T. R., & Wakslak, C. J. (2004). Profiling and police legitimacy: procedural justice, attributions of motive, and acceptance of police authority. *Criminology, 42*(2), 253–281.

U.S. Department of Justice. (n.d.). *What is procedural justice? Fact sheet*. Community oriented policing services. Retrieved from http://cops.igpa.uillinois.edu/sites/cops.igpa.uillinois.edu/files/pj_fact_sheet.pdf

United Nations Security Council. (2004). *The rule of law and transitional justice in conflict and post-conflict societies*. Report of the Secretary-General. Retrieved from https://www.un.org/ruleoflaw/blog/document/the-rule-of-law-and-transitional-justice-in-conflict-and-post-conflict-societies-report-of-the-secretary-general/

Vidmar, N. (2002). Retributive justice: Its social context. In M. Ross & D. T. Miller (Eds.), *The justice motive in everyday life*, (pp. 291–313). Cambridge: Cambridge University Press.

Viki, G. T., Fullerton, I., Ragett, H., Tait, F., & Wiltshire, S. (2012). The role of dehumanization in attitudes toward the social exclusion and rehabilitation of sex offenders. *Journal of Applied Social Psychology, 42*, 2349–2367.

Young, I. M. (1990). *Justice and the politics of difference*. Princeton, NJ: Princeton University Press.

Young, I. M. (2000). *Inclusion and democracy*. Oxford: Oxford University Press.

Zehr, H. (2015). *The little book of restorative justice*, revised and updated. New York, NY: Good Books.

SECTION II

Strategically Contemplating the 3Ps

3

POSITIONALITY

Positionality is a way of conceiving subjectivity that simultaneously accounts for the constraints and conditions of context while also allowing for an individual's action and agency. In other words, positionality asserts that the meaning of identity categories (such as race and gender) are not essential but rather are fluid and contextual. For example, there is no universal meaning for what it is to "be Black." Rather, what it means to a Black, young woman in rural Georgia in 2019 differs from what it means to be a Black, gay man in Harlem in the 1910s. At the same time, aspects of identity are not wholly determined by context but rather allow for a person's own interpretation and construction of values. In other words, social contexts and constraints do not create an identity which a person then discovers but rather form a position from which a person can craft meaning and use as a point of departure for action (Alcoff, 1988, p. 434).

It is this relation to taking action that makes positionality especially relevant to social justice. If social justice is collective and active (Chapter 2), then positionality offers a useful lens for seeing how people (including one's self) are positioned relative to one another in the social fabric and, relatedly, for identifying our margins of maneuverability for action in pursuit of justice. In this section (Chapters 3–5), we build upon the foundations laid in Section I (exploring oppression and justice) by re-theorizing three central concepts: Positionality, privilege, and power. These concepts comprise a framework for enacting inclusivity and social justice in the field of technical and professional communication (TPC) and beyond. Examining our own positionality (what our identity means in particular contexts of action) and our own privilege (the types and extents of unearned advantages we are accorded) provides keen insight into the types and amounts of power we may have for taking coalitional action in support of justice (see Figure 3.1).

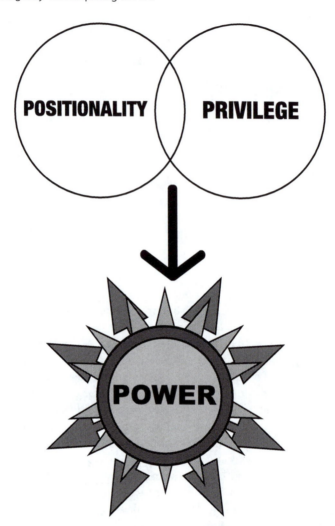

FIGURE 3.1 Relation of the 3Ps: Positionality, Privilege, and Power.

Primarily drawing upon the work of activists and scholars of color under-examined in the field of TPC, this conceptual framework of positionality, privilege, and power (the 3Ps) provides a lens useful for change-making and coalition building. In other words, understanding the 3Ps is necessary if we want to build coalitions across the field and in our local communities. As we discussed in the introduction and in Chapter 1, our field is well positioned to engage in coalitional work. For example, TPC's long history of user advocacy and intercultural communication can be augmented for social justice, but doing so requires the kind of structured reflection facilitated by the 3Ps.

What Is Positionality?

Positionality[1] asserts that aspects of identity (such as race, gender, nationality, religion, etc.) are complex and dynamic. In other words, what it means to "be a woman" or to "be American" has no single, fixed meaning but rather is

- **Relational:** It is more meaningful to consider what it means to be a person with disabilities when considered alongside what it means to be able bodied
- **Historical:** What it means to be Black in 2018 is different from what it means to be Black in 1918 or even 2008, and this historicity changes how we interpret the past and envision the future as well
- **Fluid:** What it means to be a gay man may be different when a man is in his teens compared to his 50s
- **Particular:** What it means to be a devout Hindu differs among individuals ascribing to the same religion
- **Situational:** What it means to be a woman of color is different in the boardroom than it is in the courtroom than it is in her aunt's kitchen
- **Contradictory:** What it means to be a successful technology professional may be perceived to conflict with what it means to be an immigrant, even for a person who is both
- **Intersectional:** What it means to be transgender is different for a person who is white than for a person of color and for a person with disabilities than for an able-bodied person

In threading this complex perspective on identity, positionality offers an alternative to simplistic perspectives such as essentialism, social determinism, and dyadic perspectives.[2] Essentialism is a Platonic notion that aspects of identity (such as race or gender) make a person what they are, that identity categories are the "essence" of a person. Not surprisingly, essentialist perspectives underlie scientific racism,[3] which has been used to explain away patterns of difference in wealth, education, and other factors as stemming from essential differences among groups of people (rather than oppression, inequities, and injustice). For example, as discussed in Chapter 1, essentialism is often a key ingredient in cultural imperialism,[4] an association that shows how dangerous essentialist positions can be. Yet essentialist arguments have also been embraced by some activist groups, which try to reclaim and reframe essentialist messages of oppressors: For example, women are not weak and overly emotional; they are nurturing and caring. This claim, like the one it refutes, is based on an essentialist premise. In some ways opposite of essentialism is social determinism, which argues that people are not what they are because of any innate quality of "gay-ness" or "Black-ness" or "woman-ness" or other identity markers but rather that people's identities are determined by socially and culturally prescribed designations: For example, women are emotionally expressive because that is the role prescribed for them in society. Some might describe this as the nurture perspective opposite essentialism's nature perspective. Yet, as feminist philosopher Linda Alcoff (1988) points out, neither perspective leaves room for agency, for change over time, and for other types of complexity. Similarly simplistic is a dyadic or dualistic perspective of identity: For example, a woman is either a lady or a whore. Called out and rejected by Chicana activist Gloria Anzaldúa (2007), dyadic perspectives and categorizations operate as oppressive ideologies which offer only two options: Full obedience to racist patriarchies or utter social rejection. Dyadic identities tend to be extreme and permanent, making for an effective tool of social control and oppression. In contrast to these perspectives on identity (essentialism, social determinism, dyads), positionality offers a useful tool for engaging complexly with issues of identity.

Positionality equips us to analyze the micro (i.e., the meaning of particular identity markers in particular combinations for a particular person within a particular context) within the macro-level social structure. Social structure is a multidimensional space within which members of society are positioned, and the positions stand in determinate relation to each other (Blau, 1977). As Young (2000) explains, "Structural social groups are relationally constituted in the sense that one position in structural relations does not exist apart from a differentiated relation to other positions" (p. 94). A person's position within the multidimensional social structure governs the opportunities, resources, and capital available to them, shaping numerous facets of life: For example, labor and production, desire and sexuality, rules of authority and subordination, and prestige (Young, 2000, p. 94). But it is important to note that although social structures are real in that they constrain and enable people's life chances, they are not natural in that they exist apart from the people whose choices and behaviors construct these social structures: "social structures exist only in the action and interaction of persons; they exist not as states, but as processes" (Young, 2000, p. 95). These processes, then, form a context for crafting positionality, thus influencing the meaning of particular identity markers.

Positionality allows for people to recognize, account for, and hold as true conflicting, contradictory aspects of their own identity, as well as that of others. Positionality provides a frame for understanding that, perhaps counterintuitively, many people simultaneously occupy some seemingly contradictory identities: For example, college-educated professional with mental illness and disabilities, rural Southern Christian lesbian, etc. These supposed contradictions among our identity categories create points of tension as we try to live out what it means to be supposedly contradictory things simultaneously. For example, whereas dominant perspectives may insist upon what Anzaldúa (2007) calls "an absolute despot duality that says we are able to be only one [sex] or the other," positionality accounts for complexity in which, for example, Anzaldúa (2007) occupies a both/and position, explaining, "But, I, like other queer people, am two in one body, both male and female. I am the embodiment of the hieros gamos: the coming together of opposite qualities within" (p. 41).

This "coming together of opposite qualities within" is at the heart of Anzaldúa's mestiza consciousness, which we read as a theory of positionality. She advocates for a new consciousness that breaks down dualistic thinking: A new way of seeing the world, our own position within it, and the identities of others that transform how we behave and interact. This new consciousness refuses to accept the binaries that not only sever social groups (e.g., man/woman, white/nonwhite)[5] but also place them in subject-object orientations, order them hierarchically, and strip groups of their power and humanity. The new consciousness is based on a concept of unity that is not simply the balance of opposing forces or the connection of previously severed components but rather a synthesis in which the whole is greater than the sum of its parts (pp. 101–102). She envisions this new consciousness emerging first from multiply marginalized people, those whose identity markers are not only nondominant but also clashing and contradictory. Multiply marginalized people are well positioned to develop this new consciousness because they have had to cultivate "a tolerance for contradictions, a tolerance for ambiguity" (p. 101) for their own sanity: To resolve, accept, and live out their own positionality in social contexts that prescribe categories and combinations of identity with which they do not fit.

Occupying clashing, contradictory identity markers is not easy; it can be dizzying and straining, confusing and painful. Anzaldúa (2007) speaks particularly to struggles of being mixed race:

> The ambivalence from the clash of voices results in mental and emotional states of perplexity. Internal strife results in insecurity and indecisiveness. [...] Cradled in one culture, sandwiched between two cultures, straddling all three cultures and their value systems, *la mestiza*[6] undergoes a struggle of flesh, a struggle of borders, an inner war.
>
> *(p. 100)*

And this tension emanates not only from racial identity; clashes and contradictions spark across many identity categories. For example, professor of Asian American studies Trinh Vo (2012) discusses the tensions inherent in being a tenure-track scholar and a child of immigrants. Occupying this combination of identities, she straddles cultures with conflicting norms and values: Academic culture, which requires direct and explicit self-promotion to be recognized for her accomplishments, and an ethnic and familial culture that expects humility and deference to her elders (p. 95).

In addition to allowing for contradictions, positionality also accounts for how combinations of identity markers affect meaning. For example, Anzaldúa (2007) makes it clear that to understand what it means for her to be Chicana means considering her ethnicity alongside what it means for her to be a lesbian, to be a writer and artist, to be from the Texas/Mexico border, and her identity must be contextualized within norms and myths and atrocities and beauties of the multiple cultures she navigates, rails against, and claims. Her mestiza consciousness (read as a theory of positionality) makes clear that membership in a powerful or elite social group does not neutralize the effects of one's membership in marginalized or otherwise oppressed social groups. Rather, these identity markers shape respective meaning. In other words, a privileged identity marker, such as "rich" or "famous," does not balance or cancel out all social disadvantages of less-privileged identity markers, such as "Black." Rather, each affects the meaning of the other because identity markers are not interpreted in isolation but are perceived and interpreted alongside and in light of each other. This is why positionality allows us to recognize that what it means for an unemployed man in his 20s to be Black and what it means for a famous football player in his 20s to be Black differs—and yet shares some meaning, some oppressive constraints and injustices due to shared historical and geographic context. Being attuned to positionality means recognizing that what it means to be one of the things you are—say, "professor"—is affected by other aspects of your identity such as your race, gender, age, nationality, and other factors. And for those who do not fit the normative myth of a particular identity, the fit (or lack thereof) can cause strain.

Positionality provides a lens that brings into focus some of the precarity and difficulties associated with claiming and performing identity. If the professional identity marker "professor" is associated with the racial identity marker "white" and the gender identity marker "male," then professors whose racial and/or gender identity conflicts with this normative expectation must not only fulfill official requirements for success (e.g., number of publications) but also constantly navigate murky, unspoken, and often unconscious hurdles triggered by the dissonance of their identity. And though these hurdles may be unconscious and murky, they have actual, material consequences. For example, after reviewing decades of research on student evaluations and other evaluations of academics' professional competence, professor of constitutional law Sylvia Lazos (2012) concludes,

> Unconscious stereotypical beliefs create expectations about someone before that person walks in the door. When women and minorities enter their classrooms, their students, too, have expectations about them. Their majority counterparts do not face this obstacle. As women and minority instructors labor to make their classrooms friendly and warm (so that they can get decent student evaluations), they must ponder how their conduct will be perceived by their students in the context of their gendered and raced role expectations. From the get-go, the task is daunting.
>
> *(p. 176)*

As we see, positionality places identity markers alongside each other and within broader cultural and historical contexts to demonstrate that identity has very real meanings (e.g., what does it mean to be a good teacher) with very real consequences for people's lives (e.g., garnering positive student evaluations, satisfactory annual reviews, and tenure), which are shaped by considerations of positionality (e.g., historical context, intersectionality, etc.). In the case of professorial consequences, students' bias can directly impact tenure and promotion, qualifications for teaching awards, movement up through leadership, and other measures with monetary, material consequences.

People whose combination of identity markers conflict with mythical norms often have a precarious, dangerous, and/or tense relationship with some of the social groups to which they ascribe. One example is the utter (often violent) rejection of lesbian, gay, bisexual, transgender, queer (LGBTQ) people from their racial social groups, family social groups, or community social groups: Anzaldúa (2007) explains, "As a lesbian I have no race, my own people disclaim me" (p. 102); she writes similarly about a gay man of color who is rejected, stabbed, and beaten by his "brothers." A less extreme but no-less-burdensome example is detailed by legal scholars Devon Carbado and Mito Gulati (2000). They explicate the tensions, emotional and psychological costs, and catch-22s of "outsiders" (e.g., women, people of color, gays, and other minority groups) seeking to strengthen their claim to professional identity markers (e.g., lawyer, professor, engineer). While everyone performs a "working identity" (conveying aspects of who they are as a strategy for achieving professional goals such as promotion, positive annual review, acceptance by co-workers, etc.), the psychological strain and amount of work required for individuals to perform their working identities varies not primarily by place of employment or profession but primarily by perceived fit with the qualities and characteristics that the employing organization or profession values (Carbado & Gulati, 2000). And the perceptions that count are, of course, those of people with the power to grant professional membership, increased status, or positive recognition: Disproportionately members of dominant groups.

This is where some real-life, applied implications of positionality begin to emerge. Employees whose identity markers are associated with stereotypes that conflict with values of the institution or profession must work especially hard to overcome negative default assumptions. In contrast, those employees whose identity markers are associated with stereotypes that correlate with institutional values have an advantage. Thus, what it means to be a software coder can be very different for, say, a Korean-American woman than for a cisgender white man.[7] Interplay of identity can radically affect how the same behaviors by members of the same social group (e.g., lawyers at the same firm, professors of the same rank in the same department) are interpreted, and negative stereotypes of outsiders (especially people who are multiply marginalized) often cut both ways. For example, the field of technical communication prizes technological literacy, and academic culture rewards visible scholars with international reputations. In an effort to overcome stereotypes of women as self-effacing and less technologically capable, a female tenure-line TPC professor may promote her publications, funded grants, and other accomplishments via an active, highly visible social media presence, only to be perceived as a "diva": A high-maintenance online attention seeker. An employee with a visible disability may try to dispel a stereotype of helplessness by firmly asserting his independence and self-reliance, only to be perceived as prickly and easily offended.

In the context of professional roles, performing racial identity poses challenges for employees of color not faced by white employees, particularly in institutions claiming a "colorblind" organizational culture (Carbado & Gulati, 2000). Colorblind cultures place the burden on people of color to perform their racial identity in a way that makes white people comfortable, that is, able to ignore race except in clear-cut cases of hatred and intentional harm, which can be condemned by "good" white people. How do employees of color experience the burden of colorblindness? For example, colorblindness is accorded to whites who associate with whites and to people of color who associate with whites, but not people of color who associate with each other (Carbado & Gulati, 2000). Therefore, a group of white men who regularly eat together in the faculty breakroom are seen to be reflecting the departmental value of collegiality. However, faculty women of color who go out to lunch once a month may be seen as exclusive and clique-ish: "Why isn't everyone welcome? Why do they have to have their own separate lunch meeting?"[8] These perceptions have implications for what it means to be perceived as a good employee, a collegial faculty member, a good departmental citizen, a good fit with university or department culture.

The pressure to perform racial identity in a way that makes dominant groups comfortable illustrates the reach of respectability politics (see Chapter 7). Respectability politics condemns people who do not conform to the white aesthetic and mythical norms considered to be "proper" and "respectable." Efforts to conform to these molds of respectability may include hiding or downplaying aspects of one's identity (e.g., choosing not to listen to rap music at work) and/or self-censoring (e.g., deciding not to explain why you turn down colleagues' invitation to a movie that reinscribes racial stereotypes) (Carbado & Gulati, 2000). But often respectability politics is a double-edged sword, with negative outcomes for attempting to conform to the white aesthetic *and* for refusing to do so. Case in point: Women of color wearing natural hair and African-print headwraps may be criticized for "unprofessional attire." But a woman of color in a pencil skirt (straight-cut, knee-length business skirt) is at risk of the same criticism, despite wearing the same styles as her white counterparts (see Elias, 2018). Performing racial identity in a way that is comfortable for dominant-member colleagues and supervisors can be exhausting; it is a psychological burden that is not only unshared but likely unseen entirely by members of dominant groups. So again, we see that one's specific combination of identity markers and particular contexts of action affect the meaning of identity: In these examples, what it means to occupy a particular professional role (e.g., to "be a professor").

Here, the value of positionality as a lens for justice work becomes clear. For people whose identity markers align more closely with mythical norms, what it means to be a professor may be garnering authority and respect (e.g., being called by one's title: Professor So-and-So) and enjoying more autonomy than that offered by many industry positions (e.g., selecting one's own research agenda, operating some level of control over working hours). For those whose identity markers diverge from the mythical norms, what it means to be a professor may mean being questioned ("Do you really have a doctorate?"), misidentified ("Wait, are you the professor?"), and challenged ("I'm not really sure you need to bring race into the class content, do you?").[9] The identity marker of "professor" means constant struggle against impediments large and small (read: microaggressions). And, maddeningly, these impediments are often invisible to those who don't face them. In reflecting upon this example (meaning of the identity marker "professor"), we can see connections between dissonance in identity and oppression in the form of powerlessness (Young, 1990). Powerlessness is associated with lacking status that commands respect: People are unwilling to do what a powerless person asks or to respect what she says because her authority, expertise, or influence is unrecognized or unacknowledged (p. 57). The lens of positionality can bring into focus some of the reasons multiply marginalized people may leave the academy: Why work so hard to claim and integrate an identity marker that contributes to one's powerlessness?

What It Means To "Be a Woman"

To engage in coalitional work, we must be attuned to not only our own positionality but also that of others. It is not enough to reflect upon the meaning of one's own identity but also to recognize the range of meanings across the spectrum of people within social groups. This recognition can help us to avoid unintentionally reinscribing oppression by assuming that all members of a particular group must have a similar experience: For example, "I am a woman, so I know what it means to be a woman, for heaven's sake." In fact, the identity category "woman" offers a particularly rich example to excavate for both (a) how we may reinscribe oppression by ignoring the complexities of positionality and (b) how we could coalitionally explore meanings of this identity category in an effort to center the voices and experiences of multiply marginalized members. In this section, we present some of those examples in an effort to clarify not only what positionality is but also how to use it—its relevance to the work of social justice in TPC and beyond.

The failure to consider positionality is a fatal flaw in many feminisms. For example, second-wave feminism in the U.S. in the 1960s aimed to radically transform American society to become more just and less oppressive to women, refusing to accept the low-bar goal of equality with men and instead insisting upon revolutionizing the country's social structure. Ironically, though, the failure to consider positionality crafted this feminist movement into yet another tool of oppression. As hooks (2000) recounts, this is because the white women who claimed leadership of the movement, such as Betty Friedan, cast their own experiences as those of all women, making "her plight and the plight of white women like herself synonymous with a condition affecting all American women" (p. 2). In equating white women's experience with all women's experience, white female activists obscured how they themselves reinscribed systems of oppression such as classism, racism, and, yes, even sexism (hooks, 2000). We see in this example the dangers of social justice efforts that are not intersectional. This form of feminism not only blocked women positioned more marginally in society from moving toward the center but also obscured this move by pretending not to be complicit in oppression, even while erasing the struggles, perspectives, and priorities of women of color:

> The hierarchical pattern of race and sex relationships already established in American society merely took a different form under "feminism": the form of women being classed as an oppressed group under affirmative action programs further perpetuating the myth that the social status of all women in America is the same; the form of women's studies programs being established with all-white faculty teaching literature almost exclusively by white women about white women and frequently from racist perspectives; the form of white women writing books that purport to be about the experience of American women when in fact they concentrate solely on the experience of white women; and finally the form of endless argument and debate as to whether or not racism was a feminist issue.
>
> (hooks, 1981, pp. 121–122)

In this way, second-wave feminism crafted an oppressive legacy that obscured other factors affecting the meaning of "woman" and the range and extent of how sexism oppresses individual members of this social group.

Positionality is a versatile lens for bringing injustice into focus. The example of second-wave feminism illustrates injustices caused by denying differences of positionality. Positionality also allows us to identify the injustice of victim blaming when the same patterns of behavior are interpreted differently depending on the actors' identity markers. Consider, for example, scholarly interpretations of history in which both Black 19th century women and white 19th century women occupied a dominant role in their respective homes. According to hooks (1981), many historians have blamed the "domineering Black woman" (p. 46) for emasculating Black men and therefore unraveling the fabric of Black families by taking up the dominant role in their domestic households. This interpretation ignores the responsibility of white racism and the legacy of slavery for their devastating effects on Black families, placing the blame squarely on multiply marginalized people. In contrast, white women in this period also occupied dominant domestic roles and yet were not accused of emasculating white men, despite an uptick in white men's violent efforts to cement their social control, as demonstrated, for example, by the founding of the KKK in this period. Historians recognize that white patriarchy flourished in the 19th century home and beyond. Summarizing the injustice (and illogic!) of these disparate interpretations, hooks (1981) concludes,

> It is safe to say that if white women playing a dominant role in the 19th century domestic household did not lead to the de-masculinization and undermining of white male power, the enslaved Black woman playing a dominant role in the slave household represented no threat to the already powerless Black male.
>
> *(p. 46)*

What can help us recognize the injustice of these inconsistent interpretations? Positionality. Viewing these interpretations of history through the lens of positionality allows us to see that the meaning historians ascribed to occupying a dominant role in one's household differed based on the race of the women in this role—despite their shared gender, geography, and historical context.

Honing in on the identity category "woman" also provides examples of intersectional listening, of coalitionally exploring meanings of "woman" in an effort to center the voices and experiences of multiply marginalized members. Listening, as an intentional rhetorical practice, can open space for recognizing both similarities and difference (see Ratcliffe, 2005; Starosta & Chen, 2000). Rather than a passive state, listening in this perspective is an actively engaged practice of co-constructing meaning across differences in identity and culture. One example of this engagement is a 2006 book by artist and Chicana activist Amalia Mesa-Bains and Black feminist writer and activist bell hooks. Formatted as a dialogue, the book presents their ruminations, their experiences, and their wisdom for the explicit purpose of countering simplistic narratives that pit people of color against each other or seek to erase their differences: "We do have differences, but our commonalities are just as strong, and they represent hope for resistance and freedom" (p. 3). This claiming of both difference and commonality, acknowledging the complexities of their own identities and the social groups of which they are a part, reveals how embracing a positional perspective of identity opens space for coalition building. It does so in part by refusing to demand that individuals must hold all perspectives, priorities, or experiences in common to join a coalition.

Intersectional listening invites a multiplicity of marginalized perspectives and identities to be centered and acknowledged, without demanding that they coincide, match, or align. For example, in her dialogue with Mesa-Bains (2006), hooks presents many pictures of what it means to be a Black woman. Her maternal grandmother was an "empress of domesticity" (p. 20): A woman deeply connected to nature who grew grapes and made her own wine; who could distinguish between 18th- and 19th-century antiques; who could not read or write; who had creativity, confidence, and power that emanated from her ability to grow living things. For her mother, what it meant to be a Black woman was in many ways counter to that of bell hooks' grandmother (Rosa Bell's mother): "Rosa Bell, my mama, represented the tyranny of modernity" (p. 19). She sought respectability and class mobility, trading the loud, expressive church of her upbringing for a more "seemly" congregation; marrying a man who had traveled internationally during his service in World War II; and imitating the image of white womanhood represented in 1950s magazines. The meanings of Black womanhood for hooks' mother and grandmother diverge and conflict in some ways with hooks' own identity as a Black woman, and her experience of womanhood shares some specific meanings and experiences with that of Mesa-Bains. For example, in reflecting upon their identities as women activists of color, both hooks and Mesa-Bains chafe against simplistic notions of identity in which one could not be both a serious activist and also a sexy, glamorous woman. Embracing the complexities of positionality, Mesa-Bains rejects the premise that identity must be seamless and harmonious:

> There is a point where our desire to be activists and advocates may clash with the clothes we're wearing or even the cars we may drive. At some point, questions may be asked. That's why tension is such an important word to me—sometimes I don't feel that the contradictions can truly be resolved.
>
> (hooks & Mesa-Bains, 2006, p. 17)

In this exchange, Mesa-Bains and hooks model intersectional listening: Embodying an openness to what it means for the other person to be a woman, an activist, an artist, a person of color. In listening to these stories of identity, we can hear both similarities and differences, harmoniously aligned experiences and discordant notes of supposedly conflicting truths which are none-the-less embodied, claimed, and lived out. Positionality makes space for these complexities of identity.

We note that gender identity is a particularly salient case because it reveals the discord between outward-facing identity markers and one's identity in reality. The term "marker,"[10] used often when discussing identity, reminds us that few navigate the world without our identities being read by others, and for many, our identities are misread. As Hannah Gadsby's *Nanette*[11] reminds us, a discord between perceived identity (as communicated through markers) and lived experience of identity often results in violence, marginalization, and other forms of oppression that challenge seemingly obvious identities, in this case gender (though it's applicable to many other aspects of identity like race, ability, and class). This risky discord requires that understandings of positionality be radically committed to intersectional listening, not merely because difference abounds but also because difference can be obscured from our initial views: The woman you're speaking with may pass for white but may be a woman of color; the woman you work with may live with a disability that is not apparent to you.

Widening our scope from a specific example of intersectional listening informed by positionality, we can perceive how positionality has informed feminist movements in the last two decades. Homogeneity serves those already at the center. Thus, for feminism to serve interests of social justice rather than reinscribe oppression, it must not only make space for difference but must acknowledge that those furthest on the margins can best see the changes that need to occur. In other words, the white, middle- and upper-class women who were at the center of second-wave feminism must work coalitionally with women of color, transgender women, women with disabilities, poor women. As hooks (2000) notes, it is through dialectical exchange and a willingness to engage in critical reflection that feminisms can actually offer coalitional avenues toward justice:

> There has been no other movement for social justice in our society that has been as self-critical as feminist movement. Feminist willingness to change direction when needed has been a major source of strength and vitality in feminist struggle. That internal critique is essential to any politics of transformation.
>
> *(p. xiii)*

Tracing out this example shows not only that what it means to "be a woman" differs in important ways in light of other identity factors (such as race and class) but also highlights how essential it is for those positioned at the center of society to be humble and willing to "change direction" by moving out of the center so people at the margins can move inward. In TPC academic programs, for example, this would involve shifting the balance of power away from tenured faculty members. To do so, programs may create graduate student advisory boards led by students who are members of underrepresented groups. These advisory boards could play a key role in not only recruiting efforts (i.e., improving programmatic diversity) but also informing curricular shifts, revealing microaggression in the classroom, and directing resources toward priorities of underrepresented stakeholders (i.e., cultivating a culture of inclusivity).

Retributive Justice: Which Identity Markers Confer Expertise?

Considerations of expertise are central to much of our work in TPC, and recent TPC scholarship has argued for broader recognition of the delegitimized expertise of many social groups: For example, mom bloggers (Petersen, 2014), women in the Peruvian Amazon (Dura, Singhal, & Elias, 2013), and nonelite Rwandan youth (Walton, 2016). Positionality can be useful for informing these broader notions of expertise: Not only equipping us to recognize the range and fluidity of meanings that identity markers confer but also to reason out implications of those meanings for perceived expertise and whose expertise can and should inform justice work.

As an extended example to illustrate the implications of expertise for justice work, consider the question, "Who has expertise relevant to informing notions of retributive justice?" As discussed in Chapter 2, retributive justice is concerned with according punishment that is appropriate to an offense, and it is this perspective of justice that primarily informs the U.S. criminal justice system. Those who first come to mind as experts in retributive justice may be those with certain professional identity markers. For example, lawyers and judges regularly consider what constitutes appropriate punishment for a particular crime as part of their jobs. Similarly, police officers are positioned by their profession to enact procedures and enforce laws relevant to retributive justice. Secondary groups with potentially relevant perspectives may include ordinary, law-abiding citizens. In considering this group's perspective of retributive justice, one may reason that this group doesn't "have an agenda" or that law-abiding citizens have "earned the right to an opinion" by contributing to society as productive members. Conventional wisdom (by definition, the wisdom of those whose positionality is considered to be conventional, i.e., aligning with mythical norms) dismisses perspectives of people who have been convicted of breaking the law. They have a biased perspective, conventional wisdom may assert, an assertion likely followed by respectability politics (see Chapter 7).

Yet digging into considerations of positionality reveals how essential it is for people occupying the marginal position of "lawbreaker" or "criminal" to shift to center, to be able to share their perspective of retributive justice as it is practiced in the U.S. and for that perspective to centrally inform reform efforts. Reflecting upon some of the factors affecting the meaning of identity—such as intersectional, historical, and situational considerations—suggests some of the ways meaning should shift. Considerations of intersectionality would reveal that racial bias informs who is prosecuted and who is imprisoned in the U.S. For example, although most drug users are white, those who are incarcerated for drug offenses are disproportionately people of color; in fact, three-fourths of those imprisoned on drug charges are Black or Latino (Alexander, 2012, p. 98). Thus, we see that the identity category race affects who is more easily labeled with the identity marker "criminal."

Considerations of historicity would reveal blatantly racist motivations and intentions underlying the laws and policies of the 1980s War on Drugs: For example, penalizing distribution of crack cocaine (associated with Black people) far more harshly than distribution of powder cocaine (associated with white people), coordinating a media blitz that publicized drug use as a crisis perpetrated by Black people (inventing tropes such as the Black woman as "crack whore" and Black children as "crack babies"), imposing unprecedented mandatory prison sentences for drug crimes including first-time offense for possession of any amount of cocaine base, and eliminating federal aid such as student loans for anyone convicted of a drug-related offense (Alexander, 2012, pp. 51–54). The War on Drugs triggered an unprecedented surge in incarceration rates, focused particularly on people of color. Thus, we see that historical contexts shape the meaning of the identity marker "criminal," creating legal structures which triggered the mass incarceration of people of color and rendered a group that is disproportionately (and intentionally) people of color to permanent second-class citizenship: Stripping them of voting rights, rendering them ineligible for student loans, and leaving them functionally unable to secure employment.

These intersectional and historical aspects of positionality suggest that people who have been convicted of a crime may themselves be victims of targeted, biased, and unfair laws and procedures. As such, they are likely to have important and credible knowledge to share about the justice system and about what should be considered fair punishment. As civil rights lawyer and activist for criminal justice reform Michelle Alexander (2012) summarizes:

> Those who have been swept within the criminal justice system know that the way the system actually works bears little resemblance to what happens on television and in the movies. Full-blown trials of guilt or innocence rarely occur; many people never even meet with an attorney; witnesses are routinely paid and coerced by the government; police regularly stop and search people for no reason whatsoever; penalties for many crimes are so severe that innocent people plead guilty, accepting plea bargains to avoid harsh mandatory sentences; and children, even as young as fourteen, are sent to adult prison.
>
> *(p. 59)*

Experiencing these injustices firsthand equips people with the most intimate and credible knowledge regarding how the justice system works and how retributive justice plays out—expertise no less important for its perceived illegitimacy. Inversion thesis, which is a central tenet of feminist standpoint theory, recognizes this expertise, claiming that people who are subject to systematic oppression and domination are "epistemically privileged in some crucial aspects" because their experiences confer knowledge lacked by those positioned more centrally and powerfully in social structures (Wylie, 2003, p. 339). In light of this expertise, those who lack it (e.g., ordinary "law-abiding"[12] citizens) should be willing to shift away from center, recognizing it is erroneous to assume that this privileged position confers legitimate, accurate knowledge (see Chapter 4). Instead, enlightened by considerations of positionality, those in dominant positions should intentionally make space for perspectives of the railroaded, the marginalized, and the powerless to centrally inform coalitional work focused on criminal justice reform. Organizations undertaking this work offer particularly rich sites of study for social justice-minded TPC scholars. For example, Jones (2012) sheds light on how the Innocence Project Northwest works coalitionally to shift dominant ideals about the functionality of the U.S. prison system and to center the stories, voices, and perspectives of the incarcerated while working to address wrongful conviction and its causes.

Positionality: Useful for Coalitional Pursuit of Social Justice

We close this chapter with three takeaways relevant to social justice work, the first of which is especially applicable to those of us who claim as one of our identity markers some variation of "technical communicator." As members of a field that is oddly difficult to define (Allen, 2004) but generally embraces goals such as conveying a clear message and supporting practical application (Pringle & Williams, 2005), we find it inspiring how Anzaldúa's writing style mirrors her message. To challenge dominant (and dominating) perspectives of identity, Anzaldúa coins a new genre, autohistoria, to tell the story she needs to tell, rejecting not just the static, staid forms of identity prescribed by traditional views but their static, staid genres as well. She critiques domination through language by writing in multiple languages. Rejecting "givens" of dominant culture, such as history as a linear timeline, Anzaldúa presents history as a winding, twisting loop that circles back on itself. She does not just tell us that identity is clashing, dynamic, complex, and ambiguous; she shows us by mixing languages and presenting what we read as a theory of positionality in poetry, essays, quotes— unapologetically crafting the tools she needs to build her message. And if this message is sometimes fragmented, not always clear, and certainly not straightforward, well, welcome to Anzaldúa's world. Her writing suggests that if she and other multiply marginalized folks must navigate myriad complexities and tensions in their everyday lives, then readers can certainly navigate them in her text.

In reflecting upon how well suited Anzaldúa's unapologetically unconventional form is to conveying and demonstrating her message, we see implications for technical communicators involved in socially just work. Specifically, that genres, word choice, research methods, visualizations, traditions, norms, and other tools of communication that are based on dominant ways of knowing and dominant notions of credibility may be insufficient for or poorly suited to some goals of social justice to which technical communicators can contribute. We need to draw upon a wider variety of traditions, writing forms, and ways of knowing to craft the messages of more socially just TPC. And, indeed, some scholars and practitioners are doing just that. For example, see Marcos Del Hierro's work on hiphop rhetoric: Using interactive free presentations to engage publics in the experience of knowledge making used by hiphop communities ("The Use of Hiphop Rhetoric," 2018). His work legitimizes nondominant knowledge, art, and meaning making and explicitly highlights the activism of youth of color.

In the final two takeaways, we summarize what the lens of positionality enables us to recognize and therefore to do in pursuit of social justice. First, positionality is a useful lens for viewing oneself. Positionality is a major factor in helping you to determine what types and amounts of power you have in particular situations, to understand your margin of maneuverability for action, and to see where and how you might be able to intervene in particular situations (see Chapter 6). And, second, positionality is also a useful lens for seeing other people more fully, more complexly, and more respectfully.

For example, positionality can be very useful for people who occupy positions of privilege to guard against appropriation and other violences of cultural imperialism. (For example, prompting reflection upon the meanings of culturally specific dress, objects, and symbols and how those meanings can be compromised and even erased by dominant appropriation.) Similarly, positionality can prevent people from unknowingly participating in exploitation by ignorantly commodifying artists, activists, writers, and other influential people of color without doing the due diligence of learning about and reflecting upon their positionality. For example, consider Frida Kahlo, one of the most widely recognized women of color artists. Her image is emblazoned on T-shirts and earrings, her artistry simplified to mere "magical realism" or "Mexican primitive," and her name taken up as a feminist icon (hooks & Mesa-Bains, 2006, pp. 30–37). This exploitation and "cultural strip-mining" (p. 36) overlooks complex psychoanalytic layers in her art and the focus on class in her activism— complexities, layers, histories, and nuances that emerge with considerations of positionality.

Viewing others, especially fellow coalition members, through the lens of positionality makes space for contradictions and tensions and strips away self-justification for imposing a simplified identity or agenda. Positionality slays casual allyship. Casually claimed allyship costs nothing of allies but drains the energy of oppressed people, who are expected to recognize, praise, and unoffensively educate their more privileged coalition members. Casual allyship wants to have it both ways: Claiming solidarity with oppressed people but also claiming the right to criticize, correct, lead, and/or "save" them: For example, claiming to sympathize with people of color regarding police brutality but opining that wealthy football players are in no position to protest due to their financially privileged position. Positionality asserts that contradictions can and do exist. One person's identity can (and usually does) include some powerful, privileged aspects of identity as well as some aspects of identity associated with oppression.

And the one set of identity markers does not negate the other; rather, their interaction affects the meaning of identity in context. Thus, a multi-millionaire can experience cultural imperialism, and a white person can experience powerlessness. Recognizing this truth can keep coalition members from making incorrect assumptions about fellow members based on oversimplification of their identities.

In conclusion, positionality contextualizes people in complex ways that allow for tension, for conflicting truths, for imperfection, for things that seem like they don't fit or can't coexist to do so. It opposes dumbing down, stripping away, simplifying, and cultural strip-mining. In so doing, positionality equips for the work of social justice by serving as a lens for self-reflection (for informing one's own action) and also as a tool that opens space for connection to others (for increasing acceptance and understanding). Positionality can help us to perceive ourselves and other people more fully; as such, it is a useful tool in coalition building.

Notes

1 This concept was introduced by scholars such as feminist philosopher Linda Alcoff and is usefully contrasted with other philosophical perspectives in her 1988 "Cultural feminism vs. Post-structuralism."

2 Note: These perspectives are not completely distinct, nor are they fully representative of every perspective on identity.

3 The connection between science and racism has been well-established by a range of scholars, including Fairchild (1991) and Gould (1996), among others, and so we don't choose to unpack it here.

4 See discussion of Eurocentrism and exceptionalism in Chapter 1.

5 Note: When at all possible, we have tried to avoid colonizing terms like "nonwhite," which lump all nondominant groups together under a label which manages to refer back to and name only the dominant group. In writing this book, we have struggled with the limitations of language, how the available terms can oppress by, for example, eradicating the Other.

6 A Latin American term for a woman of mixed race, especially Native American and Spanish.

7 People who are cisgender are those who identify with the gender identity they were assigned at birth: For example, a person assigned as female at birth who grows up to identify as a woman is cisgender.

8 For a discussion of why these dedicated spaces are necessary, see Blackwell, K. (2018). Why people of color need their own spaces. *The Arrow*. Retrieved from https://arrow-journal.org/why-people-of-color-need-spaces-without-white-people/

9 See Chapter 7 for more potential critiques, as well as ways to address those critiques and relevant readings for more information.

10 We thank disability rhetorics scholar Sean Zdenik for his insightful feedback on this term.

11 In her Netflix comedy special, *Nanette*, Gadsby shares personal experiences of homophobia and assault, including assault triggered by misinterpretation of her gender.

12 Please see the Chapter 7 discussion of respectability politics. As discussed in more detail there, everyone has broken a law at some point in their life, but only some are incarcerated and permanently hamstrung for it. So the trope of "ordinary law-abiding citizen" is just one more mythical norm perpetuating oppression.

References

Alcoff, L. (1988). Cultural feminism versus post-structuralism: The identity crisis in feminist theory. *Signs: Journal of Women in Culture and Society, 13*(3), 405–436.

Alexander, M. (2012). *The new Jim Crow: Mass incarceration in the age of colorblindness.* New York, NY: The New Press.

Allen, J. (2004). The case against defining technical writing. In J. Dubinsky (Ed.), *Teaching technical communication: Critical issues for the classroom* (pp. 67–76). Boston, MA: Bedford/St. Martin's.

Anzaldúa, G. (2007). *Borderlands, La frontera: The new mestiza* (3rd ed.). San Francisco, CA: Aunt Lute Books.

Blau, P. M. (1977). A macrosociological theory of social structure. *American Journal of Sociology, 83*(1), 26–54.

Carbado, D. W., & Gulati, M. (2000.) Working identity. *Cornell Law Review, 85,* 1259–1308.

Dura, L., Singhal, A., & Elias, E. (2013). Minga Perú's strategy for social change in the Perúvian Amazon: A rhetorical model for participatory, intercúltúral practice to advance húman rights. *Rhetoric, Professional Communication, and Globalization, 4*(1), 33–54.

Elias, P. A. (2018, March). What does dressing 'professionally' mean for women of color? The rules aren't the same for everyone. *Racked.* Retrieved from https://www.racked.com/2018/3/8/17096202/women-poc-office-dress-code-professional-attire

Fairchild, H. H. (1991). Scientific racism: The cloak of objectivity. *Journal of Social Issues, 47*(3), 101–115.

Gould, S. J. (1996). *The mismeasure of man.* WW Norton & Company.

hooks, b. (1981). *Ain't I a woman.* Boston, MA: South End Press.

hooks, b. (2000). *Feminist theory: From margin to center* (2nd ed.). Cambridge, MA: South End Press.

hooks, b., & Mesa-Bains, A. (2006). *Homegrown: Engaged cultural criticism.* Cambridge, MA: South End Press.

Jones, N. N. (2012). *Mediation, motives, and goals: Identifying the networked nature of contemporary activism* (Doctoral dissertation).

Lazos, S. (2012). Are student teaching evaluations holding back women and minorities?: The perils of "doing" gender and race in the classroom. In G. Gutiérrez y Muhs, Y. Flores Niemann, C. G. González, & A. P. Harris (Eds.) *Presumed incompetent: The intersections of race and class for women in academia* (pp. 164–185). Logan, UT: Utah State University Press.

Petersen, E. J. (2014). Redefining the workplace: The professionalization of motherhood through blogging. *Journal of Technical Writing and Communication, 44*(3), 277–296.

Pringle, K., & Williams, S. (2005). The future is the past: Has technical communication arrived as a profession? *Technical Communication, 52*(3), 361–370.

Ratcliffe, K. (2005). *Rhetorical listening: Identification, gender, whiteness.* Carbondale, IL: Southern Illinois Press.

Starosta, W. J., & Chen, G.-M. (2000). Listening across diversity in global society. In W. J. Starosta & G.-M. Chen (Eds.), *Communication and global society* (pp. 279–293). New York, NY: Peter Lang.

The use of hiphop rhetoric to combat the criminalization of black, brown, and red youth. (2018). *dailyUV.* Retrieved from https://dailyuv.com/949059/76730?utm_medium=email&utm_source=rev-pub&utm_content=/feed/949059/76730

Vo, T. (2012). Navigating the academic terrain: The racial and gender politics of elusive belonging. In G. Gutiérrez y Muhs, Y. Flores Niemann, C. G. González, & A. P. Harris (Eds.), *Presumed incompetent: The intersections of race and class for women in academia* (pp. 93–112). Logan, UT: Utah State University Press.

Walton, R. (2016). Supporting human dignity and human rights: A call to adopt the first principle of human-centered design. *Journal of Technical Writing and Communication, 46*(4), 402–426.

Wylie, A. (2003). Why standpoint matters. In Robert Figueroa & Sandra Harding (Eds.), *Science and other cultures: Issues in Philosophies of Science and Technology* (pp. 26–48). New York, NY: Routledge.

Young, I. M. (1990). *Justice and the politics of difference.* Princeton, NJ: Princeton University Press.

Young, I. M. (2000). *Inclusion and democracy.* Oxford: Oxford University Press.

4

PRIVILEGE

Introduction

Privilege is receiving unearned social, cultural, economic, and political advantages due to alignment with specific sociocultural identity markers. These markers can include race, gender, sexuality, religion, and economic status, among other things. People have privilege when their identity aligns with socially constructed assumptions about what it means to be "normal." That is, assumptions about what is normal and expected affect which individuals within society benefit and which individuals do not, which individuals have to work harder, and which individuals have to prove themselves. Those individuals who are most closely aligned with the socially constructed assumptions have an extra "edge." Where positionality allows us to understand the complexities of identity, privilege allows us to place that identity within social systems and understand the effects of that placement.

Interrogating privilege as layered, dynamic, and inherently connected to positionality (see Chapter 3) and power (see Chapter 5) is important for social justice and coalition building. A technical communication perspective that centers social justice (and an understanding of the human impact of our work, scholarship, and pedagogy) facilitates action and redresses inequities, and to that end, acknowledging privilege helps us to examine how ideas about normativity are embedded in oppressive thoughts and practices and to identify how some individuals and groups of individuals are pushed to the margins of society.

Privilege, or who is valued in a society, informs who can perceive the wholeness of how oppression functions in that society. hooks (1984) engages with the concept of privilege in terms of being at the center (more privilege) or at the margins (less privilege) of society. Those with relatively less privilege tend to perceive both the margins and the center of society because they are often on the outside peering in (think: a fishbowl). In contrast, those who have more privilege are often attuned only to the center, maintaining a separation of those at the margins and those at the center (hooks, 1984). hooks asserts that being at the margins means you are "part of the whole but outside the main body" (p. ix). Because individuals who are centered may not readily recognize or understand how others are affected by privilege, it may be difficult for the most privileged individuals and groups to notice others' oppressions (or how they are complicit in others' oppressions). For example, in academia, when men graduate students are more likely to be offered prestigious research fellowships while women graduate students are offered smaller assistantships, who notices? The men or the women in the department? Even though the women graduate students are part of the whole (i.e., members of the academic department), they are pushed to the margins. This separation sends a message that the women graduate students are valued less in the department and that men students are a better "fit" for research teams (Ahmed, 2017). It is this kind of subtle discrimination and inequity that emerges from privilege. The individuals who notice the subtlety of discrimination typically understand it because of their place at the margins. Recognizing privilege in this way shifts perspectives and challenges us to confront privilege as an important part of understanding oppression in technical and professional communication (TPC).

As a relative concept, privilege operates on a continuum, with some individuals having more privilege than others. Ahmed (2017) frames privilege as "an energy-saving device" (p. 125). She argues that more privileged individuals are not required to put forth as much effort as less privileged individuals:

> Less effort is required to be or to do. If you arrive with dubious origins, you are not expected to be there, so in getting there you have already disagreed with an expectation of who you are and what you can do, then an institution is the wrong shape; the jumper does not fit. You fidget to try to make it fit, but fidgeting shows all the more that it does not fit. [...] It wears out; you are worn down. When you try something on, you test the fit of a garment. Something is trying when it is subject to strain. No wonder: not to inherit privilege is trying. It can be trying to embody diversity. Your body becomes a performance indicator. You become a tick in a box. You might be one of this many students from working-class backgrounds who get into the university; one of this many people of color hired by the university; one of this many women in senior positions; one of this many students or staff with disabilities.
>
> *(p. 126)*

Ahmed makes it clear that those individuals with identity markers (embodied, material, social, cultural, and economic) that are considered the default benefit from their standing in society. This societal positioning serves as a tangible marker for who has privilege and who does not have privilege. In this way, privilege is tied very closely to positionality and power—and yet is distinct from them. As McIntosh (2009) notes, "Privilege confers dominance, gives permission to control, because of one's race or sex…Moreover, though 'privilege' may confer power, it does not confer moral strength" (p. 14). Those in power do not necessarily hold the concerns of others as important. Further, since those in power are often concerned primarily with protecting their power, the ways power is wielded—and who wields that power—may shift and change. What is normal, what is expected, shifts and changes as well. As such, the default assumptions interwoven in a society's fabric—and upon which privilege is based—are fluid and dynamic; they can change across cultures, across generations, across geographical borders, and over time. The instability of privilege can make it difficult to pin down and discuss, but it functions as a fundamental concept for understanding TPC's role in oppressive structures and our potential for intervening in injustices.

Understanding privilege, for example, provides insight into the ways that technology prioritizes particular users and in so doing, particular perspectives of the world; understanding privilege can help refocus our energies in design scenarios. Those upon whom more privilege is conferred—say educated, white men—may not realize that their designs reflect their privilege. But, as Rose, Björling, Kim, and Alvarez (2018) remind us, our responsibility as UX designers is to recognize and acknowledge that particular designs prioritize and privilege particular people and that, as such, these designs can function as exclusionary sites of injustice. This chapter explores privilege as a phenomenon that can help us understand injustices more fully; in doing so, it provides an additional framework for understanding the potential for redressing inequities in TPC.

Understanding Privilege

Scholars have long been interested in how privilege shapes society and impacts individuals. Indeed, there has been a great deal of research about what privilege is and how it functions, specifically in the U.S. However, much of this research has originated from scholars who are in positions of privilege due to their sociocultural identity markers. In other words, individuals at the center have theorized about what it must be like to be an individual or group at the margins. And, while scholars have examined privilege through theoretical frameworks like critical race theory, we have yet to see this work foregrounded in TPC. In our experience, research grounded in minority perspectives by marginalized individuals is often simply pushed aside as "race work" or social justice work—which, to some scholars, falls outside of TPC disciplinary boundaries (if this strikes you as untrue, or you're interested in why we say this, see Chapter 7). To this end, we push back against theories and conceptualizations of privilege that, ironically, define the concept only from the perspectives of those who enjoy more privilege. Instead, we ask what might privilege be like if not conceived from a Western, white, heteronormative, ableist, patriarchal standpoint?

In this book, and in our exploration of privilege as a concept, we center the voices of underrepresented scholars who can offer us experiential orienting perspectives for broadening our knowledge about how privilege frames our ways of being and existing in the world. We call on scholars like Angela Davis, Audre Lorde, Patricia Hill Collins, and Sara Ahmed as a way of grounding the concept of privilege in a minority perspective. We include multiple voices to help us construct the theoretical framework for our understanding of privilege because we acknowledge that the minority experience is not monolithic. Further, this multivocal approach assures that our framework for understanding how privilege functions in society synthesizes rather than homogenizes experiences. This framework—a minority standpoint, a marginal standpoint—allows (and argues for) a re-envisioning of how privilege works, in tension with and in conjunction with the concepts of power and positionality. We argue that any theory of power necessarily needs a theory of positionality and privilege to undergird it—and that doing so from a marginalized perspective is one step towards decolonizing the field of TPC. Further, grounding our understanding of privilege by elevating the perspectives of the traditionally marginalized resists tendencies to negate and silence the contributions of individuals whose lived experiences matter.

In TPC, as in most academic disciplines, there is an expected and traditional canon of texts that are considered foundational. Often, the texts in these canons do not include voices of the most (and multiply) marginalized and underrepresented, even though their voices contribute to a richer, more complex, and more rigorous understanding of our scholarly field. Moving to privilege perspectives of the marginalized requires a collective action that transforms our research, service, and pedagogy. This shift is epistemological in that foregrounding the knowledge and experiences of marginalized voices does more than just acknowledge a differing perspective: It amplifies coexisting and integral ways of knowing and being in the world. Moreover, this epistemological transformation necessarily impacts how we perceive privilege in society because it pushes us to listen more carefully, respond more critically, and act more cautiously.

In TPC, this practice aligns with participatory, user-centered design—but does so more radically than is often spoken about in UX discussions. Certainly, the designer and technologist have traditionally been seen as expert when compared to the user. In response, TPC scholars have called for a shift in understanding design contexts: Listen to the user and design with them. This perspective recognizes and values the knowledge of users (an epistemological shift in the design process). But whom do we mean by "users"? Are we specifically attuned to privilege: For example, the fact that certain users' perspectives are readily accepted as true and as "relevant" to design considerations, while others' perspectives are questioned or dismissed as irrelevant or outside of scope? Incorporating considerations of privilege into UX practices, therefore, can enrich and inform existing approaches such as participatory design in ways directly relevant to social justice. From a social justice framework, understanding privilege and shifting our focus towards the multiply marginalized allows us to acknowledge and make visible already existing (coexisting) ways of making knowledge, not as "alternative" knowledges but as meaningful knowledge in and of itself. By not situating marginalized ways of understanding and making knowledge as "alternative," we hold these ways of learning and knowing not as Othered but as irreducible, as valid, as significant. This kind of epistemological shift does not allow us to cast aside marginalized voices and perspectives as unimportant; it asks us to understand. As Lorde (1984) reminds us, understanding is imperative: "What understanding begins to do is to make knowledge available for use, and that's the urgency, that's the push, that's the drive" (p. 109).

Moving beyond simplistic understanding toward knowledge making (wisdom), it becomes important to critique how we engage with ideas of privilege; it is no longer enough to simply say that TPC is not neutral—we must now articulate how privilege creates an unequal foundation for users, scholars, students, and all members of our communities. We assert that knowledge about how privilege operates must be grounded in definitions and frameworks set forth by the marginalized. Because marginalized and otherwise oppressed groups have the right to claim their own narratives and their own experiences, these groups alone can articulate the experienced-based impact that privilege (as a function of oppression) has had on the social, political, economic, and cultural landscape of our human existence. These groups are uniquely positioned as experts on privilege and the impact it has on lived experiences. Further, because privilege cannot be understood without the frame of lived experiences, it follows that privilege operates in an ontological manner, a manner that frames being—both what is and what can be.

Privilege as an Ontological Paradigm

Conceptually, privilege can be understood as an ontological paradigm. Here we ask, how do we operationalize privilege as a way of being, of existing in the world? Before we explore how privilege can be characterized as an ontological paradigm, we want to provide a foundation for understanding how we intend to use the concept of ontology in this instance. In general, ontologies are a useful lens for understanding privilege because (1) ontologies help us to identify constituent components, and (2) ontologies are shared views of reality. According to Smith and Welty (2001), philosophical ontology is defined as "the science of what is, of the kinds and structures of objects, properties, events, processes and relations in every area of reality" (para. 1). In its most basic form, ontology can be understood as a way of being or a way of understanding being, as it "investigates and charac-terises the necessary structures of reality" (Bateman, Farrar, Hois, Tenbrink, & Vierhuff, 2006, p. 9). Reflecting upon ontology makes us aware that reality is both constructed and relational. Because philosophical ontology lends itself to understanding the constituent elements of concepts, "the tools of philosophical ontology have been applied to solve practical problems, for example the nature of intellectual property" (Smith & Welty, 2001, para. 18). We adopt an ontological understanding of privilege as a way to examine what "makes up" privilege, asking how this concept of privilege (or a privileged way of being) is socially constructed and designed. In this way, privilege can be considered as an ontological frame of reference that must interrogated to do social justice work in TPC.

An ontological paradigm can be described as a shared understanding of the nature of reality, as it "focuses on nature and structure of things" (Guarino, Oberle, & Staab, 2009, pp. 2–3). Individuals or groups of individuals reach a consensus on the particular irreducible parts of a concept—that is, what makes up a specific concept, what is inherent in that concept, and the constit-uent parts of that concept (Guarino et al., 2009). Wilson (2001) expands this notion of ontology, asserting that ontology is "belief in the nature of reality" (p. 175). Of importance in the definition of ontology, a shared understanding of the nature of reality, is the idea of collectivity. It follows that ontological instantiations are akin to a shared understanding of a collectively experienced reality, a constructed framework of being in the world. Ontological thinking also assumes that ways of being are a frame of reference or framework for experience.

Although experience is constructed subjectively, experience can itself be considered from a collective standpoint. For example, scholars might ask what is the Black experience in the U.S.? However, the danger in framing experience collectively is that often the collective experience is conflated with the mono-lithic. Experience, though at times collective, is not monolithic. An emphasis on collectivity helps us to understand not only how reality is constructed but also how the subjective and layered, relative nature of privilege underscores the differences in experiential realities across individuals and groups that are based on the positions of privilege that individuals and groups occupy. This holistic view of privilege, as an ontological paradigm that is simultaneously collective, subjective, and relational, acknowledges that privilege changes, transforms, and restricts. It is dynamic and shifting but ever-present as a force that signals our placement and value in society in the continuum of marginal-ized to centered.

Ontological Instantiations of Privilege

As we have established, privilege is both socially constructed and socially maintained. Following this social basis, McIntosh (2009) argues that privilege is allowed to thrive due to five main cultural myths: Meritocracy, manifest destiny, white racelessness, monoculture, and white moral elevation:

- Meritocracy assumes that there is no such thing as structural oppression and individuals can succeed based on what they do and how they behave
- Manifest destiny alludes to the rights of whites to the lands of others (especially Indigenous people) because it is God's will
- White racelessness refers to the idea that whites do not have a race and are racially unmarked because they are "normal"
- Monoculture is the idea that American culture is monolithic and experienced by all in the same way
- White moral elevation is an internalized sense of superiority by whites (pp. 2–3)

Similarly, privilege as a way of being in the world, as an ontological paradigm, can be understood in five ways of being, or ontological instantiations:

1 Othering, difference, and individualization
2 Knowledge creation and legitimization
3 Sociocultural, material, and embodied protection
4 Questioning and critical interrogation
5 Navigating the world and educating others

These five instantiations describe the concept of privilege by exploring its constituent elements. We use the word instantiation to indicate a socially constructed but very real manifestation of privilege. In the field of computer programming, "instantiation is the creation of a real instance or particular realization of an abstraction" (https://whatis.techtarget.com/definition/instantiation). The instantiations that we explore reveal how the reality and lived experiences of marginalized and oppressed populations are in tension with the reality and lived experiences of privileged populations. The instantiations listed earlier affect both the privileged and the underprivileged, albeit in very different ways. Further, each instantiation promotes our consideration of primary guiding questions, questions that ask us to think about how we center the voices and experiences of others when we engage with the concept of privilege. These instantiations are not mutually exclusive but overlapping, intersecting, and interlocking, and neither do they represent a hierarchical ranking of oppressions and microaggressions. No one ontological instantiation is more or less important than the other. This understanding of privilege eradicates what Collins (2002) calls "additive models of oppression" (p. 18), where the oppressions of multiply marginalized individuals are considered singularly and serially—for example, considering the oppressions experienced by a Black, queer woman in terms of, first, those oppressions associated with race and, then, those oppressions associated with sexuality, rather than seeing the inter-connected, interlocking, and compounding forces of race-and-sexuality-based oppressions. Instead, we acknowledge that individuals may experience all or any combination of these instantiations of privilege in varying ways, circumstances, situations, and temporalities.

Ontological Instantiation: Othering, Difference, and Individualization

Othering is a well-studied theoretical concept (see, for example, Spivak, 1985) and provides an apt framework for understanding privilege. According to Spivak, othering is constructed along three dimensions: Power, normativity, and possession (Jensen, 2011). Jensen reviews these dimensions of othering, asserting that

- The power dimension illustrates how those in power "produc[e] the other as subordinate" (p. 64)
- The normativity dimension is "about constructing the other as pathological and morally inferior" (p. 64)
- The possession dimension "implies that knowledge and technology is the property of the powerful empirical self, not the colonial other" (p. 65)

Since Spivak's characterization of othering as a "multidimensional process," a number of scholars have taken up and critically interrogated the concept in ways that more richly engage with the sociocultural dimensions of identity formation (Jensen, 2011, p. 65). Othering happens when individuals are seen as outside of the "default" or "norm" and different from what is expected in regard to the "default" sociocultural identity marker. Lorde (1984) describes the idea that there is a normal or default identity as the mythical norm. Typically, especially in the context of a Western, patriarchal, ableist, white supremacist society, bodies that are not perceived to be or identified as heterosexual, white, male, and able-bodied are othered. Due to these assumptions about what is the norm and what is "different," individuals and groups of individuals that are othered are subjected to oppression (see Chapter 1). "Hence othering concerns the consequences of racism, sexism, class (or a combination hereof) in symbolic degradation as well as the process of identity formation related to this degradation" (Jensen, 2011, p. 65). Othering is not only about markers of difference but also how that difference is acknowledged, penalized, or ignored by others. It also sets up a dichotomy and ranks the value of certain groups of people. As Lorde (1984) expands,

> Much of western European history conditions us to see human differences in simplistic opposition to each other: dominant/subordinate, good/bad, up/down, superior/inferior. In a society where the good is

defined in terms of profit rather than in terms of human need, there must always be some group of people who, through systematized oppression, can be made to feel surplus, to occupy the place of the dehumanized inferior. Within this society, that group is made up of Black and Third World people, working-class people, older people, and women.

(p. 114)

In this way, othering and difference are central foundations of privilege because individuals who are othered have less relative privilege. Moreover, individuals who are not othered or are considered the "norm" avoid the societal consequences of being different. The more categories of the mythical norm you fit into, the more you are protected. Within the privilege framework certain categories "fit" better. Take, for instance, the different experiences of a Latinx, disabled, woman professor as she enters into a classroom to teach versus those of a white, able-bodied, man professor who might enter that same classroom. In many situations, the man professor simply "fits" better than the Latinx, able-bodied woman: fits expectations, fits with others, fits the pre-existing portrait of a professor. Fit has implications for our ability to meet pre-set expectations (without critical interrogation). Students sometimes openly question the competence of a professor who is a multiply marginalized, visibly marked minority. For example, Natasha has had, on more than one occasion, students challenge her qualifications to be in a classroom (with more than one student asking her whether or not she has a PhD and is truly a professor). This type of critical interrogation occurs because of wrongly held ideas about what a "normal" PhD-holding instructor looks like, and it reflects the ways othering and difference work to instantiate privilege.

It is important to note that difference is not a problem in and of itself, but how society responds to difference is of concern, particularly because superficial acceptance of difference as individualism muddies the water of inclusion. While our Western patriarchal society heralds individualism as positive and respected, the experience of multiply marginalized populations reveals the limits of individualism as a mechanism for addressing and embracing difference. The danger of a superficial understanding of individualism is that only certain, "safe" differences are celebrated, while other differences are condemned. For example, students of color may be welcomed into academic programs (diversity) but only if their difference is limited to skin color and does not include, say, bringing disruptive ideas of research sites and questions that reflect nondominant perspectives, alternative formats of conveying scholarship, and research-sharing priorities that focus first on communities. Where individualism might celebrate diversity of ideas in the classroom, this celebration is reserved for those from privileged positions. Embracing minority students wholly (their ways of making knowledge, their ways of communication, their activism) helps academic programs progress toward inclusion as a productive, disruptive difference; otherwise, programs risk tokenizing students, accepting them primarily or exclusively because they make the program look better. This—diversity without inclusion—is oppressive and dangerous.

Privilege acts upon difference in complex and seemingly paradoxical ways: those with privilege (or whose way of being in the world is accepted without question or aligns with default assumptions) are both visible and invisible due to their sociocultural identity markers. Those with more privilege are de facto visible because they fit the "slot" and meet the norm. Their experiences and existence are seen and valued. Yet, at the same time, those with more privilege are also invisible, albeit in a very different way, because they can "fly under the radar" and do not stand out in negative or disruptive ways due to their differences. In the example above, a student who aligns with the mythical norm can more easily present alternative approaches without being seen as disruptive; rather he may be seen as an individual or innovative scholar. Importantly, those with privilege can render invisible the difference of needs, strengths, and wholeness of those unlike them, those farther removed from the mythical norm. The visibility and invisibility of difference creates the structure for privilege, particularly as privilege is constituted by the mythical norm.

In terms of race, one potential difference, whiteness, is not marked and is primarily "underexamined" (Haas, 2012, p. 284). This is true for other sociocultural identity markers that are considered to be the "norm": Male, heterosexual, able-bodied. For example, consider a white man shopping in a high-end department store who is acknowledged and left alone to browse versus a Black woman in the same high-end department store who is followed and watched with suspicion. In addition, differences may be invisible to others and yet still held against you: For example, people with physical or mental disabilities; people who are neurodiverse or neurodivergent; or people who can "pass" as other races, ethnicities, sexualities, or genders. Privilege manifests, for example, in questions like "Why are you not able to go to X meeting?", which becomes "Everyone else can go. Why can't you?" or "I could go. Why can't you?" This interrogation of difference results in marginalization of individuals and groups—one of the faces of oppression—and can easily creep into our organizational and communicative habits, functioning to marginalize those members of our organizations with less privilege. This marginalization, a refusal to center those who do not adhere to society's idea of what is normal, as well as groups that are "othered," also tracks to the idea of relative privilege within oppressed groups. That is, individuals who are part of an oppressed group may be further oppressed within their own group depending on intersecting sociocultural identity markers. For example, a Latinx transgender woman may be othered within the Latinx community due to her gender identity. And so, privilege is tricky and requires an intersectional approach to understanding its instantiations.

In summation, interrogating privilege requires that we address how difference can be ignored (marginalization). To help us think through how privilege engages with and creates experiences of being othered (or othering) and of being labeled different, we can ask ourselves the following guiding questions:

* Who is othered?
* How (in what ways) is difference celebrated or denounced?
* Whom does individualization benefit or harm?

Ontological Instantiation: Knowledge Creation and Legitimization

Another way that privilege manifests is through knowledge creation and knowledge legitimization. In other words, whose knowledge and the types of knowledge we value are grounded in ideas about whom society values and whose experiences society normalizes. Again, Lorde's concept of the mythical norm as privilege applies here because those who are most closely aligned with society's norms have their knowledge and their ways of making meaning acknowledged and validated. In other words, privilege is instantiated epistemologically.

Western, patriarchal approaches to knowledge and meaning making gathered under the umbrella of research often leave out the perspectives of the oppressed and less privileged. In *Research is Ceremony*, Wilson (2009) notes that what counts as research and, even more, what counts as ethical research (the right way to do research), is dictated by a hegemonic demographic: White men. In other words, the most privileged make the rules about what research is, how research is conducted, what is considered knowledge, and how knowledge is created and legitimized. Further, Smith explains the troublesome connections between colonization, imperialism, and research: "The term 'research' is linked to European imperialism and colonialism" (Smith, Introduction). Even normalized knowledge-making processes are flawed and grounded in systems of oppression—for example, the idea that you can observe and study other cultures to develop interventions to "improve" that culture. We have witnessed this type of "research" often in relation to medical birth control and contraceptive measures for minority women.

This approach to knowledge making (i.e., Western notions of research) not only makes assumptions that certain ways of knowing are more valuable but also that only certain ways of knowing—privileged ways of knowing—are valid. "This assumption implies that communities that did not practice western science historically lack a legitimate means of knowledge production worthy of recognition in decision making that impacts their own lives" (Jolivétte, 2015, p. xviii). Because their knowledge is not valued and does not align with more privileged forms of knowledge making, oppressed and marginalized communities are effectively shut out of making their own meanings about their own lives and experiences. Instead, meaning and "legitimized" knowledge are forced onto them by those outside of their own communities: For example, Native scholars, such as Wilson (2009), have been taught Native Studies by white men and women who relied on academic research by white men and women that reflected only white ways of learning and knowing (pp. 18–19).

Fundamentally, those with more privilege are able to validate their own ways of learning and meaning making, relaying and passing on knowledge in ways that prevent those with relatively less privilege from claiming what they know and what they have learned as knowledge. Often, this invalidation is tied to how knowledge is acquired and developed. For instance, when TPC scholars argue that knowledge is tied primarily to numbers and quantitative data, they privilege a way of knowing that can run contrary to how minority communities learn and know. Rather than excluding these knowledges, TPC scholars can and should acknowledge that minority communities have their own valuable ways of learning and knowing that serve as integral parts of the communities' existence. For example, a womanist epistemology argues that there is a clear "interdependence of experience, consciousness, and action" as a way of learning and knowing (Banks-Wallace, 2000, p. 316). Where some TPC scholars might argue that experience, stories, or action do not constitute knowledge (much less theory or data), others have highlighted experience and stories as legitimate approaches to knowledge making. For example, Sauer (1993) explored how women's knowledge about the dangers of mining represented a type of knowledge that was not considered "expertise." Women's testimonies emphasized what Sauer noted as the women's unique standards for determining danger and risk in the mines: "domestic evidence" (i.e., the amount of dust clogging a household washing machine) (p. 74). This example illustrates how experience is indeed knowledge, just as valid as numbers and statistics.

We often see this discounting of experiential knowledge in the academy, even within the field of TPC. Arguments that scholarship should be more "data-driven," "empirical," or "generalizable" are quite often thinly veiled ways of countering research methods and practices that have been invalidated because they venture too far afield of white, Western, patriarchal methods and practices. And the policing of qualitative scholarship using terms like "validity" and "replicability" do similar harm. In other words, we fail to acknowledge and value research and research methods that fall outside of the version of history that has been told by colonizers and dominant groups. For example, Haas's (2007) work presents a "counterstory" about the Western "discovery" of hypertext (p. 77). She explains how wampum belts are hypertext, demonstrating the need for challenging colonial ways of learning and knowing and dismantling oppressive ideals about knowledge making, intellectual contributions, and histories of "progress" and "innovation." Similarly, Mukavetz (2014) argues for research practices that are "rooted in indigenous and decolonial knowledges" (p. 121). Scholars like Haas and Mukavetz understand that Indigenous research practices and methods are developed, understood, and founded in Indigenous perspectives, perspectives that have not only been devalued but also too often erased. Jolivétte (2015) asserts that "all methods of producing the building blocks of our own worldview and realties must be recognized as equally valuable and relevant, if not critical, on a par with those validated and accepted in dominant institutions" (p. xviii). This assertion does not mean, as Mukavetz notes, that a scholar must be Native or "work with native peoples" (p. 121). It also does not mean that a scholar must be a minority. It simply means that scholars must value ways of learning and knowing beyond their own and challenge complicity in oppressive intellectual practices. And, importantly, more privileged scholars should take care to center perspectives of the marginalized.

In short, privilege takes for granted that the ways that one makes knowledge and meaning will be accepted and validated. Those with relatively less privilege must work harder to convince others of the validity of their arguments and the veracity of their lived experiences as legitimate ways of learning and knowing. When we consider privilege as epistemologically instantiated, we can ask ourselves these questions:

- What is characterized as research and what is invalidated as research?
- Whose knowledge is legitimized?
- What ways of knowledge creation are seen as legitimate?

Ontological Instantiation: Sociocultural, Material, and Embodied Protection

Privilege is inextricably tied to sociocultural identity markers in addition to ways of knowing because some individuals are protected (institutionally, societally, judicially) and others are less so. Specifically, how we are marked by our gender, sexuality, race, economic class, religion, body size, abilities, and other factors affects who is protected from marginalization, disempowerment, silencing, exploitation, and other oppressions (see Chapter 7). Moreover, these sociocultural identity markers affect lived experiences, increasing or decreasing opportunities to succeed within society (including who has access to quality education, well-paying jobs, transportation, and even healthy food, clean water, and effective medical care). In other words, privilege is not simply a socially constructed concept. Privilege manifests in material, tangible, and embodied ways. The more privileged are often more protected from societal ills and are insulated from various economic, cultural, political, and embodied harms.

One way we can understand how privilege protects in the U.S. is through the lens of crime and law. Consider, for instance, Angela Davis's (2012) critique of former President Clinton's crime bills, which focus on "victims of crimes" (often symbolized as white women and children) and draw on the rhetoric of Black men as perpetrators: "a black, male rapist and murderer of a white woman" (p. 24). As Davis (2012) notes, the "socially constructed fear of crime in the national imagination" is the image of a Black man (p. 24). Davis urges us to "read the racial codes embedded in the discourse around the crime bill" (p. 25):

> Intentionally making no direct allusions to race, Clinton employs a rhetoric that focuses on victims of crime. The quintessential contemporary victim is the white girlchild Polly Klaas.[1] Please don't misunderstand me. Her murder was horrible, and I convey my sympathy to her parents. What I criticize is the rhetorical manipulation of her image as a crime victim. Clinton constantly has evoked Polly Klaas, and did so in the aftermath of the initial stalling of the crime bill. Although the suspect in the Polly Klass case is a white man, there is enough socially constructed fear of crime entangled in the national imagination with the fear of black men that Richard Allen Davis, the white suspect becomes an anomaly perceived as one white face representing a sea of black men who, in the collective mind's eye, comprise the criminal element.
>
> *(Davis, 2012, p. 24)*

At its foundation, Davis's analysis emphasizes how Black men, when contrasted with white women and children, are less protected in the criminal justice system (and in fact are often characterized as the demographic that the U.S. criminal justice system protects others from) and thus often experience treatment that criminalizes them simply based on their race and gender. Where Tamir Rice can be gunned down in a park because of a toy gun; Dylann Roof, protected by his privilege, can be taken away in handcuffs and offered a fastfood stop on his commute to prison. In examples like these, we understand that the demographic with relatively more privilege (by and large, white men) makes the laws about who should be protected and whom society needs to be protected from. Further, because of this rhetorical positioning of Black men as criminals, Black men experience higher rates of incarceration, police brutality, state-sanctioned murder, and capital punishment (Thurau & Wald, 2018).

Aligning certain less-privileged groups with "deviant" behaviors (e.g., calling out entire groups of people as criminals, promiscuous, prone to anger, unintelligent) clearly has a negative impact on the lived experiences of already-marginalized groups. In the same vein, this rhetorical devaluing of groups also provides the more privileged with protections, including protection from scrutiny and protection from being assumed to fit stereotypes of an entire minority group (e.g., all Asians are good at math, all gay men are into fashion, all Latinas are fiery). When Stephen Paddock, a white man, committed mass murder in Las Vegas, NV, in late 2017, social justice activist Shaun King noted that, despite the crime Paddock committed, he was not scrutinized or named a terrorist, largely due to his race and gender. If a minority, particularly a Muslim

American, had committed the same crime, they would have been labeled a terrorist, and many would have drawn parallels between the individual and their race, gender, and/or religious affiliation. King (2017) asserts,

> What we are witnessing is the blatant fact that white privilege protects even Stephen Paddock, an alleged mass murderer, not just from being called a terrorist, but from the anger, rage, hellfire, and fury that would surely rain down if he were almost anyone other than a white man. His skin protects him. It also prevents our nation from having an honest conversation about why so many white men do what he did, and why this nation seems absolutely determined to do next to nothing about it.
>
> *(https://theintercept.com/2017/10/02/*
> *lone-wolf-white-privlege-las-vegas-stephen-paddock/)*

Even as we understand the implications of privilege as protection from a legal and political perspective, there are numerous mundane examples of how privilege functions as protection from oppression. These protections affect even commonplace, everyday activities, including shopping in a market or applying for a job. Take, for instance, Austin Channing Brown's (2018) parents' explanation for why they named her, a Black woman, "Austin." When Brown asks her mother why she'd selected the name Austin, her mom replies,

> We knew that anyone who saw it [the name Austin] before meeting you would assume you are a white man. One day you will have to apply for jobs. We just wanted to make sure that you could make it to the interview.
>
> *(p. 15)*

As Brown notes, her parents' awareness of how privilege protects in sociocultural, material, and embodied ways led them to try to extend that protection to their child by bestowing upon her the "cultural cash of a white, male name" (p. 23). Additionally, the material protections of privilege extend even to basic human needs. For example, the water crisis in Flint, MI, exemplifies how a city that is majority Black and poor (i.e., lacking racial and class privilege) struggled to have city and state officials acknowledge the harmful levels of lead in the water system. Flint's residents were ignored and silenced during and after the water crisis, while city officials attempted to hide that the water was not safe (https://www.independent.co.uk/news/world/americas/flint-water-crisis-michigan-racism-city-mayor-karen-weaver-police-a8369981.html). Even more disturbing, the residents remain without clean water at the time of this writing (nearly four years after they were exposed to lead and other contaminants in the water supply).

Quite simply: Privilege protects. The privileged are most often those heard, protected, and defended. When we consider privilege as instantiated as socio-cultural, material, and embodied protection, we can ask ourselves: Who is protected, and who is not?

Ontological Instantiation: Questioning and Critical Interrogation

Those with relatively more privilege often struggle to acknowledge that the lived experiences of those with relatively less privilege may differ greatly from their own, and part of our argument in this chapter is that critical awareness of one's own privilege is necessary for social justice work in TPC. When a critical awareness is absent, some may view the experiences of the less privileged with suspicion. This suspicion manifests when a privileged person questions the validity of others' claims about what it means, how it feels, and how it affects them to move through the world with less privilege. In other words, those most impacted by marginalization, discrimination, and other forms of injustice are questioned and interrogated, even asked to "prove" that they have experienced oppression or to justify certain behaviors or attitudes. This questioning and critical interrogation can manifest in two specific ways: Proof/evidence questionings and normative/deviant questionings.

Proof/evidence questioning occurs when the less privileged are asked (usually by those with more privilege) to prove that they have been impacted by or experience(d) oppression. One prominent example of this type of questioning is commonly called "playing the race card." Colloquially, "playing the race card" refers to using someone using race to justify their actions or beliefs when race is not perceived to be relevant to a situation or issue. We typically see this term used in a manner that delegitimizes claims that someone has experienced bias due to their race (e.g., the claim that John played the race card by arguing that he was passed over for the job because he is Black). The lived experience of the individual experiencing racism is quite directly called out as incorrect, inaccurate, a misunderstanding. The phrase "race card" is a metaphor that "attempts to discredit any racialized suffering that can be turned to advantage now that colorblindness is supposedly in effect" (Williams, 2002, p. 4). By deploying this term, people reveal their underlying assumption that race does not matter and demands further evidence of wrongdoing. Dei, Karumanchery, and Karumanchery-Luik (2004) argue that the race card metaphor indeed functions as a rhetorical device with the sole purpose of delegitimizing claims of racism and injustice. When one is accused of "playing the race card," the onus is put on the accused to then prove or provide evidence that race was truly at play and that it was not a figment of the accused's imagination (when the accused is told, "You are being too sensitive"). Accusing someone of "playing the race card" assumes a certain strategic, nefarious motivation for a person who claims to experience racism, and this metaphor reframes racism and racial discrimination as a game (not reality) with winners or losers (Dei, Karumanchery, and Karumanchery-Luik, 2004). Instead, people accused of playing the race card are accused of using their claims of racism as a way of leveraging some material, social, political, or economic reparation. This rhetorical move trivializes the effects of racism on lived experiences, forcing those impacted by such discrimination to prove that their claims of racism are not a tool that they are just using to get ahead.

Questioning and critical interrogation in the form of asking for proof of discrimination requires those most harmed to do the work of defending themselves. Further, experience is rarely accepted as valid proof in these instances: Simply arguing that there is bias or that discrimination was experienced is never enough. We see here that the request for evidence and proof has clear ties to privilege via knowledge legitimization (discussed earlier in this chapter). It asks, how can you know that what was experienced was oppression? Moreover, when an answer is received, those who lack relative privilege often find that their knowledge is not respected or recognized. This is the basis of the recent #metoo movement, wherein women have built collective knowledge to withstand the white male privilege that constructs the criminal justice system. Those who are relatively less privileged, who encounter bias and discrimination on a regular basis, have necessarily learned to cope with inequity and inequality and are the true "experts" in oppression. Yet, these marginalized groups are the very ones whose "expertise" is being questioned.

Another way questioning and critical interrogation manifests is through ideals about what is normative and what is deviant. Normative/deviant questioning occurs when those with more privilege question people, behaviors, beliefs, and attitudes that are seen to be outside of the accepted "norm." Someone may ask, for example, "Why would a man paint his nails red?" Or even "Why is he so fat? I'm concerned for his health." This type of questioning can be more insidious (and considered a microaggression) when it is couched as curiosity or concern rather than blatant discrimination. Critical interrogation only masquerades as curiosity and concern ("wanting to understand" or "inviting another perspective"). In actuality, the person posing the questions is asking the Other to provide justification for deviating from the norm. To draw on Lorde's mythical norm, the questioner is concerned that the Other is not white enough, male enough, heterosexual enough, financially secure enough, lean enough, etc. Rather than accepting the Other for who they are, the questioner interrogates the Other's very existence by being critical of the way that the Other experiences and engages with the world around them. Privilege reifies norms and allows innocent queries about any deviation from those norms.

The need or obligation to provide proof or evidence of oppression and the responsibility of justifying one's way of life forces an undue burden, a need to defend one's existence, on oppressed and multiply marginalized groups: "This is how racism works: it blocks the possibility of living an undefended life" (Laird,

2015). This is, similarly, the case for other types of oppression and discrimination: sexism, ableism, heteronormativity, and so on. When we consider the privilege of questioning and critical interrogating others, we must ask ourselves:

- Whose perspectives and experiences are questioned, interrogated, and criticized?
- Who must defend and justify their existence?

Ontological Instantiation: Navigating the World and Educating Others

Privilege allows some individuals to live a life unburdened by the obligation to justify their existence and to navigate a world designed for and dictated by a group of which you are a member; those without that privilege face undue demands of personal responsibility in a world designed without them in mind. Following Ahmed (2017), we might think about this as strain: a strain on the body, a strain on emotional and mental health, a strain on our families. Ahmed (2017) likens the struggle to manage one's own existence against dominant ideals and norms to wearing an ill-fitting garment: The less one matches the dominant model, the worse the fit and greater the strain. "Something is trying when it is subject to strain. No wonder: not to inherit privilege is strain" (p. 126). She further notes that embodying your own diversity (p. 126) and being questioned about your existence as a minority is strain (e.g., being questioned about whether she, as a marked minority, is really a professor). She notes that when questioned about your identity, "You have to make a declarative statement," and, even more, "you might have to continue making that statement" (p. 127). In this way, the marginalized must prove over and over again that they belong. They have to state that they have the right to be and to exist as they are. The privileged, in contrast, are not responsible for justifying their existence. This obligation, this strain, falls on the shoulders of the already oppressed (see Chapter 7). Being called to explain experiences, beliefs, and ways of life becomes another jab at the marginalized as they move throughout the world, requiring them to gird themselves against continuous critique. It becomes an existential responsibility for the marginalized to validate themselves and then, in turn, to make evident this validation to those around them. It's like having a badge checked at the door to gain admission while the privileged blithely sail through. Lorde (1984) explains that, "Traditionally, in American society, it is the members of oppressed, objectified groups who are expected to stretch out and bridge the gap between the actualities of our lives and the consciousness of our oppressor" (p. 114). Privilege is not needing to bridge that gap.

Because the world is designed for particular groups, systematically oppressed groups must do the extra work, learning not only to navigate a world that is structured by oppression but also mitigating their own oppression by altering who they are or how they navigate the world around them. For example, in the context of racial marginalization, racial minorities must know and be familiar with white culture and whiteness. This knowing is their obligation, while white people do not have to, unless they choose to, develop an understanding of any cultural, racial, or ethnic group outside of their own before they can move through spaces and places crafted for whiteness—in fact, white folks who do know nondominant traditions often expect to be celebrated and acknowledged by minority groups. The same holds true for other minorities. Consider, for example, how most spaces and places are designed with able-bodied folks in mind. It then becomes the responsibility of those with disabilities to figure out how to navigate the space and/or communicate the lack of accommodations. They must do extra work to be in the space. Another example of how this ontological paradigm of privilege manifests is in the way groups are challenged to use language. Consider the October 2018 example of a white woman verbally attacking two women for speaking Spanish to one another as they shopped in a store in Colorado (https://www.cnn.com/2018/10/05/us/colorado-woman-defends-two-friends-speaking-spanish-trnd/index.html). The lack of linguistic privilege, along with the implied intersecting racial difference, marked them as Other, triggering abuse that questioned their right to exist in that space. This example illustrates one way that strain manifests for minorities and the marginalized who are expected to mold themselves to fit an idealized (read: white, Western, heteronormative, patriarchal, "neurotypical", and able-bodied) existence. Lorde (1984) reminds us that

> in order to survive, those of us for whom oppression is as American as apple pie have always had to be watchers, to become familiar with the language and manners of the oppressor, even sometimes adopting them for some illusion of protection.
>
> *(p. 114)*

In addition to holding the marginalized responsible for managing and mitigating their own oppression, privilege also assumes that the marginalized are obligated to educate others about oppression. When privileged allies, well-meaning liberals, and individuals who identify as social progressives become aware of oppression and injustice, too often these groups rely on the marginalized to explain what privilege is and how it functions. The oppressed are tasked with explaining how and why you should not disadvantage people, as the burden to reveal privilege falls to those who lack it. For instance, consider safe spaces for minority groups. The minorities that the spaces are created to protect are questioned about their motivations for creating such spaces, chided for the "exclusionary" and "gatekeeping" implications of such spaces, and interrogated about the need for such spaces (see Chapter 7). The very groups that the spaces are created for must educate, inform, and explain to others (even those who have self-identified as allies) why marginalized groups need safe spaces to exist without questioning and without critique. These groups must take on the responsibility to call out the oppression, create spaces free from said oppression, and then defend the spaces that they created from claims of exclusion and discrimination.[2] How exhausting! Lorde (1984) notes that fighting against oppression for marginalized folks is a "constant drain of energy" (p. 115); inheriting less privilege requires more mental, physical, economic, and emotional energy.

When we critically address the burden of a responsibility to justify and validate one's own existence and right to simply be, we ask,

- Who must expend their energy?
- Who must experience strain to be in different spaces and places?
- Most importantly, who is expected to shoulder the responsibility for recognizing, revealing, rejecting, and replacing oppression?

Conclusion

Here's the thing about privilege: It impacts everyone. Those who are most privileged very rarely recognize the effect that privilege has on their lives; their experiences; and how they view, understand, and exist in the world. However, those with relatively less privilege, and especially those of us who are multiply marginalized (e.g., myself: A fat Black woman), are keenly aware of how privilege informs our ways of being in this world. Privilege allows one group of people to be easily believed, valued, unquestioned, protected, and unburdened by the responsibility of justifying who they are and how they are. Those of us farther from Lorde's mythical norm—

The Black, Latinx, Hispanic, Asian, Indigenous folx
The fat, obese, curvy, thick, big folx
The folx with disabilities, mental illnesses, and the neurodiverse
The women folx
The trans, gender-fluid, gender-nonconforming folx
The poor folx
The homeless folx
The atheist, agnostic, "outside" of the Judeo-Christian religious orientation folx
The immigrant folx
The gay, lesbian, bisexual, asexual, queer folx
The folx who occupy spaces between the categories above

—understand that privilege veils oppression in such a way that it is insidiously imbued in assumptions about others and the world around us, in our ontological assumptions, in our understanding of what it fundamentally means to be. It is necessary for us, as scholars, to remove the veil (Williams, 2010) of privilege that enables our complicity in oppressive practices.

As a field, TPC aspires to be a discipline uniquely attuned to the human experience. We even embed the words "human" and "experience" into our disciplinary areas of expertise (e.g., human-centered design, user experience). If we, as scholars in TPC, are truly concerned with humans and the human experience, we cannot with clear conscience say that oppression of others is outside the scope of our disciplinary domain. In fact, as a discipline that, at least in theory, has human need and human experience as a core consideration, it would be at odds with our own conceptualizations of TPC work if we members of the field failed to consider how people live in, exist, and experience the world around them. To this end, developing a more complex understanding of privilege and how privilege relates to how individuals design, interact with, and deploy texts and technologies that impact their experiences is essential to TPC scholarship and practice. We cannot, as a field, afford to ignore the ontological impact of privilege. If we were to treat privilege as an essential concept for solving problems in technical communication, what would have to shift, and what would that shift look like? We propose that such a shift could start with critically reflecting on our positionality, accounting for our privilege, and reconceiving power to illuminate how and where we can intervene in injustice through coalitional action.

Notes

1 Polly Klaas was a 12-year-old California girl who was kidnapped and killed in October 1993.
2 Lest we think this is a problem that only exists outside of TPC, one need only recall the resistance to WomeninTC both when it first began and even now, in its 6th year. Men and women alike demanded an explanation for why women would possible need a safe space to talk about their concerns; meanwhile, the 2019 luncheon drew record attendance from women in the field.

References

Ahmed, S. (2017). *Living a feminist life*. Durham, NC: Duke University Press.

Banks-Wallace, J. (2000). Womanist ways of knowing: Theoretical considerations for research with African American women. *Advances in Nursing Science, 22*(3), 33–45.

Bateman, J., Farrar, S., Hois, J., Tenbrink, T., & Vierhuff, T. (2006). *Augmenting the generalized upper model for spatial language*. Technical report, SFB/TR8 Collaborative Research Center for Spatial Cognition, Bremen, Germany.

Brown, A. C. (2018). *I'm still here: Black dignity in a world made for whiteness*. New York, NY: Convergent Books.

Collins, P. H. (2002). *Black feminist thought: Knowledge, consciousness, and the politics of empowerment*. New York, NY: Routledge.

Davis, A. Y. (2012). *The meaning of freedom: And other difficult dialogues*. San Francisco, CA: City Lights.

Dei, G. J. S., Karumanchery, L. L., & Karumanchery, N. (2004). *Playing the race card: Exposing white power and privilege* (Vol. 244). New York, NY: Peter Lang.

Guarino, N., Oberle, D., & Staab, S. (2009). What is an ontology? In S. Staab & R. Studer (Eds.), *Handbook on ontologies* (pp. 1–17). Berlin, Heidelberg: Springer.

Haas, A. M. (2007). Wampum as hypertext: An American Indian intellectual tradition of multimedia theory and practice. *Studies in American Indian Literatures, 19*(4), 77–100.

Haas, A. M. (2012). Race, rhetoric, and technology: A case study of decolonial technical communication theory, methodology, and pedagogy. *Journal of Business and Technical Communication, 26*(3), 277–310.

hooks, b. (1984). *Feminist theory: From margin to center.* Cambridge: South End Press.

Jensen, S. Q. (2011). Othering, identity formation and agency. *Qualitative Studies, 2*(2), 63–78.

Jolivétte, A. (Ed.). (2015). *Research justice: Methodologies for social change.* Bristol, UK: Policy Press.

King, S. (2017, October 2). *The white privilege of the "lone wolf" shooter.* Retrieved from: https://theintercept.com/2017/10/02/lone-wolf-white-privlege-las-vegas-stephen-paddock/

Laird, N. (2015, April 23). *A new way of writing about race.* The New York Review of Books. Retrieved from https://www.nybooks.com/articles/2015/04/23/claudia-rankine-new-way-writing-about-race/

Lorde, A. (1984). Age, race, class, and sex: Women redefining difference. In B. K. Scott, S. E. Cayleff, A. Donadey, & I. Lara (Eds.), *Women in Culture: An intersectional anthology for gender and women's studies,* (pp. 16–22). Chichester, West Sussex: John Wiley & Sons.

McIntosh, P. (2009). *White people facing race: Uncovering the myths that keep racism in place.* Retrieved from https://www.whitworth.edu/cms/media/whitworth/documents/administration/diversity-equity--inclusion/peggy-mcintosh-white-people-facing-race.pdf

Mukavetz, A. M. R. (2014). Towards a cultural rhetorics methodology: Making research matter with multi-generational women from the Little Traverse Bay Band. *Rhetoric, Professional Communication, and Globalization, 5*(1), 108–125.

Rose, E. J., Björling, E. A., Kim, A., & Alvarez, N. Y. (2018, August). Usability testing with teens: Adapting human-centered design and UX methods. In *Proceedings of the 36th ACM International Conference on the Design of Communication*, Milwaukee, WI.

Sauer, B. A. (1993). Sense and sensibility in technical documentation: How feminist interpretation strategies can save lives in the nation's mines. *Journal of Business and Technical Communication, 7*(1), 63–83.

Smith, B., & Welty, C. (2001). Ontology: Towards a new synthesis. *Formal Ontology in Information Systems, 10*(3), iii–x.

Spivak, G. C. (1985). The Rani of Sirmur: An essay in reading the archives. *History and Theory, 24*(3), 247–272.

Thurau, L. H., & Wald, J. (2018, September 14). Police killings, brutality damaging mental health of black community. *USA Today.* Retrieved from https://www.usatoday.com/story/opinion/policing/spotlight/2018/09/14/police-brutality-damaging-black-communitys-mental-health/1218566002/

Williams, L. (2002). *Playing the race card: Melodramas of black and white from Uncle Tom to OJ Simpson.* Princeton, NJ: Princeton University Press.

Williams, L. F. (2010). *Constraint of race: Legacies of white skin privilege in America.* University Park, PN: Penn State Press.

Wilson, S. (2001). What is an Indigenous research methodology? *Canadian Journal of Native Education, 25*(2), 175–179.

Wilson, S. (2009). *Research is ceremony: Indigenous research methods.* Manitoba: Fernwood.

5

POWER

In the past two chapters, we have defined, theorized, and exemplified the importance of two terms that have been generally under-discussed in technical communication: Positionality and privilege. These terms serve as the foundation for understanding this chapter, which focuses on a term well explored by technical communication scholars: Power. Power has long been theorized both within and outside of technical communication, but the purpose of this chapter is not to offer an exhaustive report on theories of power.[1] Neither is the purpose to review all the ways technical communicators have used the term power. Rather, this chapter seeks to answer this question: Given what we know about positionality and privilege, how might technical communicators conceive of power so as to address inequity, oppression, and other injustices? And what theory or theories of power help with this work?

Inherent in this question is the assumption that technical communicators need to reconceptualize power in order to do coalitional, intersectional social justice work, that coalitions and intersectionality demand a particular framework for understanding power. Indeed, we argue that an individual's positionality and privilege in any given situation helps to define and determine how power can be understood and deployed for good. In other words, while power is (of course) dynamic and shifting, the ways privilege and positionality work to shift the experiences of power and oppression help us approach toward inclusion in meaningful ways. Our approach to understanding power focuses specifically on the pursuit of justice and in so doing, challenges existing theories of power used in technical and professional communication (TPC) in a number of ways:

- In building from theories of positionality and privilege, we take the inequities produced by systems of oppression as an assumed backdrop for understanding power

- We embrace epistemologies that build theory from experience and story-telling, understanding that theories of power must take both a macro and a micro view, must tack in and out of the lives and bodies of systemically and systematically oppressed individuals in order to see the systems of oppression at work

Neither of these are in and of themselves exclusive to our approach nor completely new. But the field of TPC has yet to fully articulate the implications of oppression and experiential knowledge making on its theoretical landscape. In this chapter, we extend these implications and consult a theory of power that explicitly accounts for how power enables and constrains coalition building, social justice, and advocacy. By relying on Patricia Hill Collins, a sociologist and Black feminist theorist, we explore an approach to power that focuses specifically on redressing injustice and prompts us to shift epistemological frames as we do so.

This chapter does double duty: (1) Providing a viable theory of power for technical and professional communication (TPC) scholars who hope to enact social justice and build coalitions and (2) critiquing approaches to power that have historically not considered privilege and positionality. As such, this chapter functions as a form of institutional critique, which Porter, Sullivan, Blythe, Grabill, and Miles (2000) define as a rhetorical methodology for making change. We follow Niemann (2012), who writes that the authors included in the *Presumed Incompetent* collection deserve for their work and experiences to be theorized. In making this claim, she encourages a shift in how theory works and is made. She writes:

> A viable theory must include scrutiny of the roles of institutionalized power and privilege and societal mores, history, and values in generating and exacerbating the realities these women have lived. A theory that can serve as a foundation for change must reflect lessons from the extensive social science research on racism, sexism, classism, heterosexism, stereotypes, group dynamics, cognitive distortions and the role of socioecological forces in individual and group behavior toward members of historically underrepresented groups.
>
> *(p. 447)*

This chapter forwards a framework for power that keeps experiences of marginalized group members in view and works from those experiences. This stance shifts our framework from an idle, neutral theory of power to a theory of empowerment. Our approach to understanding power and empowerment in this chapter draws explicitly on Patricia Hill Collins's Black feminist approach to theory, eschewing forms of theory that have been privileged and valued in TPC in the past. Traditional theory making often relies on elaborate macro-level views of how the world works, rarely taking the time to tap into experiential and lived knowledges (a cornerstone of Black feminist epistemology), often privileging a sort of navel-gazing that can trap or stabilize theories and disallowing the movement from lived situations to lived theory, the kind of movement necessary if we are to work coalitionally to address injustices. Rather than mere theory, we seek a living theory that values knowledge as experiential and lived and "does not separate politics from living" (Frye ctd in Ahmed, p. 214). As we discuss in Chapter 4, we embrace the need to consider experience as a form of knowledge and work to adopt an approach to theory in TPC that is dynamic, that accommodates shifts, and that works in situ to provide a foundation for action. By privileging experience, we attempt to remove barriers between politics and living. As a Black feminist perspective acknowledges, the political is personal. Early work on power did the important work of connecting TPC to politics (Barton & Barton, 1993; Sauer, 1993; Slack, Miller, & Doak, 1993). But we also need to connect politics to living and, more specifically, TPC to living and to experiences. Few have connected lived experience to the TPC landscape. But, doing so is essential for revealing in new ways how power, privilege, positionality, and politics are connected to TPC. This book is a modest step toward making these connections explicit and moving us toward addressing the inequities revealed when these connections are illumined.

From Power to Empowerment in Technical Communication

For all its periodic appearances in the scholarship of our field, power has been under-explored and certainly under-theorized from particular viewpoints: Those of multiply marginalized people. Barton and Barton's 1993 special issue serves as a representative example of this scholarship in terms of its contributions and its shortcomings. This special issue does some very important work: It intentionally contributes to the field's understanding of power and professional communication through a range of field-relevant topics using different theories of power (Barton & Barton, 1993, p. 6). For example, Sauer's article uses feminist theory to push back against dominant, exclusionary technical discourses and epistemologies, identifying the potential value of women's ignored and discredited expertise. Slack et al. (1993) use Foucauldian and mass communication theories to frame three potential positionalities for technical communicators, each with increasingly expanded power. Katz (1993) explores relationships among Aristotelian rhetoric, praxis, ideologies, and power to frame communication breakdowns between interests of the state and its citizens regarding the location of a radioactive waste storage facility.

As a whole, the special issue rejects the myth of neutral professional communication, specifically acknowledging our field's historic connection to industry and the "power attendant to a capitalistic economy and its institutions" (Barton & Barton, 1993, p. 5). In various ways, the scholarship acknowledges complicity of our profession in oppressive structures. And this was an important step.

However, these articles, like many others in the field, fail to name structures and practices as oppressive, fail to connect TPC to systems of racism, sexism, ableism, and others in the way that Niemann (earlier) articulates. For example, Slack et al. (1993) point out that a goal (if not the goal) of organizational politics (i.e., how organizations engage in the "ongoing process of negotiating power relations," per Coole & Frost, 2010, p. 18) is to obscure how organizations actually work. But the scholarship stops short of digging into what that means: How organizations use power to obscure the way they work, from whom those processes are obscured, and the oppressive outcomes experienced by particular groups of people. Their analytical work helps us identify some problems with power relations, but nonetheless leaves those who are oppressed in the margins and maintains a veil over the most important impact of the power relations often at work in technical communication: It functions to dominate and oppress.

To engage in the work of justice, we need theories of power imbued with understandings of oppression, theories that centralize the experiences of multiply marginalized people, who are in the best position to see those oppressive structures that block empowerment (see Chapter 4). Rappaport (1987) describes empowerment as "both individual determination over one's own life and democratic participation in the life of one's community, often through mediating structures such as schools, neighborhoods, churches, and other voluntary organizations" (p. 121). In other words, empowerment is not just an individual concept, wherein a person either is empowered or is not. Rather, empowerment also signals an organizational and structural framework that enables focuses on justice as a central project. As we consider how to engage power in TPC, then, we argue that we also need theories of power that confront the various types of privilege and positionality that enable and constrain empowerment, change, and social justice.

More recently, critical theories of power, particularly as they have been used in technical communication, have provided an entry into the work we forward here. As Jones (2016) explains, "[T]echnical communication scholarship has addressed issues of power and ideology and has examined how these concepts impact how communication is created (Dragga & Voss, 2001), transformed (Slack, Miller, & Doak, 1993), and used to create rhetorical and material conditions (Scott, 2003)" (p. 346). And, indeed, some scholars have committed themselves to the kind of advocacy Jones imagines for technical communicators, moving the field toward empowerment and activism. Simmons (2008) critically examines the way power emerged in an environmental justice case to argue for shifting the processes for public decision-making. Her understanding of power, built from Foucault, provides a framework for institutional critique and rhetorical action: We can shift the ways public participation occurs if we take seriously the way processes are imbued with power. And, she argues, we should advocate for shifting power toward those who have traditionally been excluded from decision-making in order to make the process more ethical and just.

Like Simmons, we adopt theories of power so as to understand the position of those who have been excluded and marginalized; we embrace theoretical perspectives that enable the pursuit of social justice. But we do not ascribe to the belief that just any theoretical approach will do, and we are hesitant to pursue social justice with theories that don't share the priority of empowerment. "Theory does not develop out of the air," Grosz reminds us. "It is not the result of 'great ideas', 'brilliant minds', or 'astute observation'…it is the result of the interwoven and mutual defining set of relationship between one theory or discourse and many other" (p. 59). To Grosz's list, we might add that theory arises out of lived experiences as well. If, as Jones and Walton (2018) suggest, "social justice research in technical communication investigates how communication broadly defined can amplify the agency of oppressed people—those who are materially, socially, politically, and/or economically under-resourced," then any theory of power must keep systems of oppression in view in order to empower. What does that theory of power look like? What experiences and relationships ought to be brought into consideration? How do we account for power in mundane interactions and experiences, like language use, daily practices, and interpersonal relationships?

First, a theory of power that considers oppression must account for the range of systems that oppress. That is, oppression must be understood as intersectional and as constructed across a range of systems. Foucault's theory of power, much embraced in our field, helps demonstrate the ways that power functions within systems and that it need not be executed by a person. His theory of power has been fundamental to our understanding of the ways institutions and organizations maintain and enact power relations. Grabill and Simmons (1998), for example, use Foucault to argue for a field-changing articulation of risk as rhetorically constructed. They write, "Foucault also argues that by understanding the ways in which power is exercised, and looking for gaps in this system, we can work toward resisting, even altering these unequal power relations" (p. 417). We agree that Foucault has been helpful in clearing the way for some important empowerment work in the field of technical communication. But his theoretical frame has not sufficiently prepared us to grapple with the intersectional experiences of people from multiply marginalized positions. And, importantly, his theory doesn't move us to explicitly understand opportunities for redressing inequities in active ways. A theory that leads to the empowerment of those who are marginalized prioritizes activism, social action, and the demarginalization of nondominant groups.

Second, a theory of power that seeks to empower also builds from the experience of the oppressed, builds from the margins, as many Black feminists attest. If theoretical approaches are developed by those in power, they risk misunderstanding needs and contexts for TPC work; misapplying theory or solutions; or doing further damage to those at the margins. hooks (2000), for example, critiques early forms of feminism which worked to address sexism to the exclusion of other forms of oppression experienced by Black women. Because of their privilege (see Chapter 4), white women's theories of oppression were inadequate for describing and overturning systems of oppression that worked against the empowerment of Black women. hooks specifically argues that the theories of power embraced by bourgeois white women simply replicated the forms of power that built the patriarchy: Domination and control. Reconceiving theory from the margins allowed for feminists to "redefine power positively with new organizational strategies: rotating tasks, consensus, emphasis on internal democracy" (hooks, 2000, p. 90). Without a commitment to working from outside of the dominant frame, feminist movements could do little to effect change.

Noble (2018) similarly demonstrates the ways theorizing from the margins shifts our understanding of topics. As a technologist focused on strategies that will "eliminate social injustice and change the ways in which people are oppressed with the aid of allegedly neutral technologies," she analyzes and understands artificial intelligence through the lens of Black feminism, which

> challenges the dominant research on race and gender, which tends to universalize problems assigned to race or Blackness as "male" (or the problems of men) and organizes gender as primarily conceived through the lenses and experiences of White women, leaving Black women in a precarious and understudied position.
>
> *(p. 33)*

By working from the margins, Noble is able to poke holes in the seemingly neutral algorithmic rhetorics dominating search engines. Like Noble, we adopt a Black feminist approach to power because we (like Black feminists) are not attempting to shift power as the end goal; rather, the end goal of this project is to achieve equity for those who are not part of dominant groups and address the forms of oppression that emerge from practices in TPC. This goal, achieving equity, requires that we not seek to re-purpose, re-envision, or replicate power wielded by white patriarchal and hegemonic structures. Instead, this goal requires us to work arduously to avoid the pernicious pull of dominant conceptions of power that, as Lorde poetically states, threatens to "corrupt as poisonous mold" (Lorde, 1978).

In taking seriously the way privilege and positionality affect our theoretical horizons, we also suggest that our own theoretical work—for example, the work we're doing in this book—requires an openness about our goals as well as our privilege and positionality. Otherwise, we risk implying neutrality or, worse, monolithic dominance over other approaches. We work overtly from marginalized frameworks not to be neutral, monolithic, or all-encompassing, but rather to be targeted and focused on goals of advocacy and social justice.

When suggesting that we build theory from a particular position, we adopt a critical methodological approach that has been widely accepted in qualitative field methods: That our positionality and subjectivity matter to the development of a research project. This is also true as we develop epistemological approaches and theoretical perspectives. Field researchers are trained to discuss the ways their own assumptions and practices affect their research site and participants, with the assumption that no researcher is neutral and that no researcher leaves a field site unaffected (Tracy, 2012). Although field researchers are called to articulate their position and subjectivity in their methods sections (see, e.g., Powell & Takayoshi, 2012), too few theorists do the same (though Royster and Kirsh provide one excellent example we can model). It seems to us that theories (of all sorts, but particularly theories of power) in the 20th century have not "come clean," as feminist methodologists say, about their positionality. As such, they appear neutral, ontologically innocent, and applicable to all projects and all cases. But theories emerging from the proverbial center (as opposed to the margins) are not neutral[2]—especially theories of power. Theories of power are not ontologically innocent. And so we argue that there's no way to talk about power, to theorize it, from a neutral position. In order to expand our foundations for justice, we purposefully choose theories throughout this book that are developed from the margins. And we argue we ought to do the same with theories of power because those writing from privileged positions reflecting much of the mythical norm necessarily construct theory differently than those who occupy the margins. Theories of power that emerge from the margins reflect a different view of power and oppression because they assume a need to empower. This is what is needed for the project of an inclusive, socially just technical communication.

Patricia Hill Collins, Black Feminist Epistemology, and Domains of Power

Although power is theorized by a wide range of scholars of color, Patricia Hill Collins (2008) offers a Black feminist approach to understanding power that specifically pursues empowerment—indeed, her approach to empowerment grows out of her understanding of Black women's activism, which she suggests is more complex and less visible than typical approaches that tend to be identified through their location in public and political realms (pp. 217–218). Rather, Black women's activism emerges not only as a form of institutional transformation but also as a struggle for group survival; she argues that addressing oppression and systems of domination as a Black woman sometimes includes direct confrontation of oppressive structures and other times includes "strategies of everyday resistance" (p. 225). In developing a theory of power that honors both of these approaches, Collins provides us with a theory that mirrors the kinds of social justice work technical communicators are often positioned to do—advocating for lived experiences of resistance as a model for change.

Because of her overt focus on activism, Collins's theory of power provides technical communication with a way to consider new strategies and experiences of power, empowerment, and disempowerment. It is tempting, as we say in the Introduction and in Chapter 6, to believe that technical communicators committed to social justice should be able to address all forms of oppression or to openly resist all injustices at all times—and that there is a right way and a wrong way to do it. But this is not our position: Rather (like Patricia Hill Collins), we think addressing oppression can happen in small, indirect ways. For some of our colleagues—those who are first generation college students, transgender, or otherwise multiply marginalized—simply existing and persisting is a challenge to the systems of oppression around us in part because existing and persisting often requires building or supporting coalitions. Others with more privilege can and must do more to make the field and the work we do more inclusive. We consult Patricia Hill Collins's matrix of domination and theory of power to offer a framework for understanding power because it provides multiple approaches to building an inclusive form of technical communication. As in previous chapters, we deliberately and reflexively work with theories from women of color—theories that have yet to dominate the bookshelves of colleagues across the field of TPC. This citation practice honors our efforts toward inclusion as both a practice and an ideal.

When Collins offers up her theory of power, she does so in pursuit of empowerment of Black women and other multiply marginalized populations. She writes, "Rethinking Black feminism as a social justice project involves developing a complex notion of empowerment" (2008, p. 308). So, too with TPC: Rethinking TPC as a social justice project involves developing a complex notion of empowerment. The theory of power and empowerment that Collins articulates invites complexity and generative new linkages among technical communication, activism, and social justice. "Just as oppression is complex," Collins writes, "so must resistance aimed at fostering empowerment demonstrate a similar complexity" (p. 308). This is where Collins's theoretical foundation extends the important work already done by scholars in technical communication we discuss earlier. We work to build from approaches that offered a cultural studies approach to TPC. These early integrations, like *Critical Power Tools*, for example, offered important strategies that "help[ed] us and our students review technical communication as regulated by and enacted as power" (Scott, Longo, & Wills, 2007, p. 13); we now move from review and understanding to a more overt approach that resists oppressive power structures in all their complexity.

Collins's theory of Black feminist offers us vantage points from which to understand both oppression and power, one vantage point of which we address throughout this book: That power dynamics underlie what counts as knowledge. Her theory of power further explicates the other: That Black feminism requires "a fundamental paradigmatic shift in how we think about unjust power relations" (p. 291). When we consider power in this chapter, then, we aren't thinking about all power relations; rather, we are working to understand those that are unjust, unequal, or oppressive.

In *Black Feminist Thought*, Collins (2008) conceptualizes power in two ways: As a relationship between groups (where change in power results from human agency) and as shifting collection of forces (where change in power shifts in relation to an individual). "One way of approaching power," she writes, "concerns the dialectical relationship linking oppression and activism, where groups with greater power oppress those with lesser amounts" (p. 292). This "have or have not" approach highlights the way some groups have privilege and others have less, the way some can move through the world with ease and others cannot (see Chapter 4). In this view, those with less power could ostensibly gain more power or those with more power can oppress those with less power. While power might not be literally possessed (a critique waged by postmodern theorists, to be sure), this conceptualization allows for groups to articulate limited mobility and difference across social spectrums and helps reveal the relationship between oppression and resistance: Resistance and activism can shape and reshape oppression.

But this approach can also reveal competing efforts toward social change or resistance. This is a particularly important note to make for coalitional work. Theoretically, the conceptualization of power as a dialectic between oppression and activism forces coalitions to confront the problems that arise with difference of experience, both material and embodied. Indeed, as Collins describes, "[D]ialectical analyses of power point out that when it comes to social justice, groups have competing interests that often generate conflict" (p. 292). We perceive these conflicts as generative: They allow for the kinds of tensions that arise in coalition building (see Chavez, 2013) and embraces difference among coalition members. But understanding Collins's approach to power as relational also helps assuage some of the problems that in-group differences can make because it implores us to consider difference across groups and because it implores us to consider positionality and privilege.

Collins encourages us to understand the embodied, constantly shifting approach to power that emerges when we understand it as "an intangible entity that circulates within a particular matrix of domination to which individuals stand in various relationships" (p. 292). The various relationships referred to invite all of us to consider how "individual subjectivity frames human actions within a matrix of domination" and, in turn, invites both privilege and positionality to be seen as meaningful parts of power and oppression (p. 292). It isn't merely that power is distributed across networks (a theory adopted by many technical communicators) but that the constant shifting of power (sometimes brought about by activism and resistance) necessarily shapes Black women's (and we would argue all those who are marginalized) self-definition, relationships with oppression, and relationships with others.

> Because oppression is constantly changing, different aspects of an indi-
> vidual Black woman's self-dimensions intermingle and become more sa-
> lient: her gender may be more prominent when she becomes a mother, her
> race when she searches for housing, her social class when she applies for
> credit, her sexual orientation when she is walking with her lover, and her
> citizenship status when she applies for a job.
>
> *(p. 293)*

In this view of power, the relationships between systems of oppression and the
individual shift from context to context. "In all of the contexts," Collins continues, "her position in relation to and within intersecting oppression shifts" (2008,
p. 293). Not only is power itself dynamic, but so is the relationship between the
oppressed and the system of oppression. For those technical communicators
who have adopted theories of power that see it as shifting, then, Collins helps us
to realize that power analyses that overstabilize the relationships of individuals
(or that flatten out hierarchies completely) may not provide meaningful, intersectional, or coalitional approaches to social justice and change. But the good
news is that as we continue to contemplate the empowerment of others and the
establishment of coalitions, technical communicators can meaningfully engage
with the distributed system of power and seek to shift it when the distribution
of power is asymmetrical, uneven, or inequitable. But in order to do so we must
consider oppression as relational and power as always shifting.

Collins's two approaches to power acknowledge complexity, multiplicity,
tensions, and contradictions, accepting both that power relations shift across
networks and that they shift with individual subjectivity. This approach embraces and values difference. As Lorde (1984) and others have demonstrated,
differences enrich our experiences and enable an intersectional approach to
understanding feminism, lived experience, and activism. An intersectional approach developed from dialectical and relational analyses of power motivates
action and decision-making: Where oppression can be identified, so too can an
activist approach shift power and resist oppressive structures.

We find Collins's theory of power compelling and useful because she accepts
that both of these theoretical approaches to power (dialectical and relational)
have value and can be deployed for activist and empowerment ends. "Both of
these approaches remain theoretically useful because they each provide par-
tial and different perspectives on empowerment. Unfortunately, these two
views are often presented as *competing* rather than potentially *complemen-
tary* approaches" (p. 294, *emphasis original*). Her central problem with pitting
these ideas against one another is that neither helps activists and social
justice-minded scholars fully conceive of empowerment and change: "[N]either
is sufficient." We agree.

Further, we suggest that technical communicators interested in empowerment, inclusion, and coalition building should engage with power as both

a dialectical and as relational, as a dialectical system where individuals and groups can enact change and as a relational, shifting system of positionality and privilege. In our daily work as administrators, practitioners, community-based researchers, and citizens, technical communicators engage in a struggle to tack in and tack out of the systems of power and oppression that both enable and constrain their ability to work. When a community-based researcher, for example, enters into a community, Collins's nondichotomous approach to power shines a light on the need for researchers to perceive how power relations are constructed and also how power is wielded. We must ask who holds the power in this community, how power is distributed, and what is the process for shifting power. As discussed in Chapter 6, technical communicators need concrete actions that reorganize power systems so that multiply marginalized members of our communities (including our academic community) are empowered and included. The sort of tacking in and out that we suggest, drawing on Royster and Kirsch (2012), requires us to understand what Collins calls the "four interrelated domains of power…the structural, disciplinary, hegemonic, and interpersonal domains" (p. 295). These domains of power explain the ways oppression works, reveal various sites of resistance and allow us to consider intersectional coalition building, positionality, and privilege as central parts TPC.

Structural

The structural domain of power "encompasses how social institutions are organized," drawing attention to the fact that social institutions repeatedly subordinate not only Black women, which Collins focuses on, but also other members of marginalized social groups (p. 295). In other words, this domain is infrastructural. Social institutions are, in fact, built by humans, but they are developed over the course of decades with no singular control or power mechanism. As Bowker and Starr (2000) explain,

> In the past 100 years, people in all lines of work have jointly constructed an incredible, interlocking set of categories, standards, and means for interoperation infrastructural technologies. We hardly know what we have built. No one is in control of infrastructure; no one has the power centrally to change it. To the extent that we live in, on, and around this new infrastructure it helps form the shape of our moral, scientific, an esthetic choice.
>
> *(p. 319)*

The structural realm of power is often invisible and therefore seems inarguable. This is the point Noble (2018) makes as she describes the ways algorithms function to describe and create the world. Though algorithms span both structural and disciplinary domains of power (they are, after all, "loaded with power" (p. 171)), the algorithms function to transmit knowledge in a structure pre-determined by the developer as they order the world and make some versions of the world visible. If these are the only versions "retrieved" by the algorithm, then the other perspectives on the world remain invisible, hidden, and suppressed. The difficulty with this domain of power is that the undergirding ideologies of the structures and infrastructures are difficult to identify and connect. And yet, theorizing power within the structural domain requires us to acknowledge that infrastructures and organizations are imbued with values—often white supremacist and patriarchal values. As such, our policies and procedures require careful consideration and analysis that assume they reproduce existing social values. Importantly, these social values include those we specifically adopt and own up to as well as those that perniciously seep into our organizations.

In this domain of power, technical communicators must attune ourselves to the built-in and historical power relations that oppress individuals and social groups through structures that organize the world and the country. Williams (2010) provides a particularly salient example of this kind of TPC as she examines the ways Texas Black Codes maintained racially motivated forms of discrimination across the state. Even now, we can continue to see the oppressive, racist hierarchy established and maintained by those laws, which effectively structured the state's system of authority to keep Black citizens at the margins. When we begin working with the structural domain in mind, then, we look toward the ways technical communication organizes the worlds around us. Collins explains that when we work in the structural domain, we must work to address "forms of injustice that permeate the entire society [that] yield only grudgingly to change" (2008, p. 296). The difficulty of shifting structural forms means that we must work toward shifting policies and procedures but not rely exclusively on the changes in the structural domain, which is only one part of the matrix of domination.

Disciplinary

The disciplinary domain for power is closely related to the structural, but is more overtly procedural, rather than infrastructural (think how an organization runs rather than how an organization is structured). Although laws may shift, the implementation of those laws may not be so quickly enacted or, because of the disciplinary domain of power, they might not be enacted at all. Collins draws specific attention to the way power relations rely "on bureaucratic hierarchies and techniques of surveillance" (p. 289) to control individuals or groups. As such, the disciplinary domain can shift the ways technical communicators think about documentation, enrollment policies, and other forms of reporting that might unwittingly expose members of the community to undue scrutiny and function as an oppressive activity. This form of "discipline" echoes the disciplinary realms Foucault (1979) articulates in Discipline and Punish, in which he reminds us that institutions of education and jailing produce and reproduce systems of power.

In addition to educational or carceral contexts, even more seemingly harmless governmental or bureaucratic procedures function to reproduce oppression and injustice. Simmons's (2008) work in environmental justice provides a good example of this domain of power and oppression. Simmons's *Participation and Power* explored the official policy of the National Environmental Policy Act of 1970, which requires the inclusion of citizens in any major environmental decision or change. In the case she studied, a VX nerve agent needed to be disposed of and, per this policy, citizens were talked with and a number of public meetings were held. From a structural approach, this policy worked to advocate for citizen involvement. The implementation, however, functioned to further marginalize citizens and dismiss their concerns. As Simmons explains, this was a form of pseudo-participation—not the sincere participation that would ensure public safety—and potentially approved risking citizen health and safety by ignoring citizen concerns and erasing them from the official documentation. These citizens, who were already excluded from early decision-making, remained at the margins of decision making, demonstrating the way that procedures themselves can, "reproduce intersecting oppressions" in the way they're executed and/or "mask their effects" (p. 289). This case, like other environmental justice cases like the Dakota Access Pipeline, remind us that those who have more power and privilege seldom fall prey to the procedures of environmental decision-making.

For Collins, the disciplinary domain requires us to consider not only organizational processes but also surveillance practices that can harm individuals forced to engage with bureaucracies and other governmental organizations. As such, the disciplinary domain can shift the ways technical communicators think about documentation, enrollment policies, and other forms of reporting that might unwittingly expose members of the community to undue scrutiny and function as an oppressive activity. Scott (2003) offers an example of the ways technical documents—in his case HIV tests—function as a form of surveillance. Although HIV tests provided some semblance of empowerment for those tested, "[c]ase identification, especially when it involves name-based reporting, allows for various forms of institutional surveillance and regulation" (p. 52). Scott clarifies that while HIV tests provide important knowledge for the person tested, positive cases, which had to be reported to public health officials, often resulted in long-term scrutiny, surveillance, and/or being labeled high-risk. Scott's nuanced reading of HIV testing and the potential for home testing represent the kind of activist work we support—and the kind of change and empowerment that can occur when TPC members interrogate the disciplinary domain of power.

Hegemonic

The hegemonic domain of power is the most abstract because it "deals with ideology, culture, and consciousness" (Collins, 2008, p. 301). The assumptions we make about how others should behave and how the world should be structured are not developed out of our own certainty and experiences alone. Rather, our expectations are set by cultural and ideological currents that inform our understanding of the world and, in many cases, imbue our consciousness. Given that it requires technical communicators to scope out to the level of culture and ideology, this domain of power might appear the least readily accessible and pertinent to TPC. But, as Collins notes, the hegemonic domain "aims to justify practices in [the structural and disciplinary domains] of power" (p. 302). She writes, "By manipulating ideology and culture, the hegemonic domain acts as a link between social institutions (structural domain), their organizational practice (disciplinary domain), and the level of everyday social interaction (interpersonal domain)" (p. 302). Because the U.S. and most Western cultures were built on white supremacist, colonial, patriarchal values (see Chapter 7 for concerns about this claim), our work reflects and reinforces these values unless we are working specifically to resist and reform our practices.

TPC must engage with the hegemonic domain if we are to understand how we inadvertently reinforce and build oppressive structures. This domain of power reflects the important work already being done in TPC, particularly, for example, by J. Blake Scott, whose work we reference earlier. HIV home testing kits tacked in and out of the hegemonic domain to expose the ways cultural assumptions about morality and bodies imbued forms of technical communication. Explicitly considering the hegemonic domain of power can reveal normalizing assumptions of sexuality, morality, and human bodies, assumptions rooted in heteronormativity and ableism. Another example of TPC scholarship working at the hegemonic domain of power is Jennifer Sano-Franchini's (2017) examination of double eyelid surgery. She reveals how racialized experiences shift our understanding of user experience design, arguing

> that UX designers need to look beyond traditional UX methods in order to better understand race and user experience, as these methods have evidently been limited for addressing such issues. Part of this is because users are not always self-aware of the racial implications of their experiences or interactions—hence, the term "unconscious bias"—nor are they always reflexive about how race functions systemically, across large patterns of experience.
>
> (p. 34)

In contextualizing double eyelid surgery within broader cultural patterns of racism, Sano-Franchini's work reveals some of the ways power operates in the hegemonic domain.

Despite these examples, we find this domain of power under-researched and under-acknowledged in TPC, but we remain committed to understanding hegemonic power through both expanding the theoretical scope of TPC as well as the practical scope of TPC. Indeed, technical communication forms and reforms expectations for norms, bodies, and power relations.

> An all important feature of the hegemonic domain of power lies in the need to continually refashion images in order to solicit support for the U.S. matrix of domination. Not just elite group support, but the endorsement of subordinated groups is needed for hegemonic ideologies to function smoothly.
>
> *(Collins, 2008, p. 303)*

This feature of hegemonic power reminds us that one form of resistance and activism in TPC is to expand the knowledges accepted and studied within the field. As we discuss later, we can and should adopt a wider view of knowledge including lived experiences, embodied knowledge, and narrative/storytelling approaches. This work opens up technical communicators to studying the hegemonic domain of power, reminding us that traditional boundaries of TPC limit our ability to address structural and disciplinary power systems.

Interpersonal

The interpersonal domain

> operates by seducing, pressuring, or forcing African American women, members of subordinated groups, and all individuals to replace individual and cultural ways of knowing with the dominant group's specialized thought—hegemonic ideologies that, in turn, justify practices of other domains of power.
>
> *(p. 306)*

This domain of power is particularly tricky and demands that technical communicators confront privilege and positionality (both their own and that of others) as they move toward empowerment and coalition building as central to their daily work. This is the domain of microaggressions and daily work that, when not tended to, reifies structures of oppression and exclusion. Collins explains,

> Whereas the structural domain of power organizes the macro-level of social organization with the disciplinary domain managing its operations, the interpersonal domain functions through the routinized, day to day

practices of how people treat one another (e.g. the micro-level of social organizations). Such practices are systematic recurrent and so familiar that they often go unnoticed.

(p. 306)

For example, across the university, women continue to shoulder the burden of service work, specifically taking on emotional and administrative labor that men counterparts are not expected to do (El-Alayli, Hansen-Brown, & Ceynar, 2018; Guarino & Borden, 2017). These daily practices of caretaking and administration reflect and extend from hegemonic and cultural expectations tied to gender and women's work.

The challenges to shifting this domain of power include implicit bias, ethics of expediency, and the American values of individualism (discussed in Chapter 4) that imbue our schools, programs, and community organizations. Often, we harbor implicit bias against particular members, and that bias emerges in insidious, barely-even-noticeable ways: We become unknowing agents of the system of oppressions we have grown up in. And, of course, because we rely on an ethic of expediency (to echo Katz, 1992) in most bureaucracies and jobs, it's difficult to slow down and consider how our interpersonal relationships tack in and out of other domains of power. In this domain, privilege can go unnoticed and underexamined. "Although most individuals have little difficulty identifying their own victimization within some major system of oppression...they typically fail to see how their thoughts and actions uphold someone else's subordination" (p. 306). Our positionality and privilege, in other words, often conceal the ways power functions in the interpersonal domain.

Domains of Power in TPC

While many TPC projects function in one of the domains of power, an approach to coalitional, intersectional social justice prompts us to be aware of all domains and to consider how we might address or perpetuate injustices within and across the domains of power. These domains of power allow us to examine power and power relations systematically without losing sight of any of the domains in which oppression occurs. This is important if we want to understand how to redress inequities and seek justice. Injustice, like power, functions ideologically and culturally, procedurally and managerially—at both the macro level and at the micro level. Too often, it's easy for even those invested in socially just practices to ignore the interplay of the domains of power. The strength of Collins's framework is that it reveals the ways domains of power intersect, compound oppression and influence one another. Our arguments about oppression, power, and injustice, in other words, are strengthened when we envision how one domain of power influences the other, when we are vigilant about connecting microaggressions with policy, relating cultural "norms" with hegemonic structures. For example, in Lubbock, TX, official city policy held that African American citizens could not own land south of 19th street, the road where Texas Tech University is located, up until 2006, when it was officially off struck from the city ordinances. In a class discussion, some students suggested that since the policy wasn't really enforced, the policy didn't really make much of a difference anyway. Yet, when Kristen worked through the demographic data with students and showed the persistent segregation and discrimination that continued in the city, it became clear that the policy had long-lasting effects across interpersonal, structural, and hegemonic domains (Foster, 1974). In this way, we offer Collins as a heuristic approach for thinking through how we navigate systems of power and oppression throughout our work as a means of redressing injustices.

In other words, in any technical communication project, technical communicators work across the four domains of power. Think, for example, about the way an instruction set might be developed for a new technology. Traditional approaches to TPC might adopt an instrumental approach to considering the power at play in the development and use of an instruction set: The instruction set offers the user the opportunity (or power) to engage with the technology. In this view, an effective instruction set allows the user to engage with the technology in the way the technology designer intends. And yet we know that instruction sets affect and are affected by all four domains of power. They often preserve the dominant, macro-level organizations in that they preserve the relationship between expert and novice, a power dynamic technical communicators are invested in dismantling through user-centered design (Johnson, 1998) but that continues to be maintained. In part, the user-centered design approach has worked toward dismantling the structure of power between expert and novice by working at what Collins calls the disciplinary level: Process and procedures that maintain the organization of power. By flattening the hierarchy between designer and user, an instruction set may become a document that upends or addresses the disciplinary and/or structural domains of power. Selber (2010), for example, notes the ways that instruction sets can be created in an open, user-generated format. Traditionally, however, instruction sets are developed as one-way documents that impart knowledge to the user, reflecting the process of designing technologies and documents in the disciplinary domain and seeking to control the behavior of the user. It is easy to recognize from the example of instruction sets how seemingly neutral technical communication genres work across the structural and disciplinary domains of power: Technologies and their instruction sets structure power and the design of both uphold power structures.

But instruction sets also reflect cultural and ideological domains of power as well. Particularly as instruction sets begin to interact with bodies, we can see the ways that instructions are normalizing constructs, making assumptions about how bodies work and how we relate to technologies (and thus function in the hegemonic domain). A ready example of this might be instructions for inserting tampons. As a technology, tampons play an important role in the lives of individuals negotiating their menstrual cycles. Most tampon instruction sets suggest that users put their leg up on the side of a toilet or bathtub to access their vaginal entry. Yet, people of various abilities and sizes may not find that suggestion accommodates their bodily constraints. In this way, the instruction set reinforces cultural assumptions about bodies and how they should work. Especially with tampon instructions, instruction sets can structure micro-level interactions and experiences as well because they are often imbued with everyday exclusive practices. When an instruction set, for example, deploys pronouns so as to be inclusive—using he or she or they—the instruction set adopts the "everyday practices" of gender inequity, marginalizing those whose gender does not conform to this binary.

An instruction set—or any document, process, or interaction in technical communication—cuts across the dynamic, shifting domains of power. It would be a mistake to believe that we can or should choose just one. Rather, we must commit to interrogating all domains of power, seeing our positionality and privilege as cross-cutting various realms. In Table 5.1, we lay out some examples from existing research that seem to exist in a particular domain, but we acknowledge that the domains interconnect, pushing and pulling on one another at each moment.

Before finishing our discussion of the way TPC works across the domains of power, we think it's important to note that one struggle with using the domains of power is that language use—a central concern of technical communicators—extends throughout all of them. Naming matters, language structures our worlds,

TABLE 5.1 Domains of Power and Field-Specific Examples

Domain of Power	Location	Example from TPC
Structural	Macro-level of social organization	The design of algorithms (Noble, 2018); state and national policies (Koerber, 2013; Williams, 2010)
Disciplinary	Processes, procedures	Procedures for hiring, tenure, or promotion (Ranney, 2000); processes for decision-making (Simmons, 2008)
Hegemonic	Ideology and culture	Conceptions of normativity (Dolmage, 2014); Maps (Barton & Barton, 1993);
Interpersonal	Microlevel of social organization	Interactions between clients and technical communicators (Walton, 2013); classroom and meeting behaviors (Patterson, 2016; Haas & Eble, 2018); language use (Gonzales & Zantjer, 2015; Young, 1990)

A note of caution: This kind of chart suggests that these examples exist exclusively in one particular domain, but the domains are interrelated. This is what makes examples like Williams's Texas policies particularly salient: While it would be easy to assign this to the structural realm, where rights are structured by policy, the policies merge into the hegemonic realm, where ideological and cultural values become powerful domains of TPC work.

and small interpersonal norms, like the ways gender is constructed as binary or fluid reflect the hegemonic domain, co-construct the patterns of power, and function to structure algorithms, forms, and other kinds of documents. Indeed, exclusion and marginalization happens through language use and through norms of language. In *Inclusion and Democracy*, Young (2002) provides a helpful example about the way language functions to exclude particular people. "A norm of 'articulateness,'" she writes, "devalues the speech of those who make claims and give reasons, but not in a linear fashion that makes logical connections explicit. A norm of dispassionateness dismisses and devalues embodied forms of expression, emotion, and figurative expressions. People's contributions to a discussion," she writes, "tend to be excluded from serious consideration not because of what is said, but how it is said" (p. 56). Young's example provides a salient connection to the work that technical communicators do with language. In our concerns with clarity and coherent arguments, we may knowingly or unknowingly contribute to the exclusion of particular perspectives, groups or individuals, and it reminds us that as we develop an approach to TPC that seeks inclusion, justice, and empowerment, our language use can and should be tended to.

Gonzales and Zantjer (2015) provide one example of the way that a focus on inclusion can shift the language practices adopted across domains of power. They developed a study of multilingual users' translation practices, and in so doing they move the field from translation practices to localization practices, arguing that understanding the localized practices of multilingual users can deepen our understanding of translation practices. Where nonlocalized translation practices may rely on structural or disciplinary domains of linguistic power, Gonzales and Zantjer gather experience-based, localized examples and develop new frameworks for understanding translation practices that are multidimensional, more nuanced than existing frames, and that empower the multilingual user rather than make them subject to existing practices. This provides one example of the way that a justice-oriented, inclusive understanding of TPC can shift language use across domains of power.

How are the Domains of Power Connected to Intersectional Coalition Building?

A central argument we make in this book is that the work of TPC needs to be intersectional and coalitional. Patricia Hill Collins's domains of power help us ground the work of intersectional coalitions, allowing us to make two arguments about how intersectional coalitions work to address injustices: (1) Since injustice and oppression occur across the domains of power and create the norms, standards, and infrastructures of our society, intersectional coalitions are needed to shift these often invisible domains of power, and (2) the four domains reveal how important lived, embodied experiences and epistemologies can and should be to our understandings of power.

Collins suggests that the domains of power are interlocking, intersecting, and interrelated. We agree. That is what makes shifting power relations so difficult. But the domains of power help us see more clearly how power "works as a mode of directionality" (p. 43). In *Living a Feminist Life*, Ahmed explains that norms structure our lives, creating patterns, paths, and flows that direct our actions, our lives. "A norm," she writes, "is also a way of living, a way of connecting with others over or around something. We cannot 'not' live in relation to norms." Unless resisted against, actions in the four interrelated domains of power reinforce norms, policies, and procedures of oppression. And resistance is difficult, especially as an individual activity. The way Ahmed describes power as directionality, however, suggests that coalitional approaches to change can recreate new directions, new norms, and new forms of resistance. She writes, "Note here how collectivity can become a direction: a clearing of the way as the way of many" (p. 46). Collective labor can clear the way for others. Across the domains of power, we can see, for example, how heteronormativity (Ahmed's example) has been established as the collective path. Policies restricting marriage and adoptions suggest that we ought to organize families around heterosexual couples; at the disciplinary level, the procedures for securing benefits, for example, are created for heterosexual couples. Heteronormative ideology imbues our cultural touchpoints and dictates how we treat one another on an interpersonal level.

But if collective labor clears the way for unjust systems of power and oppression, we believe that coalitional work can shift the pathway, easing the progression for those who historically have been shoved down a path of norms that oppress them. An intersectional coalition can redress inequities across the domains of power, shifting norms and connecting with struggles across intersecting systems of oppression. As the Combahee River Collective[3] teaches us, coalition building as a form solidarity can "strengthen the political commitments from other groups by getting them to recognize how the different struggles were related to each other and connected under capitalism" (Taylor, 2017, p. 11). Building coalitions requires an understanding of the way power functions across domains; coalition members cannot excuse themselves from understanding the way they wield power in any of the domains Patricia Hill Collins articulates. This includes the interpersonal.

The second way Collins's four domains augment the pursuit of socially just TPC through intersectional coalition building is by demanding attention to the hegemonic and interpersonal domains of power. This becomes important, in part, because it invites coalition members to build from lived experiences of hegemony, structural oppression, and marginalization. Members of intersectional coalitions are responsible for understanding the struggle of other members and other coalitions. We might connect this to what Ahmed (2017) calls the collective [feminist] snap. Ahmed articulates snapping as the action tied to a breaking point: "Snap: when she can't take it any more; when she just can't take it anymore. Speaking sharply, speaking with irritation" (p. 190). A collective snap is shared, listened to, and sometimes occurs across individuals. In the example Ahmed gives, the film A Question of Silence (dir. Marlene Gorris, 1982) offers a snap not just as a single breaking moment but a connected experience of women enduring the patriarchy. These collective snaps, recognition and reckoning with the experience of oppression, demand an attention to the stories, experiences, and bodies of coalition members. A contemporary example of collective snap might be the way the #metoo movement, which was coined by African American activist Tarana Burke in 2006 and eventually gained significant traction in 2016 when the phrase was applied to victims of Harvey Weinstein, among other Hollywood sexual abusers. In sharing a single story of sexual harassment or assault, survivors invited and joined a collective snap seeded in experiential truth, lived experiences, and a story-based knowledge that, with the support of other #metoo members, cannot be denied.[4]

Historically, lived experiences and bodies have not been understood as central or important sites of study for TPC, even though for Black feminists (and other scholars of color) these are locales of power, resistance, theory-making, and language use. When we examine power as it exists in the interpersonal, we are invited to acknowledge the ways TPC affects and is affected by lived experiences and bodies. It also provides an additional site of knowledge making in TPC. Patricia Hill Collins's epistemological framework requires lived experiences to be included in the epistemological landscape—lived experience is knowledge making. Intersectional coalitions in TPC require technical communicators to listen for the collective snap, to honor lived experiences as part of the work, and to embrace new epistemological approaches.

When intersectional coalitions shape the direction of the field, new priorities and forms of social justice emerge. For example, although we have seen some integration of material, embodied rhetorics in the field of TPC, the importance of embodied anger and rage has not been a part of this discussion. This is a curious omission, given that women of color have long been theorizing and describing anger or rage as a party to their work and experience (Cooper, 2018; Lorde, 1988; Ore, 2015), and certainly no technical communication system that includes humans is devoid of these emotions. In many sites of public technical communication that Kristen has researched, anger and rage are an integral part of the problems technical communicators are challenged to consider, accommodate, and communicate, especially as they are tied to oppression and racism. When working with citizens on planning projects, for example, citizens often reveal important emotions about political, technical, and scientific information: Rage, anger, regret, sadness. Because these emotions are of import to citizens, they can and should shape our understanding of technical communication, yet TPC scholars have rarely addressed these embodied experiences at all. Drawing on Black feminist theories and other intersectional approaches provides an impetus for including anger and rage as productive and important parts of our theory-building. Lorde (1988) is instructive here: "Any discussion among women about racism must include the recognition and the use of anger" (p. 128). Lorde's point helps in two ways: First, that intersectional coalitions (if they are to work effectively) require that knowledge be made across the domains of power and that members of the coalition engage with embodied pains of oppression and injustice; second, that as TPC engages with issues of oppression and injustice, new sites of power must be prioritized in order to redress inequities.

How Are Positionality and Privilege Connected to the Domains of Power?

Collins's domains of power demonstrate the importance of integrating positionality and privilege into the field's framework for understanding social justice, empowerment, and privilege. Both positionality and privilege affect the margin of maneuverability for any individual actants, and both function across domains of power. Without an articulation of those domains, we may fall short of the ways we are collectively and personally responsible for how we empower and disempower others through our work in the classroom, public sphere, corporate sphere, and discipline. That said, we want to emphasize that power is dynamic and unstable and that power relations are often in flux. This is one of the reasons we insist on pairing power with privilege and positionality.

Privilege and positionality, as terms related to power, demonstrate the dynamic, unstable nature of power and its domains. At any one time, individuals, coalitions, organizations, and so on may be interacting with power in many ways, in many forms, and across many domains—and Patricia Hill Collins approach to power helps us understand this in new ways. Chavez (2013) suggests we think about this as interactionality. Interactionality "moves away from the linear metaphor and highlights the complicated and dynamic way in which identities, power, and systems of oppression intermesh, interlock, intersect, and thus interact" (p. 58). We deploy the 3Ps as a way to explore the same interaction, but more slowly and with a reverence for the difficulty that many of us have in understanding our own complicity in oppressive structures. We think that an inclusive approach to TPC requires a kind of accountability that hasn't yet been articulated: The 3Ps help us consider what this looks like within the unstable, dynamic systems of power we work in as technical and professional communicators.

In other words, our theory of power, positionality, and privilege implore technical communicators to consider their own individual positions within the matrix of domination, oppression, and injustice in addition to institutional, structural, and cultural power relations. Doing so allows us to address the problems we face as technical communicators: Problems with diversity and inclusion, yes, but also problems with document design, problems with editing, problems with intercultural communication, problems with health communication. These wicked, complex problems require theoretical perspectives that can motivate and inform solutions. In taking seriously the way privilege and positionality work in the development of TPC theory, we commit to acknowledging the limits of the mythical norm and the potential for expanding our ability to achieve social justice by working from the margins.

As an approach to technical communication, we offer the 3Ps as a theoretical framework that supports inclusive, socially just practices. This approach to 3Ps has some clear takeaways:

- Technical communicators need to acknowledge and recognize the limits and breadth of their own power
- Technical communicators function across domains of power in most projects; choosing to examine just one domain can function to exclude important steps toward social justice
- Technical communicators must interrogate their approach to social justice through a coalitional, collective sense of accountability
- Technical communicators should engage genres, word choice, research methods, visualizations, traditions, norms, and other tools of communication that draw from nondominant ways of knowing and notions of credibility in pursuing goals of social justice
- Technical communicators must embrace complex perspectives of identity, recognizing that positionality often involves occupying seemingly contradictory positions. This recognition is essential for informing coalitional work
- Technical communicators should also reflect upon their own positionality in complex ways so as to evaluate their margin of maneuverability to engage in actions supporting social justice
- Technical communicators must acknowledge that privilege is an ontological paradigm that affects individuals' experiences of and interactions with their world and thus should be a consideration for our field's research, pedagogy, and practice
- Technical communicators should examine how privilege impacts us all in varied ways and interrogate how privilege is simultaneously collective, subjective, and relational

These are lofty goals. In some ways, they set us up for failure. They require constant reflection on our own behavior and a tireless pursuit of a world that doesn't yet exist. And, we might add, a vision of the *field* that doesn't yet exist. But they paint a picture of the field we believe in—and the only one that we can live with. There is no form of TPC that functions outside of the four domains of power; therefore, no practitioner or scholar in TPC should excuse themselves from engaging with oppression, injustice, and social justice in their work.

Notes

1 See, for example, Stewart (2001) and Grosz (1990).
2 Here, we note the regular resistance we've experience citing Black feminists in TPC journals: "Why distract with the racial issue if you're not focused on race?"; unsurprisingly, we've received little resistance to using Foucault or Latour in our articles.
3 The Combahee River Collective was a collection of Black feminists who worked coalitionally to address the oppression of Black women and others in the U.S. This group provided one of the earliest examples of how and why intersectional coalitions are needed to redress injustices. Their organization produced the Combahee River Collective Statement, which outlined a Black feminism that was radically intersectional and it called for collective solidarity.
4 Though we do write in the wake of the appointment and contested approval of Justice Brett Kavanaugh to the Supreme Court, testament (we think) that the collective snap has limits and that there is still much more work to do to advocate for lived experience as a form of knowledge-making.

References

Ahmed, S. (2017). *Living a feminist life*. Durham, NC: Duke University Press.
Barton, B. F., & Barton, M. S. (1993). Modes of power in technical and professional visuals. *Journal of Business and Technical Communication, 7*(1), 138–162.
Bowker, G. C., & Starr, S. L. (2000). *Sorting things out: Classification and its consequences*. Cambridge, MA: MIT Press.
Chávez, K. R. (2013). *Queer migration politics: Activist rhetoric and coalitional possibilities*. Chicago, IL: University of Illinois Press.
Collins, P. H. (2008). *Black feminist thought: Knowledge, consciousness, and the politics of empowerment* (2nd ed.). New York, NY: Routledge.
Coole, D., & Frost, S. (2010). Introducing the new materialisms. In D. Coole & S. Frost (Eds.), *New materialisms: Ontology, agency, and politics* (pp. 1–46). Durham, NC: Duke University Press.
Cooper, B. (2018). *Eloquent rage: A black feminist discovers her superpower*. New York, NY: St. Martin's Press.
Dolmage, J. T. (2014). *Disability rhetoric*. Syracuse, NY: Syracuse University Press.
Dragga, S., & Voss, D. (2001). Cruel pies: The inhumanity of technical illustrations. *Technical Communication, 48*(3), 265–274.
El-Alayli, A., Hansen-Brown, A. A., & Ceynar, M. (2018). Dancing backwards in high heels: Female professors experience more work demands and special favor requests, particularly from academically entitled students. *Sex Roles, 79*(3–4) 136–150.
Foster, R. L. (1974). *Black West Prairie: A history of Negroes in West Prairie, Texas to 1940* (Unpublished master's thesis). Retrieved from the Texas Digital Library.
Foucault, M. (1979). Discipline and punish, trans. Alan Sheridan. *New York: Vintage, 5,* 368–382.
Gonzales, L., & Zantjer, R. (2015). Translation as a user-localization practice. *Technical Communication, 62*(4), 271–284.
Grabill, J. T., & Simmons, W. M. (1998). Toward a critical rhetoric of risk communication: Producing citizens and the role of technical communicators. *Technical Communication Quarterly, 7*(4), 415–441.
Grosz, E. (1990). Contemporary theories of power and subjectivity. *Feminist Knowledge: Critique and Construct,* 59–120.

Guarino, C. M., & Borden, V. M. (2017). Faculty service loads and gender: Are women taking care of the academic family? *Research in Higher Education, 58*(6), 672–694.

Haas, A. M., & Eble, M. F. (Eds.). (2018). *Key theoretical frameworks: Teaching technical communication in the twenty-first century.* Logan, UT: Utah State University Press.

hooks, b. (2000). *Feminist theory: From margin to center.* Cambridge, MA: South End Press.

Johnson, R. R. (1998). *User-centered technology: A rhetorical theory for computers and other mundane artifacts.* Albany, NY: SUNY press.

Jones, N. N. (2016). The technical communicator as advocate: Integrating a social justice approach in technical communication. *Journal of Technical Writing and Communication, 46*(3), 342–361.

Jones, N. N., & Walton, R. (2018). Using narratives to foster critical thinking about diversity and social justice. In A. Haas & M. Eble (Eds.), *Key theoretical frameworks for teaching technical communication in the 21st century* (pp. 241–267). Logan, UT: Utah State University Press.

Katz, S. B. (1992). The ethic of expediency: Classical rhetoric, technology, and the Holocaust. *College English, 54*(3), 255–275.

Katz, S. B. (1993). Aristotle's rhetoric, Hitler's program, and the ideological problem of praxis, power, and professional discourse. *Journal of Business and Technical Communication, 7*(1), 37–62.

Koerber, A. (2013). Breast or bottle?: Contemporary controversies in infant-feeding policy and practice. Columbia, SC: University of South Carolina Press.

Lorde, A. (1978). *The collected poems of Audre Lorde.* New York, NY: W. W. Norton and Company.

Lorde, A. (1984). *Sister outsider: Essays and speeches.* Trumansburg, NY: The Crossing Press.

Lorde, A. (1988). *A burst of light: Essays* (Vol. 131). Ithaca, NY: Firebrand Books.

Niemann, Y. F. (2012). Lessons from the experiences of women of color working in academia. In G. Gutiérrez y Muhs, Y. Flores Niemann, C. G. González, & A. P. Harris (Eds.), *Presumed incompetent: The intersections of race and class for women in academia* (pp. 446–499). Logan, UT: Utah State University Press.

Noble, S. U. (2018). *Algorithms of oppression: How search engines reinforce racism.* New York, NY: NYU Press.

Ore, E. (2015). "They call me Dr. Ore." *Present Tense, 5*(2), 1–6.

Patterson, G. (2016). The unbearable weight of neutrality: Religion & LGBTQ issues in the English studies classroom. In J. Alexander & J. Rhodes (Eds.), *Sexual rhetorics: Methods, identities, publics* (pp. 134–146). New York, NY: Routledge.

Porter, J. E., Sullivan, P., Blythe, S., Grabill, J. T., & Miles, L. (2000). Institutional critique: A rhetorical methodology for change. *College Composition and Communication, 51*(4), 610–642.

Powell, K. M., & Takayoshi, P. (Eds.). (2012). *Practicing research in writing studies: Reflexive and ethically responsible research.* New York, NY: Hampton Press.

Rappaport, J. (1987). Terms of empowerment/exemplars of prevention: Toward a theory for community psychology. *American Journal of Community Psychology, 15*(2), 121–148.

Ranney, F. J. (2000). Beyond Foucault: Toward a user-centered approach to sexual harassment policy. *Technical Communication Quarterly, 9*(1), 9–28.

Royster, J. J., & Kirsch, G. E. (2012). *Feminist rhetorical practices: New horizons for rhetoric, composition, and literacy studies.* Carbondale, IL: Southern Illinois University Press.

Sano-Franchini, J. (2017). What can Asian eyelids teach us about user experience design? A culturally reflexive framework for UX/I design. *Rhetoric, Professional Communication, and Globalization, 10,* 27–53.

Sauer, B. A. (1993). Sense and sensibility in technical documentation: How feminist interpretation strategies can save lives in the nation's mines. *Journal of Business and Technical Communication, 7*(1), 63–83.

Scott, J. B. (2003). *Risky rhetoric: AIDS and the cultural practices of HIV testing.* Carbondale, IL: Southern Illinois University Press.

Scott, J. B., Longo, B., & Wills, K. V. (Eds.). (2007). *Critical power tools: Technical communication and cultural studies.* Albany, NY: SUNY Press.

Selber, S. A. (2010). A rhetoric of electronic instruction sets. *Technical Communication Quarterly, 19*(2), 95–117.

Simmons, W. M. (2008). Participation and power: Civic discourse in environmental policy decisions. Albany, NY: SUNY Press.

Slack, J. D., Miller, D. J., & Doak, J. (1993). The technical communicator as author: Meaning, power, authority. *Journal of Business and Technical Communication, 7*(1), 12–36.

Stewart, A. (2001). *Theories of power and domination. The politics of empowerment in late modernity.* London: Sage.

Taylor, K. Y. (Ed.). (2017). *How we get free: Black feminism and the Combahee River Collective.* Chicago, IL: Haymarket Books.

Tracy, S. J. (2012). *Qualitative research methods: Collecting evidence, crafting analysis, communicating impact.* Chichester, West Sussex: John Wiley & Sons.

Walton, R. (2013). Stakeholder flux: Participation in technology-based international development projects. *Journal of Business and Technical Communication, 27*(4), 409–435.

Williams, M. F. (2010). *From black codes to recodification: Removing the veil from regulatory writing.* Amityville, NY: Baywood.

Young, I. M. (1990). *Justice and the politics of difference.* Princeton, NJ: Princeton University Press.

Young, I. M. (2002). *Inclusion and democracy.* Oxford University Press on Demand.

SECTION III
Building Coalitions

6

COALITIONAL ACTION

At the heart of this book is the belief that technical communicators can and should build coalitions and that through intersectional, coalitional approaches to technical and professional communication (TPC), we can address issues of inequality and oppression. But we also believe that we need practical strategies and tactics for getting this work done. In this chapter, we offer four steps for redressing inequities in our daily work. These four steps—Recognize, Reveal, Reject, and Replace (the 4Rs)—provide a heuristic for action that extends from the theoretical foundation laid in Section II. Our action items for redressing inequities should include:

- Recognizing injustices, systems of oppression, and our own complicities in them
- Revealing these injustices, systemic oppressions, and complicities to others as a call-to-action and (organization/social/political) change
- Rejecting injustices, systemic oppressions, and opportunities to perpetuate them
- Replacing unjust and oppressive practices with intersectional, coalition-led practices

The bulk of this book has been about *recognizing* the injustices and oppressive systems embedded in our work as technical communicators, and this chapter extends that discussion into on-the-ground scenarios. But we ask for more than mere recognition. Mere recognition, much like surface-level representational diversity, is insufficient (see Chapter 7). These four actions may seem chronological: First, you do this and then, you do this. And that's true: It's impossible to reject and replace injustices if you can't recognize them. (That's why we've spent so much time developing a language and framework for helping technical communicators recognize our complicities in injustice and oppression.) But the 4Rs will also attune you to the kind of coalitional work that is being done in the field, across the U.S., and around the world, where there are existing groups and individuals working to reject and replace unjust and oppressive behaviors. This framework, then, isn't asking you to combat all forms of oppression alone; rather, we offer this also as a guide for joining other coalitions, building genuine allyships, and working toward sustainable practices of activism.

Throughout this chapter, we focus on turning technical communicators' attention to the need for orienting social justice work through intersectional coalition building, a term that deserves a proper introduction. We are convinced by Black feminist, queer, and other marginalized scholars who already engage in coalitional work and assert, as they have for quite some time, that (1) our feminisms and activisms are ineffectual if they do not engage with oppression through an intersectional perspective, acknowledging that those who are multiply marginalized contend with different lived experiences of oppression that are not well served by handling oppression with a razor-like focus on one oppressive system (like sexism), and (2) our approach to activism and social transformation should engage with coalitional thinking: Working collectively to understand oppression and spur change. Here's how these convictions guide our work:

- Any analysis of oppression and plan for change should consider intersecting systems of oppression, never satisfied with redressing injustices through a singular framework
- As we do the work of recognizing, revealing, rejecting, and replacing, we should be guided by coalitions and collectives in the decisions we make about how to move forward, use language, and prioritize actions
- As a member of a coalition or as someone who is looking to join a coalition, we don't always get to determine our own direction; instead, we look to those already engaged in a coalition or in the work of redressing inequities

This coalitional approach requires those who are not living at the intersections of oppression to approach change-making with humility; to listen more than they speak or lead; and to sometimes divest themselves of self-serving plans, ideas, and ways forward. In other words, the important thing about intersectional coalition building is that the right answer, the next step, is localized and should be driven by the collective agenda and the experiences of those who have been and continue to be multiply marginalized. Fundamentally, it is multiply marginalized groups that have demonstrated the need for coalitional action, and their voices and priorities should centrally inform those actions.

In this way, we address one of the central concerns we (and many others) have about a social justice orientation to TPC: Anyone can claim they're working toward their version of justice. We unapologetically demarcate ideological requirements for engaging in social justice, demanding first that the field develops intersectional understandings of oppression and second that it works toward building coalitions that acknowledge and address intersectional oppressions (see Chapter 7). We follow Chavez' (2013) vision of coalitions as "less an existing thing or relationship…and more as a possibility for coming together within or to create a juncture that points toward…change" (p. 146). We assert that coalitional thinking and inclusive coalitions are necessary for change because they can shift and change quickly and because they engage difference and different goals without rejecting them. An intersectional coalition for TPC responds to oppression without prescription, assuming that the complexity of activism, power, and domination (as Patricia Hill Collins demonstrates and as Karma Chavez asserts below) is dynamic and shifting:

> People's lives are not comprised of singular identities or concerns…As queer women of color feminists have always shown us, oppression and privilege, power and identity, domination and liberation are experienced in people's lives in vastly complicated ways. We need equally complicated understandings of how people who are committed to social change work to confront these material and symbolic conditions.
>
> *(Chavez, 2013, p. 149)*

The 4Rs respond directly to the need for complex, inclusive, intersectional approaches to doing social justice in TPC. But, as technical communicators who like to get work done, we do not shy away from the need for a practical heuristic for thinking through organizational contexts. After all, one of the objectives of this book is to help TPC scholars and activists directly address issues of inequality and injustice in their daily work in organizations and corporations.

As discussed in Chapter 2, how we define justice matters for addressing inequality and injustice. We find Young's (1990) faces of oppression useful as tools for breaking down the world around us and its matrix of domination (see Collins, 2002, pp. 277–288) because it moves from the theoretical to the lived. But theories of power, oppression, privilege, and positionality do not go far enough in helping technical communicators know what to do about injustice and oppression. We assert that, depending on their privilege and positionality, people have relatively more or less power to enact change once they've recognized the ways in which their programs or workplaces perpetuate injustices. As newly tenured professors, we are sensitive, for example, to the limits of what untenured and early-career faculty can say or do if they hope to keep their jobs. But we are also convinced that across TPC, more effort can and should be made to address inequities—many members of the field can be doing more with their power and privilege from their positions within organizations and situations. This is particularly true for het-cis white men and women, who in different ways have been sitting on the sidelines and assuming a false sense of neutrality that is complicit in oppression and injustice.[1] For some, perhaps this inaction is because those from privileged positions may struggle to recognize injustices and oppression when they occur (see Chapter 4), whereas multiply marginalized members of the TPC community are often questioned about whether or not they can know for sure that a microaggression is *really* a microaggression (even though their lived experience makes them experts at recognizing discriminatory and unjust practices). The first challenge, then, is ensuring that injustices are recognized and named as such. In the first two sections of this book, we've written a good deal about understanding oppression and injustice. Here, we get down to the nitty gritty: *How do we recognize acts and practices of injustice and oppression, and what do we do about them?*

A note to allies: Before moving on to the heuristic for action, it warrants a note that when (multiply) marginalized individuals with relatively less power or privilege say that injustice and oppression are occurring, those individuals should be trusted and listened to. Skepticism about stories of injustice may seem "balanced" or "fair" as a measure of objectivism, particularly in the face of bureaucracies—indeed, skepticism has been heralded as a prudent check and balance that ensures that, for example, Supreme Court Justice nominees don't have their "lives ruined" by one (or three) victim's claims. As discussed in Chapter 2, we want to move past conceptions of justice as fair or balanced and instead consider how our work might center the experience of multiply marginalized members (who, for the record, do not consider skepticism either fair or balanced). As such, we suggest that we cannot begin the work of shifting the field toward inclusion by doubting stories of microaggressions, institutional oppression, and procedural injustices. If colleagues or students from (multiply) marginalized positions present stories of injustices they have experienced, the response of an ally is to affirm and act appropriately. What does that kind of response look like? We suggest treating those stories like an improv actor treats narratives on stage (Poehler, 2014): Yes, and…

> Yes, and…how are you feeling?
> Yes, and…how can I help?
> Yes, and…I agree with you: that's not how we act.

If we want to be allies, we must all commit to learning more about injustices from those who experience injustices. Even those of us who experience our own forms of oppression can and should listen, learn, and engage with others whose experiences of injustice are different from our own. Which means your conversations cannot include the phrase: "Yes, but…" "But" doesn't listen; "but" tells your listener they aren't welcome; "but" is (often) a tool of oppression and/or microaggression; "but" erases experiences. And if no one is telling you about injustices, that (of course) doesn't mean injustices aren't happening. How, then, do we recognize injustices? Begin, we suggest, by centering the experiences of multiply marginalized folks. What do we mean by centering?

Perhaps, as technical communicators, the easiest way to think about centering is to talk about users in UX design contexts. Take, for example, the design of a website. When we're consulting with clients at the beginning of UX testing for a website, we often ask them about their users and/or intended users. If we're working with a nonprofit that supports pet adoption, they'll list users like families, moms, college kids. These users are at the center of the nonprofit's world: They're the people considered first in the development of the website. When, however, you're talking through user considerations and then question whether the nonprofit wants to test for blind users, the clients are hesitant: "Do we...do we really need to do that? How expensive would that be?" This is an example of the people who live at the margins of this particular (and most) design project. We know from disability studies scholars (Dolmage, 2008; Palmeri, 2006; Zdenek, 2015) that the world is designed for the able-bodied person. Ableism centers the experiences of able-bodied individuals, leaving those with disabilities at the margins. So, in design terms, we might ask, "Who is this space, place, program, technology designed for? And who simply must make do?" Dolmage (2008) critiques retrofitting, an approach to complying with the Americans with Disabilities Act (ADA) that adds design elements like a wheelchair ramp at the back of the building rather than including accessible elements in the building's design from the beginning because retrofitting continues to marginalize those with disabilities rather than assuming their experiences and engagements should be accommodated and considered from the start. To design for those with disabilities is to center them, to ask, "How is this design decision affecting these particular users?"

When we ask you (or, all of us) to center the experiences of those who are marginalized, we want to make clear that both privilege and positionality can dictate who gets marginalized in the contexts of our programs, classrooms, communities, and workplaces. In faculty ranks of the academy, for example, non-tenure track faculty members experience marginalization in various ways: Their organizational status dictates their position on the margins. As we have discussed in previous chapters, others experience marginalization—and are quite often multiply marginalized—because of race, gender, sexuality, ability, religion, or class and any combination of the preceding list. In the context of multi-national and cross-cultural research, these considerations become even more complex, particularly when U.S.-based researchers are working with vulnerable populations in the Global South (see Chapter 7). In other words, our academic programs, research contexts, and other communities are filled with people whose experiences have been all but ignored because systems of oppression have dictated what Audre Lorde (1984) calls a mythical norm (see Chapter 4) and centered some experiences over others. As we begin the process of attuning ourselves to injustices, then, we would do well to consider the way the mythical norm has shaped the assumptions we make about the places we live and work. How might centering those whose bodies and experiences challenge the idea of the mythical norm shift or change your decisions, your practices, your assumptions?

Recognizing Unjust Practices, Behaviors, and Systems

The difficult part about the work of recognition is that marginalizing already marginalized groups of people might not appear to you (or to others) as an act of oppression. But as Moore (2017) writes, designing for inclusion challenges us to consider the ways the mundane work we do might be exclusionary and, in being exclusionary, contribute to systems of oppression. In transportation planning projects, the system goes something like this:

PUBLIC OFFICIAL (FRED): "We need to do public engagement to get federal funding to build this railroad in X spot." [X spot often is through poor neighborhoods—after all, who would displace booming economic sites in a city?];

ENGINEER (PHRED): "Okay. Well, when should we do it?"

PUBLIC OFFICIAL: "I think we should do it soon, so how about in 3 weeks?"

ENGINEER: "Okay. My kids have softball practice at 6:30 pm on Thursdays, though, so we need it to be done by 5:00. So...let's have a public meeting from 3:30–5:00?"

PUBLIC OFFICIAL: "Or can we just do it after the city council meeting on that Wednesday morning. We'll all be there anyway because we have to give that presentation to the council. The meeting is scheduled for 9:00 am. Should be done by 10:15, so we can just do it at 10:30 am in the same room."

ENGINEER: "Good plan."

PUBLIC OFFICIAL: "Alright. Let's be sure Lisa gets the meeting published on the website. And we'll have her put some fliers up at the library and City Hall."

ENGINEER: "K. Let me know when you want to work on the presentation."

Is this unjust? Or oppressive? I am sure that the public official and engineer would say no. But are they contributing to systems of oppression? Seems likely. At the center of their decision-making is their own priorities: Ease, convenience, getting the project done on time, and so on. Citizens' experiences, concerns, ease, and convenience are pushed to the margins: Can citizens make it to a 10:30 am meeting at the City Hall downtown to discuss a railroad displacing them to a new neighborhood? Only if they're not working. And have daycare. And have transportation. And know about the meeting. So the meeting will be held, citizens from already privileged positions will come learn about the way a new railroad will bring in additional economic growth and cost relatively little once the federal funding kicks in. In the Environmental Impact Statement, Fred and Phred (the engineer and public official) will report having the full support of citizens. By the time local community members (who were working during this meeting) hear about the project, Fred and Phred will be shocked (if not downright annoyed) at the resistance they receive, and even though they may sincerely care about the citizens' concerns, they'll already have the federal dollars, which can only be used for this very particular project in this particular location. And so members of the community will be bought out of their houses, using a range of tactics, and they will be forced to relocate.

This scenario (and scenarios like it) happens in cities all over the nation (see Moskowitz, 2017; Rothstein, 2017). Phred and Fred's actions are perfectly defensible if we're not working to center the experiences of marginalized citizens, valuing those most at the margins and considering their experiences before others. And Phred and Fred would likely be offended if we said, "You contribute to the oppression of citizens in your community." But these small acts happen not only in transportation and urban planning but also in our academic programs, in our organizations, in our communities, and in our classrooms. Technical communicators make decisions every day that will either contribute to systems of oppression or resist and reject them; and, we argue, often technical communicators take the position of Phred and Fred: "I'm not contributing to sexism or racism or [fill in system of oppression]."[2]

By centering the experiences of multiply marginalized individuals, we become better at recognizing how our daily, mundane practices contribute to the marginalization, exploitation, and powerlessness of others. In this scenario, if Fred and Phred had centered citizens from multiply marginalized positions, they would have made different choices. And this is why we offer the 4Rs: Recognizing how we might be contributing to systems of oppression is not enough; it doesn't prepare us to shift our actions. Instead, it helps us see that the systems, organizations, and institutions where we work prioritize particular experiences and groups of people. When that prioritization gets built into our policies, procedures, and daily routines, those who are already marginalized struggle to be heard, valued, or treated fairly.

Revealing Injustices and Oppression

Revealing injustices and oppression to others is the next step toward addressing social justice in the field of TPC (and more generally), and it is difficult to articulate clear and straightforward strategies for revealing, since so much about how, when, and to whom we reveal unjust practices depends upon context and our own positionality. The more power and privilege you have in any given situation, the less risky your revelatory work will likely be. Take, for example, Greg. Greg has a PhD in Biomedical Engineering and is teaching a class on biometrics. In a classroom setting, Greg notices that his men students in a group consistently ask the lone woman student to do note-taking while they work on the assigned project. In this case, the teacher can often more easily discuss the microaggression and tie it to systems of injustice than the woman student can. The woman student's position as a student makes it risky to raise concerns, but Greg's ability to intervene is less risky.[3] Our point here is that in this case Greg has relative power and privilege, as well as a responsibility to reveal injustice and oppression. After you've recognized an injustice or an oppressive behavior, your next question is strategic: What can I, given my positionality in this moment, organization, or institution, do to address this problem? In the classroom case, Greg has more direct agency in the moment and can stop to immediately address the problem, revealing the microaggression and moving on to reject it—and perhaps replace it.

It may seem like "revealing" is closely tied to "reporting," but we shouldn't confuse the two. Reporting injustices, hate crimes, Title IX violations, and other forms of injustices is really important. And sometimes, the most appropriate approach to revealing is to file an official report. But reporting is reactive and is often tied to institutional mechanisms that work against the victim. For example, at many universities, the Title IX reporting office is run by the same attorney who is responsible for defending the university against lawsuits tied to Title IX and are thus embedded in the matrix of domination at both the structural and disciplinary domains. In contrast, "revealing" explores a coalitional approach to exposing systems of oppression and acts of microaggression, injustice, or discrimination (among others).

Revealing an injustice is a call to action, an investment, and a coalitional move on either end (either in the revelatory act or in the act of hearing, recognizing and accepting). Revealing injustices (however big or small) is a call to action. Sometimes that action is to engage another person in recognizing how an injustice perpetuates oppression or how an organization is complicit in the oppression of particular groups or individuals. And sometimes that action is listening. Here, Indigenous storytelling scholars are instructive, in that they reveal that the act of telling is a doing, an assembling, an act of making (Sullivan & Legg, 2018); this makes even the act of hearing a revelation an active engagement. In addition, at times, revealing an injustice calls for an overt action in the world: A decision to make change together and to invest in rejecting and replacing the behavior, either on a personal, institutional, social, or political level. As a coalitional act, revealing an injustice invites the listener to strategize for change together rather than alone. As the hearer of a revelation, individuals are meant to choose: Are we in this together or not?

In the Phred and Fred scenario, Lisa, the technical communication consultant working on this project, may decide to tell Phred and Fred, "I can put this on the website, but I'm wondering if you've thought about members of the 12th Street community, many of whom will be affected by this but might not be able to make this meeting." This move does not necessarily reveal the system of oppression at work here, but Lisa's act of revealing surfaces the immediate problem: Excluding those most affected from the decision-making process, leaving them at the margins of decisions, and making them subject to rather than participant in the kinds of world-making that powerfully shapes cities. If Phred and Fred are invested in inclusion and inclusivity, this may be a fairly simple move, which prompts them to say, "Oh! Thanks for bringing that to our attention. Do you have a suggestion?" Or "Can we do a survey of that neighborhood to find out what time works?"

Buuuuuuuut, in our experience that is not often how these acts of revelation go. Lisa is likely to be met with resistance:

— "But it still meets the requirements for public involvement, right?"
— "Well, if it's important to them, they'll make it. If not, that's not our fault."
— "We've already made the schedule and decision, Lisa. Just post the date and let us worry about the rest of it. You're just the communications person."

At this point, Lisa has some decisions to make. Does her revealing need more explanation? More depth? More attention? Does she need to include Phred and Fred's bosses? Does she need to just go directly to, say, the 12th Street neighborhood herself and tell them about the project and why it's important?

For the purposes of this introduction to the 4Rs, let's assume, though, that Lisa gets affirmation from Fred and Phred: "Oh, no! What will we do!? We don't want to exclude people from important justice-related decisions." At this point, Lisa has both recognized the injustice and then revealed it to others.

Rejecting Oppressive Behaviors and Structures

But, of course, revealing is not enough if our objective is to build coalitions; we must also refuse to support the behaviors and structures that oppress groups of people and leave them at the margins. Revealing and rejecting can sometimes occur in dialogue: For example, Kristen reveals to Natasha an injustice or a microaggression, and in response Natasha shares in the rejection of that injustice. Because Natasha and Kristen are part of a coalition already, each rarely has to work to help the other recognize the ways microaggressions operate—but the act of rejection necessarily requires recognition.

What does rejection look like? In some cases, rejection is performative—an utterance. Kristen is often caught saying, "That's not how we act." This is, in many ways, a coalitional statement. If a student of color talks with one of us about unjust policies in our departments, we'll often respond with, "Wait. That's not how we act!" That kind of phrase signals a rejection of behavior. But we prefer a more active form of rejection, especially for those with relative power. For example, in an administrative situation where a colleague of color has been asked (yet again) to represent the department at a diversity luncheon or on a hiring committee, rejection is more than agreeing with the colleague that the practice is unfair. Rejecting it is also speaking up and saying, "Actually, this won't work," and then offering a solution. What is difficult about rejection is that, like revealing, the rhetorical work shifts and changes depending on how power, privilege, and positionality operate in the particular situation. Sometimes, our relative powerlessness renders us capable only of acknowledging that we reject the behavior because we, too, are in a precarious, marginalized position. In other words, rejecting practices, behaviors, and injustices is a risk, especially for the multiply marginalized.

In the case of Phred and Fred, Lisa has begun the work of rejecting behavior that contributes to systemic oppression. When her engineering buddies agree to recognize the behavior as problematic, she can then go to work rejecting (and replacing) the behavior more overtly. In deciding that the timing of the public meeting is exclusionary, Phred, Fred, and Lisa have collectively rejected the decision and are ready to replace it with an alternative (if also imperfect) decision. We want to note here the cycle of the 4Rs and the way it can serve as a foundation for building allies and coalitions for change: Individuals can rarely reject, let alone replace, unjust practices alone, and recognition on one person's part is often prompted by another's revealing.

When one person (Lisa) recognizes an injustice, she then reveals it. That revelation then invites Phred and Fred to recognize an injustice. Once they, too, recognize it, the cycle begins again. Perhaps they are the sole decision-makers in this project and therefore need not reveal the problem Lisa has identified, but it's likely that Phred and Fred will then need to communicate the problem to a larger team, if and when the rejection of their decision requires the team to work outside normal business hours, or to their families, when their rejection requires them to miss a family dinner or softball practice.

Replacing Oppressive Behaviors and Structures

The final act here is replacing oppressive behavior, structures, or decisions. In some domains of power, replacing is about personal change: "I've recognized this microaggressive behavior and so will not do it again. Instead, I will stay silent, affirm, and listen." But the hard work of replacement—deciding what to do instead—often means

- shoring up additional resources
- challenging power relations or meaningful personal relationships
- restructuring organizations through new policies and procedures

In the Phred and Fred scenario, Lisa's attention to the exclusion of the 12th Street community and their affirmative response means very little if not followed by a meaningful replacement that addresses the concern. For Lisa, Phred, and Fred, who at this point have rejected the behavior, the options are many, but the consequences could be high stakes. They might, for example, plan to reschedule the meeting for another time, only to realize that there isn't actually a single time that works for all stakeholders. If they're working to center the experiences of those who are traditionally left out, they may decide to privilege the 12th Street community over other stakeholders. But this prioritization may require additional resources to:

- Learn more about the community's needs and preferences
- Pay engineers overtime for working outside of standard business hours
- Rent a room in a location that's nearer to that community

It's important to note here that it's possible that given the constraints of the project, these additional resources might not be available. Another strategy for replacement, then, would be to consider how to integrate these resources next time. This is imperfect. It still leaves the 12th Street community without an advocate, but looking toward the future allows for replacement to take on an organizational approach rather than a one-off change to the solution.

Building strategies for replacement requires a particular attention to coalitional thinking. Often, an individual can work to recognize, reveal, and reject an oppressive or unjust practice, behavior, or process. But, unless the sole context is an individual's own behavior on an interpersonal or introspective level, replacement requires the consultation of others, the humbling of one's own idea about what should happen and how a problem should be addressed in light of what others say. In this way, replacement is a building and a re-building activity that can—even if well intentioned—result in further exclusion or oppressive behavior if not planned collectively with intersectional thinking at the forefront.

Applying the 4Rs: Technical Communication Case Studies

We have briefly reviewed the 4Rs (recognize, reveal, reject, replace) as an introduction to practices for technical communicators invested in social justice, coalition building, and change. Now, we operationalize them more thoroughly in two cases that demonstrate how technical communicators can use them as a heuristic for decision-making and change. If Porter et al. (2000) are correct, that critique needs an action plan, then this is our action plan:

1 **Critical Context Analysis:** Seek to understand the levels at which the problem is functioning. This step helps technical communicators to recognize overdetermined oppressions and to pinpoint where they may be able to intervene.
2 **Coalitional Action:** Understand the technical communicator's margin of maneuverability in regard to the 4Rs, that is, based on their privilege and positionality, how they can wield power to take action.

Scenario #1: Technical Communication Intern at a Nonprofit Organization

A nonprofit organization in the Global South offers financial services such as microloans to unbanked rural community members. The organization headquarters are in the national capital, but loan officers live and work in small villages throughout the country. The national leaders recognize the richest, most detailed knowledge that should drive organizational decision-making resides at the lowest levels of the organization (an inverted organizational hierarchy typical in humanitarian organizations). The national leaders regularly seek information about community members—their needs, priorities, strengths, and resources—from community loan officers. But most of this rich knowledge remains in the heads of loan officers, while their paperwork (which contains just a modicum of this information) is slow to make its way to the capital due to poor road conditions, isolated rural communities, and the expense of physical travel. Once paperwork does arrive, it's not always useful for organizational decision making: Handwritten responses can be difficult to make out; forms are not always fully filled out; and it is labor intensive to compile information and seek patterns useful to inform decision making at the national level.

Despite these challenges, it becomes clear to the organization's national leaders that community members are requesting additional services that align with the organization's mission. But legal approval to offer expanded financial services requires a complex regulatory application and review process at the national government level, and part of this process will require more detailed information about community member needs and priorities. So the nonprofit leadership team at the national capital decides to digitize the current paper-based system. Their goal is to preserve what works about the current workflow while changing the medium to better allow the expertise and rich community knowledge of village-based loan officers to inform the major decisions the organization faces regarding expanded services.

The nonprofit organization raises money to purchase a computer for each village office and to hire developers to design a distributed computer-based system compatible with the constraints of the local infrastructure. The organization also brings on a technical communication graduate student from a U.S. university, Marcus, as a summer intern. As the developers begin backend work, Marcus is tasked with traveling the country to inform loan officers of the coming system, which could give them more input into what expanded services the organization should prepare to offer, as well as enable them to provide key information for the upcoming government application and review process. He is also asked to review the paper forms with loan officers and solicit their input regarding any changes that should be made to the digital version to make it easier to use and more appropriate for the loan officers' work and the communities they serve.

Everything seems great until Marcus meets with loan officers at one of the first villages he visits. Midway through his explanation, Marcus is startled when a loan officer stands up and starts yelling at him: This "great solution" would halve the number of people loan officers could help. Their clientele is poor; transportation is difficult, time-consuming, and expensive. Loan officers don't meet with community members at the nonprofit's local office (for heaven's sake); they travel to people's homes, which typically are also their place of business. The community members most in need of financial services are often the least mobile. If people have to physically visit the nonprofit offices to apply for microloans (or other services), those most in need will be least likely to apply. Alternatively, if loan officers continue meeting community members at their homes, the loan officers will have to write information by hand first and then travel to the office and type it into a computer, which could double their time spent recording information. They'll do half the good they can now.

Now what?

Technical Communication Intern at a Nonprofit Organization: Critical Context Analysis

Before considering how the 4Rs (recognize, reveal, reject, replace) could guide Marcus in moving forward, let's put this scenario in context (much as Marcus might do if he had read this book). Using Patricia Hill Collins's (2002) matrix of domination (discussed at length in Chapter 5) as a framework, we become aware of various systems of oppression at work in specific ways. Importantly, as Collins (2002, p. 277) notes, the matrix of domination not only reveals how interlocking, mutually reinforcing domains of power serve to oppress but also how they can be used to facilitate empowerment. In other words, using this framework scaffolds an understanding of historicized contexts, norms, and constraints that may be flattened, conflated, or unaddressed altogether by more common frameworks of our practice (e.g., traditional usability approaches), and it also highlights points at which we technical communicators can take coalitional action within a particular situation. Situating our particular technical communication workplace within the matrix of domination and situating ourselves according to the 3Ps, we propose, can better equip technical communicators for coalitional action.

In reflecting upon Marcus's workplace, the structural domain of power helps us identify the political and institutional forces that converge to create a need for the nonprofit organization's financial services. Mainstream financial resources are withheld from many poor, rural community members in the Global South, creating a need for alternatives outside of mainstream banking, such as microloans and cooperatives. Also relevant to this scenario is the nonprofit organization's location in the Global South, where colonialism only recently has shifted its form from outright governmental rule to indirect control through international institutions such as the United Nations and World Bank. Marcus might note that these international institutions are involved in regulating "development" organizations, including many of those which are locally led such as the organization where he's interning. Additionally, these international institutions and the national government inform the regulatory application and review that his organization must undergo to offer financial services requested by marginalized rural community members. It is important to note that Marcus need not be able to change factors at this level of the matrix for an analysis to be relevant; analysis at the structural level reveals to him a historicized context directly affecting his work by setting in motion (and by constraining) the project he was hired to join.

Were Marcus to reflect upon the hegemonic level, he may recognize that private donors, primarily located in the Global North, also form matrices of domination relevant to his work environment. Based on models of charity (as discussed in Chapter 2), traditional donor relationships preserve power imbalances that allow donors to drive activities and priorities of nonprofit organizations by providing or withholding funding and by setting requirements and limitations on the use of that funding. Driven by "common sense" ideas such as holding nonprofit organizations accountable for using donations "efficiently," this domination enforces cultural hegemony in the priorities, programs, and processes of many nonprofit organizations. This analysis allows Marcus to recognize that a face of oppression, cultural imperialism, is incorporated into the financial model of the nonprofit industry. A financial model that likely affects decisions about his project: For example, perhaps constraining the types of devices that project funding can be used to purchase.

Finally, the interpersonal domain of power is also at work in Marcus's dilemma. Despite the shared nationality of community-level loan officers and the nonprofit's leadership team in the capital city, and despite the inverted hierarchy of humanitarian organizational culture that at least partially informs day-to-day decisions and interactions, interpersonal domains of power threatened to render community loan officers powerless. Marcus now realizes that, faced with an information gap at the organization's headquarters, the leadership team failed to recognize that village loan officers had expertise and knowledge vital to the early envisioning of potential solutions. This lack of recognition threatens oppressive outcomes: Loan officers may lose autonomy in their work tasks, as well as their ability to serve the most vulnerable, marginalized community members (ironically, a service at the heart of the organization's mission). Without Collins's matrix of domination as a framework to prompt reflection upon interpersonal domains of power, however, this oppression could be (and was!) overlooked by the stakeholders who weren't threatened with powerlessness or marginalization, stakeholders including Marcus.

This multi-level analysis of relevant power domains is useful, but we suggest it should not fully comprise the "critical analysis" component of our action plan. In addition to using a framework such as Collins's matrix of domination to reflect upon the broader context, we recommend that Marcus also use the 3Ps to situate himself within this context: What relevant privileges has he been accorded? What are some meanings of his identity markers within this context, and how does that positionality affect his power to take action? Guided by the 3Ps, Marcus may note that he occupies a position of some privilege, in terms of nationality and education level. His national identity aligns with those in positions of power over the funding of the organization, though he does not directly represent donors. His specialized education affords some privilege, positioning him as a credible professional with relevant expertise, despite significant gaps in his knowledge and experience. However, his amount of power in the organization is relatively small. After all, he is an intern, which is not only a low-level role but also a temporary one. He concedes that he's not positioned to directly enact or enforce organizational change, since he is not in a leadership role and will not even be associated with the organization when the summer ends. This brief analysis suggests some of the ways that the 3Ps can clarify for Marcus some resources he may be able mobilize, as well as some risks and constraints limiting his margin of maneuverability, in terms of the 4Rs.

Technical Communication Intern at a Nonprofit Organization: Coalitional Action

Returning to Marcus's dilemma, we might suggest several possible paths forward for Marcus, informed by the analysis earlier. Here is one way he may choose to respond to the loan officer's revelation:

> Dismayed, embarrassed, and apologetic, Marcus thanks the loan officer and her counterparts, requesting more information about their process, their needs, and their recommendations. The next morning he contacts the national leadership and requests permission to cut short the village visits and head back to the capital to share some important news. Based on his conversations with the loan officers, it is clear that the computer-based system would be problematic as currently envisioned, but Marcus suspects that shared desktop computers would be cheaper to acquire and maintain than mobile technology such as smartphones or laptops, especially if the organization has to purchase one device per loan officer rather than one device per local office. He isn't sure what kind of flexibility the donor funding will allow regarding device purchases, nor does he know how this news could affect the timeline for developing the new system (not to mention the regulatory application and review process). But the loan officers tell him that a digitized system of some kind seems promising, and they make several suggestions for streamlining digitized forms and ensuring appropriate answer choices. Marcus spends the long ride back to the capital working on a presentation for the leadership team that he hopes will convey the threats of the system as originally designed and will pose some potential, if partial, solutions based on input and recommendations from loan officers.

Let's use the 4Rs break down what's happening here. Until the loan officers reveal it to him, Marcus does not recognize the likelihood that the computer-based system would perpetuate oppression, nor even that the design process is exclusionary. (After all, when he joins the organization, he does not ask where or how the idea for the computer-based system arose.) However, when the loan officers reveal the oppressive potential of the new system—marginalizing those most in need of microloans by requiring applicants to travel to the local office—Marcus recognizes the truth they reveal to him. His positionality within the nonprofit organization does not allow him to reject or replace the computer-based system, but it does offer a margin of maneuverability to credibly reveal the system's oppressive potential to those who may have that power. In other words, rather than dismissing the loan officers' revelation or recognizing the oppressive potential but keeping silent, Marcus chooses to share unwelcome news and make recommendations unsought by those who hired him. He chooses to reveal the system's oppressive potential to those who may have the power to reject and replace it.

This example makes clear the essential role of coalitions. Marcus is not even aware of the oppressive potential of the computer-based system without the perspectives of others, let alone able to suggest potential solutions. Similarly, the organization's leaders cannot identify the most-appropriate, most-needed new financial services alone. They must draw upon the expertise of loan officers, who themselves are guided by local community members—especially those who are most vulnerable and most marginalized. Designing socially just solutions and engaging in socially just decision making requires a coalitional approach in which the perspectives of the most marginalized are centered.

This scenario also makes clear that we won't always get it right, that the matrix of domination is powerful and insidious, at times perpetuated even by those committed to pursuing social justice. After all, the players in this scenario had good intentions, shared values, a socially just organizational mission, and an organizational culture conducive to supporting social justice. But they still came perilously close to designing and adopting a technology that would directly undermine their own organizational mission, hobble the autonomy of key employees, and threaten the access of the most marginalized community members to the financial services they sought. This danger brings home the importance of using the 4Rs as an intentional heuristic for action, supporting sustainable practices of activism.

What might that look like over the long term? Marcus could shift his own practice in several ways, moving forward. For example, when joining projects mid-stream, he can make a habit of seeking out the "before story": How did this project originate? Who was involved in not just early envisioning of solutions but also in identifying and defining the problem? Who was left out of this early definitional and envisioning work? As he asks these questions, he would be attuned to seeking out the perspectives and contributions of those on the margins. When joining pre-existing projects, Marcus may be especially attuned to the matrix of domination, using this framework to examine aspects of context (especially historicized aspects) that may not be apparent when structured by different frameworks. When he works on projects from inception, he can intentionally and habitually engage in participatory and coalitional strategies, such as seeking out a variety of types of knowledge to inform design and doing so from the stage of defining and identifying problems, not waiting until the solution-design stages. In his user research, he may look beyond the TPC discipline to identify methods well suited to coalitional approaches: For example, positive deviance and participatory action research. Other shifts could be more subtle: For example, approaching the visits with village loan officers as primarily a listening-and-learning task, rather than primarily a presenting-and-informing task. As his career progresses, Marcus may seek opportunities to enculturate the next generation of technical communicators to inclusive, participatory practices, opportunities like teaching university courses as an adjunct Professor of Practice from industry. In his courses, Marcus might draw upon participatory models, using tools like the Value-Sensitive Design Envisioning Cards[4] to prompt students to think about long-term, indirect, and unintended effects or outcomes of their designs. In these ways, Marcus could operationalize the 4Rs, incorporating them into his professional practices—not to ensure that he never again finds himself complicit in oppression. But rather to cultivate humility and an openness to recognizing injustice, as well as coalitional, strategic employment of revealing, rejecting, and replacing unjust practices.

Scenario #2: Technical Communication Scholar in an Academic Program

Let's do it again: This time using a very different scenario to trace out critical context analysis and coalitional action for technical communication work. A junior scholar, who is a woman of color (let's call her Julie), serves as the faculty advisor for her university's student chapter of the Society for Technical Communication (STC). The student chapter STC frequently partners with the university's Access and Diversity Center, as well as the Black Student Union and the Latinx Student Union, to provide TPC-relevant support such as designing promotional materials for events. One of their longest-standing collaborations is a blog that the STC developed several years ago, which provides a space for students who are members of underrepresented groups to share experiences, connect, and tell their stories. The blog has become a gathering place of sorts, and all posting privileges by members must be approved by Julie. The blog is now in its fourth year.

When the English Department (the TPC program's home department) changes web-hosting platforms, the director of the TPC program, George, approves the IT team to move over the blog's hosting as well. (After all, it's more efficient to have all sites and services in one place.) In the process, George, a senior scholar who happens to sit on Julie's promotion and tenure committee, also approves changes to the blog's permission settings, removing restrictions for posting privileges on the blog. (The new platform is much more streamlined now, and setting up an approval process like the previous one is a bit tricky with this new platform.) These backend changes all occur unbeknownst to Julie until she reads a department-wide email announcement from the IT team about the new web hosting. When Julie contacts the IT team to ask whether the new hosting platform will affect the blog, they assure her that George, in his role as program director, has given them all the information they need. "No need to worry," the IT team writes, "The blog has been moved over, and the transition was seamless. You're welcome! If you need anything, just contact George; all changes need to go through him." Julie wonders why she was left out of this process: Why didn't the IT team contact her? She's on record with the department as the blog's faculty administrator. Why didn't George defer to her, as the blog's administrator and the student club's adviser? Were these intentional slights? Does this reflect on the director's perception of her abilities? With effort, she tries to shake it off.

However, when Julie goes in to check the blog, she notices that posting privileges are now wide open. Her STC students maintain the blog's design, updating features and other tasks, but the junior scholar herself has administered posting privileges for several years now. She knows from direct experience how important it is to review and approve submissions and posting permission requests to protect the student community that gathers on this blog. Julie contacts her senior colleague to request changes to the permission settings, but George brushes off her request, explaining that this way is more streamlined and isn't it more inclusive, too? Surely, she wouldn't want to be exclusionary in a space that's supposed to be about promoting diversity. Why does she feel the need to be a gatekeeper and control who gets to participate?

This scenario presents a differently complex set of relationships and problems. In this scenario, we might consider both George's and Julie's positionality.

Technical Communication Scholar in an Academic Program: Critical Context Analysis

Julie understands a few things about the context already: (1) That students of color are potentially at risk when their private space becomes public; (2) that she has a certain amount of power as their advisor and the blog administrator; and (3) that she has less institutional power than George and, of course, needs George's support for tenure and promotion.

This scenario functions at several levels of domination, but the disciplinary domain is particularly notable. The academy structures power relations through its policies and procedures, particularly (for this scenario) tenure-and-promotion procedures. Because Julie is an untenured faculty member, the power relationships between her and George are asymmetrical, with George having direct power over Julie. Because she is in her third year and the policy is that she can be released from her contract at the end of her third year, Julie is particularly aware of the power George has (as the director of the program) to affect her life. Although there is an Office of Institutional Diversity at her university, the office can do little in tenure-and-promotion cases—after all, who is the Office of Institutional Diversity to interfere with "purely scholastic" endeavors like tenure and promotion.

But, as the many authors in *Presumed Incompetent* (2012) report, women of color in the university are often met with skepticism, challenged when their white counterparts would not be, and subject to unwritten rules and expectations. For Julie, this means that the disciplinary domain wanders into the interpersonal in ways that are difficult to reveal to those who are not attuned to problems of exclusion and microaggression. Although George has always been collegial, Julie wonders if George has excluded her from the decision-making process because she is a woman of color.

When she considers her own privilege, positionality, and power, Julie is unsure what to do. She has very little institutional capital and, as a Black woman, worries about the ways her complaints might be read: She doesn't have the privilege of being assumed competent, level-headed, and intellectually valuable. She is untenured, with only two other untenured faculty and 12 senior faculty, so she is not well positioned to change the culture of the program.

Technical Communication Scholar in an Academic Program: Coalitional Action

What is Julie's margin of maneuverability? How should she proceed, given the context she's working in? Here, the 4Rs (recognize, reveal, reject, replace) are instructive. Because she's recognized the potential problem with the blog already, the next step is to reveal the problem to another person. Especially given her limited power in the situation, moving straight to rejecting the problem or replacing it could be a risk. Revealing is a coalitional activity, an act that seeks others who can or will work with her to address the problem, so when Julie attempts to reveal the problem to George (only to be rebuffed), a new contextual element emerges. Julie understands that George, effectively, is not an ally, much less a member willing to work coalitionally.

A note about Julie's first reveal: Her first move was to reveal the problem (at least in part) to George. Given that George has taken official (or unofficial) control of the blog and STC chapter at large, this seems like a reasonable and safe move. Revealing the problem over George's head (or even laterally) can be risky, given Julie's position in the university. When Julie brings the problem to George, he has an opportunity to recognize the two potential problems or injustices: (1) That he has inadvertently (after all none of this is intentional) ignored Julie's authority in the institution, failing to include her in the decision-making and (2) that he has contributed to the institutional problems facing students of color and ignored the fact that their marginalization requires protected spaces, wherein their experiences are centered and valued. George—perhaps because he doesn't understand the problem (and refuses to listen) or perhaps because he's wrapped up in his assumptions about how improving efficiency and streamlining technology are valued/valuable—rebuff's Julie's concerns, demonstrating that he is unwilling to participate in coalition with Julie.

Given George's response, Julie is back to the beginning. And now she's worried that George might retaliate if she goes against his suggestions. What are her options?

1   Reveal to Someone Else: She can go above George's head to the chair or the associate dean in the Office of Institutional Diversity
2   Reject and Replace the Technology: She can go to IT and have the technological processes shifted

Both of these are risky moves, so Julie begins the process by moving outside of her institutional context and revealing to coalitional allies who will understand her intersectional concerns. Revealing the problem to an external, uninvolved coalition allows Julie to strategize, to be reassured that she's making the right decision, and to collectively develop an action plan.

In a meeting with coalitional allies, her colleagues ask a series of helpful questions:

"Why are you worried about George retaliating?"

It turns out, George has a rumored history of claiming to be pro-inclusivity and supportive of students and faculty of color but undercutting their efforts if they don't align with his values.

"How are you feeling about the situation now that it's a few days out?"

The sting of being left out of the process has worn off, but Julie is still worried about all the work the STC students and she have been doing to promote inclusivity and create a safe space for students of color to join the field of technical communication. The blog functions as sounding board with some personal concerns already posted: Worries about microaggressions, for example, and problems with understanding teachers' expectations.

"Do you know anyone in IT who might understand the problem the way you do?"

Julie has had coffee with Manny, a staff member who has been involved in Diversity Week with the STC, and though she doesn't know him well, she suspects he'd understand the problem. And, though he doesn't have a lot of privilege or power, his position in the department gives him access to the technology. He could probably make the changes without anyone knowing.

The coalitional meeting helps Julie come up with a plan:

1   For now, ignore the situation with George, knowing that George can't be depended on to address concerns about oppression, injustice, or inclusivity
2   Reveal the problem to Manny and gauge whether he can recognize the problem too. If he does, then they can work together to replace and reject the public setting and permissions process that leaves students vulnerable to outsiders from the STC inclusivity initiative

This scenario provides fodder for shifting practices in TPC in a number of ways. The first is that changes to technologies and procedures are not neutral, and considering those who are already marginalized helps us recognize the effects of technology in meaningful ways. Banks (2005) notes that mere access to technology is insufficient when we don't consider the critical sociocultural aspects of technology deployment. In other words, in order for a technology to function as purposeful, usable, and useful with and within a community, technology access must be transformative. The technology must be relevant to the community's social goals, needs, and wants and the community's local and contextually unique affordances and constraints. Further, the technology must not reinforce or reify existing oppressions. As Noble (2018) reveals in *Algorithms of Oppression*, the very development of both front end and back end technologies constructs and reconstructs the world's existing oppressive structures.

The second is that inclusive decision-making processes—assuming that Julie (in this case) has valuable knowledge in the situation and should be included—can help prevent these problems. This implies that TPC as a field should tend to its practices of knowledge legitimization, particularly by acknowledging, inviting, and accepting the different ways that knowledge is made (both experiential and disciplinary). Patricia Hill Collins, among others, provides a framework for rethinking epistemological frameworks and, as Moore (2018) suggests, this revised approach to knowledge making can augment our TPC practices. As such, this scenario suggests a need for expanding our knowledge bases and knowledge making through reading, citation, and listening practices. Who are we reading? Citing? And listening to? How are our patterns contributing to the marginalization, delegitimization, devaluation, or suppression of our colleagues who, like Julie, already work and live at the margins?

Finally, we want to note that coalitional and inclusive work is not all-access work. In this scenario, George adopts what he believes to be an inclusive approach, expanding the reach of the STC blog and including all students. But this, as Julie knows, is a mistake. Although we do promote inclusivity, we want to be clear that not all spaces are for all people: Especially people who benefit from ableist, white supremacist and patriarchal systems that center particular experiences while marginalizing others. George Yancey, in describing "The Ugly Truth of Being a Black Professor in America," articulates this particular point well. He writes,

> I have often heard white people express the feeling of being somehow left out from black spaces, which are necessary for black sanity precisely because of white racism. It is as if white people are driven by a colonial desire to possess everything.

While we don't suggest that George is intentionally asserting a colonial desire to possess everything, it's easy to see how this colonial influence creeps into non-intersectional approaches to inclusivity. When Agboka (2013) and Haas (2012) talk about decolonizing the field of TPC, they mean not only with our research and teaching but also in institutional contexts like the one described here: Our technology use, decision-making procedures, and daily activities also require a decolonizing framework.

Conclusion

This chapter and these scenarios have proposed several strategies for how we can proceed as technical communicators in our work to redress inequities and address oppression. The scenarios and heuristics are imperfect but useful tools for structuring decision making in a way that is not merely ethical—but also just. As you move into the world (your programs, your offices, your classrooms), we know you will be met with resistance, skepticism, and sometimes hostility. We certainly have been. And we know this is a risk you take in order to move the world along a more inclusive, socially just trajectory. In anticipation of those experiences, we provide you with a final chapter that helps you address critiques and questions—combative and honest queries alike.

Notes

1 This is an uncomfortable claim but an important extension of the previous three chapters.

2 This is particularly true when Phred and Fred are instead Phran and Fran, women who consider themselves to be feminists. But hooks (among others) has already articulated the problems with feminism's history; and we need only consider the U.S. presidential election of 2016, the Women's March of 2017, or the election of Doug Jones* to understand that feminism often does not engage in intersectional, coalitional work and has long failed to center the experiences of the most vulnerable in the U.S. This also occurs with liberal progressives, for example, whose own self-identification can get in the way of listening and centering the positions of the

marginalized. While it seems we're vilifying particular groups, we hope it's clear that we're calling in those (feminists, too) who seek to engage in just practices and asking us all to reconsider how we might be carrying out that work.

*During a special election in 2017, Doug Jones, a democrat, was elected to the Alabama State Senate. Jones ran against republican senator, Roy Moore. Moore, a former judge who previously served as a justice for the Alabama Supreme Court (and had been twice suspended from his position as justice) was accused of sexual misconduct during the election. In addition, Moore made racially insensitive remarks during his campaign, was alleged to have ties to white supremacist groups, was a vocal in his anti-gay stance, and has been noted as being opposed to allowing Muslims to serve on Congress. Despite this, Moore received 48.4% of the votes, with Jones winning the special election with 49.9% of the votes. Jones's victory is largely attributed to the votes of African American women. According to a Newsweek.com article (2017), it is estimated that 98% of Black women voted for Jones, while 63% of white women voted for Moore. Further, the article reports that only about 30% of white voters overall voted for Jones.

3 It's important to remember (as we discuss in Chapters 3–5) that privilege and positionality work in tandem, which means that sometimes despite being in a position of authority in a classroom, as in this example, a person from marginalized positions may also face risks in revealing this kind of microaggression. They may be more likely, for example, to be read as an angry feminist or angry Black woman—and those comments may show up in their teaching evaluations or be reported to upper administration.

4 The Value-Sensitive Design Envisioning Cards were developed by the Value Sensitive Design Research Lab at the University of Washington; the purpose of the cards is to help designers better account for human values in their work.

References

Agboka, G. Y. (2013). Participatory localization: A social justice approach to navigating unenfranchised/disenfranchised cultural sites. *Technical Communication Quarterly, 22*(1), 28–49.

Banks, A. (2005). *Race, rhetoric, and technology: Searching for higher ground*. Mahwah, NJ: Lawrence Erlbaum Associates.

Chávez, K. R. (2013). *Queer migration politics: Activist rhetoric and coalitional possibilities*. Champaign, IL: University of Illinois Press.

Collins, P. H. (2002). *Black feminist thought: Knowledge, consciousness, and the politics of empowerment*. New York, NY: Routledge.

Dolmage, J. (2008). Mapping composition: Inviting disability in the front door. In C. Lewiecki-Wilson & B. J. Brueggemann (Eds.), *Disability and the teaching of writing: A critical sourcebook* (pp. 14–27). Boston, MA: Bedford/St. Martins.

Gutiérrez y Muhs, G., Niemann, Y. F., González, C. G., & Harris, A. P. (2012). *Presumed incompetent: The intersections of race and class for women in academia*. Logan, UT: Utah State University Press.

Haas, A. M. (2012). Race, rhetoric, and technology: A case study of decolonial technical communication theory, methodology, and pedagogy. *Journal of Business and Technical Communication, 26*(3), 277–310.

Lorde, A. (1984). *Sister outsider*. Trumansburg, NY: Crossing.

Meza, S. (2017, December 13). *Who voted for Doug Jones? White women back Roy Moore*. *Newsweek*. Retrieved from http://www.newsweek.com/doug-jones-roy-moore-alabama-senate-race- Special-election-results-demographics-746366

Moore, K. R. (2017). The technical communicator as participant, facilitator, and designer in public engagement projects. *Technical Communication, 64*(3), 237–253.

Moore, K. R. (2018). Black feminist epistemology as a framework for community-based teaching. In A. M. Haas & M. F. Eble (Eds.), *Key theoretical frameworks: Teaching technical communication in the twenty-first century* (p. 26). Logan, UT: Utah State University.

Moskowitz, P. (2017). *How to kill a city: Gentrification, inequality, and the fight for the neighborhood.* New York, NY: Hachette Book Group.

Noble, S. U. (2018). *Algorithms of oppression: How search engines reinforce racism.* New York, NY: NYU Press.

Palmeri, J. (2006). Disability studies, cultural analysis, and the critical practice of technical communication pedagogy. *Technical Communication Quarterly, 15*(1), 49–65.

Poehler, A. (2014). *Yes please.* New York, NY: Harper Collins.

Porter, J. E., Sullivan, P., Blythe, S., Grabill, J. T., & Miles, L. (2000). Institutional critique: A rhetorical methodology for change. *College Composition and Communication, 610–642.*

Rothstein, R. (2017). *The color of law: A forgotten history of how our government segregated America.* New York, NY: Liveright.

Sullivan, P., & Legg, E. (2018). Storytelling as a balancing practice in the study of posthuman praxis. In K. R. Moore & D. Richards (Eds.), *Posthuman praxis in technical communication* (pp. 21–45). New York, NY: Routledge.

Young, I. M. (1990). *Justice and the politics of difference.* Princeton, NJ: Princeton University Press.

Zdenek, S. (2015). *Reading sounds: Closed-captioned media and popular culture.* Chicago, IL: University of Chicago Press.

7

CRITIQUES AND RESPONSES

Introduction

Advocating for inclusion and social justice in technical communication practices comes with particular challenges and invites particular critiques. Indeed, we expect that some readers will challenge and critique the ideas we present in this book. Like many other technical and professional communication (TPC) scholars who engage in social justice work, we want to address the critiques and questions that emerge for readers and skeptics. But we find anticipating these critiques while introducing our theoretical framework undercuts the argument and, more importantly, decenters the work of scholars of color and social justice advocates. It is intentional that here at the end of the book—the margins, you might say—is where we address critiques which are often grounded in white supremacist, patriarchal assumptions. Following Delgado and Stefancic (2012), we gather the critiques and challenges we have already faced (and some we have only indirectly encountered) into one space. In doing so, we equip advocates of inclusion and social justice with responses to common critiques of this work. Similarly, this chapter also engages with critiques and questions that readers might have as they move through the text. We provide these critiques and responses in the spirit of hooks' "talking back" (hooks, 1994). For hooks, talking back is empowering because it allows individuals' voices to be heard in a powerful and positive manner, not feeling beholden to agreeing with or acquiescing to dominant ideals or narratives. We keep our remarks here fairly brief so that the answers are usable, but we also provide suggestions for additional texts that might deepen readers' understandings of the responses we offer.

THEY SAY: It's hypocritical to call for inclusivity of all perspectives and then create dedicated space for marginalized voices (i.e., the "all lives matter" or "white student union" argument).

WE SAY: This kind of critique is concerned exclusively with the experiences of dominant groups—a critique that maintains the marginalization of social groups by focusing on equality rather than equity (see Chapter 2). Dominant perspectives crafted current institutions; social norms and institutions (as control agents) are created to preserve the privilege of dominant groups. There is not a need for dominant voices to also get dedicated space. The space is already theirs by default. See this excerpt from an interview with Angela Davis and Elizabeth Martinez (1998); this is Martinez speaking:

> People ask, 'Why can't we all see each other as human beings? Why do we have to emphasize these differences?' or 'Why do we need feminism? Why can't we just have humanism? Doesn't talking about racism and the different races just perpetuate the problem?' This negates the structures of power that determine human relationships in this society in a way that is deadening for a great number of people, mostly, but by no means exclusively, people of color. You can't just say, 'Let's all get along' until we get rid of those structures.
>
> *(p. 303)*

As technical communicators move toward social justice and inclusion, the need to address power structures and systemic oppression will be fundamental to our success. And, importantly, we will discover that dedicated spaces become more necessary, not less, as we develop an inclusive, diverse, and representative field.

The suggestion that we should not need dedicated spaces or that we should all just get along reflects troubling perspectives of our current political moment—an academic variation of the argument that we are in a post-racial society and that we should not "see color." Bonilla-Silva (2002) calls this "color-blind racism." Color-blind racism, or arguments that we should not see color, are insidious in that these arguments appear to be calls for inclusivity. However, color-blind racism only further marginalizes people of color by assuming that there is no inequality, inequity, or oppression and that systemic racism and discrimination do not exist:

> To deny race and ignore the existence of racism actually causes harm to people of color because it a) falsely perpetuates the myth of equal access and opportunity, b) blames people of color for their lot in life, and c) allows Whites to live their lives in ignorance, naiveté, and innocence.
>
> *(Neville, Gallardo, & Sue, 2016)*

The move to rebuff efforts to enclave or group around identity or experience threatens all types of nondominant groups, including but not limited to women; lesbian, gay, bisexual, transgender, queer (LGBTQ) people; and people with disabilities.

Ultimately, we assert that genuine inclusion does not mean we ignore issues of discrimination and oppression. Moreover, inclusion does not and should not require assimilation. Dedicated spaces for marginalized groups create a place of respite for these groups who are constantly bombarded with discrimination, racism, and marginalization and pressure to assimilate or be faced with retaliation. Living in a white supremacist, patriarchal society means that minority and marginalized individuals must always be aware of how they present themselves and how they are perceived (e.g., code-switching, code-meshing, and cultural dress). We can especially appreciate the need for dedicated spaces for marginalized populations when we take into account the violence and oppression that we witness (and that people of color in particular) experience for simply existing in predominantly white spaces. To reference a few contemporary examples:

- Two Black men arrested for "trespassing" (read: sitting) in Starbucks in April 2018
- Two Indigenous men questioned by law enforcement for making a white woman "nervous" on a college tour at the University of Colorado, Boulder in May 2018
- Two Black men asked to leave an L.A. Fitness location in Secaucus, NJ, by management and reported to law enforcement in April 2018
- A Black man followed to his own apartment and contacted by law enforcement due to a white woman feeling "uncomfortable" in October 2018

Dedicated spaces for marginalized groups are places where individuals can gather and just be, a much needed break and protection from white gaze.

Further Reading

Bonilla-Silva, E. (2014). *Racism without racists: Color-blind racism and persistence of racial inequality in America* (4th ed.). Lanham, MD: Rowan & Littlefield.

Neville, H., Gallardo, M., & Sue, D. W. (2016). *The myth of racial color blindness: Manifestations, dynamics, and impact.* Washington, DC: American Psychological Association.

Tatum, B. D. (2017). *Why are all the black kids sitting together in the cafeteria? And other conversations about race.* New York, NY: Basic Books.

THEY SAY: The U.S. is a post-racial and/or post-feminist society. After all, Barack Obama was elected president; Mary Barra was CEO of General Motors; Hillary Rodham Clinton won the popular vote in the 2016 presidential election.

WE SAY: No. This kind of critique aims to close off discussions about systems of oppression, but it just doesn't follow that one exception—one powerful, wealthy, and/or successful member of a nondominant group—can serve as evidence proving that an entire system of oppression has been eradicated. Particularly when repeated patterns of oppression play out—such as police-perpetrated killings of people of color. As writer and activist Ta-Nehisi Coates points out, such critiques as the previous one aim not just to prevent conversations about race but also to close off pointed, necessary questions, such as, "How can it be that, with regularity, the news describes the shooting of an unarmed African Americans by the very police officers sworn to protect Americans?" And, in any case, our goal shouldn't be to become a post-racial or post-feminist society. Assimilation is not the answer: Erasure of difference is a strategy of colonialism and cultural imperialism. Rather, we should pursue the goal of a post-racist (and post-sexist) society. The rare female CEO or politician of color does not make untrue the persistent, widespread, often deadly evidence that the goal is unmet.

Importantly, this argument has imbued the field of technical communication, as scholars of color have risen to leadership. This attitude and critique result in programs believing that one star queer scholar is "plenty" for the field, that the one Black woman and indigenous scholar running ATTW is evidence that the field has changed and need not be committed to post-racist and post-sexist practices, and that Women in Technical Communication is unnecessary because of the mere number of women in the field. In other words, it may seem that these critiques and perspectives, regardless of how large they loom in the world, are unlikely to pervade our field and academia at large. But this is naive at best and oppressive at worst.

Further Reading

Coates, T. (2015, July/August). There is no post-racial America. *The Atlantic.* Retrieved from https://www.theatlantic.com/magazine/archive/2015/07/ post-racial-society-distant-dream/395255/

THEY SAY: If people would just do what's right/follow the rules/not break the law, then they wouldn't be harassed/arrested/killed/locked into poverty.

WE SAY: This kind of argument is based on "respectability politics" (a term coined by Evelyn Brooks Higginbotham, a professor of History and of African and African American Studies at Harvard University). Respectability politics shifts blame for oppression onto the oppressed by claiming that they must behave better to get treated better. It is a compelling argument, especially to people blind to their own privilege, because it suggests that individuals are to blame for their own second-class citizenship. But that's not true. As legal scholar and activist Michelle Alexander (2010) points out, every one of us has broken the law, and if the worst offense you've ever committed was merely speeding 10 miles over the limit on the highway, you have put more people at risk than someone smoking marijuana in her own apartment. And yet in the U.S., there are people (disproportionately people of color) serving life sentences for first-time drug offenses (p. 215). All humans err. All humans break laws. But only some humans are arrested, incarcerated, permanently branded a felon, stripped of voting rights, and rendered functionally unemployable. Disproportionally, those humans are members of minority groups, especially people of color.

Also, we point out that doing everything right is no guarantee of freedom from oppression (including fatal violence). Consider the 2016 murder of Philando Castile by a Minnesota police officer. Castile met all the requirements of respectability: A man beloved at the elementary school where he worked; following all traffic laws as he drove; with a legal permit to carry a weapon; compliant, polite, and calm when pulled over by a police officer. He was shot seven times within 40 seconds of being pulled over. The police officer was acquitted on all charges for the killing because his defense rested upon fear: The police officer said he feared for his life, so it was legally justifiable to kill Philando Castile. When people of color are targeted, harassed, arrested, and killed, the system is not malfunctioning; it is designed to oppress.

And, lest we academics think we are not complicit in this particular problem, we authors point out respectability politics pervades our own universities and organizations. Extending from white supremacist assumptions, this system of oppression (which killed Philando Castile) is the same system of oppression that causes little Black boys and girls to be expelled from school and Black scholars to be told they are "unprofessional" for their dress or language use. It is the same system of oppression that argues that if women would just be collegial and adhere to tenure and promotion policies, then they won't face problems with tenure and promotion. One need only read the Writing Program Administrators' listserv for pushback against Vershawn Ashanti Young's 2019 CCCC Call for Proposals (among other conversations) to admit that we, too, as (often) liberal and well-meaning scholars engage in our own version of respectability politics.

Further Reading

Alexander, M. (2012). *The new Jim Crow: Mass incarceration in the age of color-blindness.* New York, NY: The New Press.

THEY SAY: But aren't these just personal concerns?

WE SAY: No. Oppression is systemic—built into society at multiple levels and in myriad ways. Racism. Sexism. Heteronormativity. Ableism. These are not just personal concerns; these are systems of oppression that target people with particular identity markers, not only taking an emotional and mental toll but also limiting people's potentialities in very practical, material ways. Take, for example, mortgage loans. Oppressive practices such as redlining (i.e., refusing to approve a loan to people who live in poor areas) lead to clear and widespread patterns of rejecting loan applications from people of color (see the Center for Investigative Reporting's 2018 study of 31 million mortgage records). Certainly, a woman of color who cannot purchase a home for her family experiences personal concern over the oppression that limits, blocks, threatens, and devalues her day-to-day life. But this oppression is not just a personal problem.

One of the suggestions we make in this book is that those with relatively more privilege and positionality must take seriously the personal concerns of less privileged people so as to recognize and reject systems of oppression. When we bracket off personal experiences, valorizing the rational over the experiential, we miss opportunities to redress inequities in our academic programs and daily practices. Our willingness to accept the relationship between personal experiences and systemic oppression is foundational to our ability to effectively move toward inclusion and socially just technical communication.

Further Reading

Collins, P. H. (2002). *Black feminist thought: Knowledge, consciousness, and the politics of empowerment*. New York, NY: Routledge. (See especially the matrix of domination and four domains of power in Chapter 12.)

THEY SAY: I think justice is important, of course, but I don't like to get political, especially in my work life.

WE SAY: We suspect that this objection—a disinclination or distaste for "getting political"—stems less from misunderstanding how justice, oppression, power, and politics are linked and more from a privileged reluctance to engage with uncomfortable realities. But if we give the objector the benefit of the doubt regarding their motives, then we would simply assert: Justice and politics are fundamentally linked. Talking about justice requires talking about oppression (see Chapter 1), and when we closely consider how oppression works, we can perceive what Patricia Hill Collins (2002) calls the matrix of domination: Interlocking, mutually reinforcing domains of power. Politics is about power:

- politics is "an ongoing process of negotiating power relations" (Coole & Frost, 2010, p. 18)
- politics is "who gets what and why" (Mills, 1997, p. 31)
- politics is the "struggle over the resources and arrangements that set the basic terms of our practical and passionate relations" (Unger, 1987, p. 145)
- politics is "the activity through which relatively large and permanent groups of people determine what they will collectively do, settle how they will live together, and decide their future" (Pitkin, 1981, p. 343)

In other words, politics is how people work out who gets the power to do what (and to whom). That process is directly in the scope of justice considerations; if you care about justice, you have to get political.

Further Reading

Young, I. M. (1990). *Justice and the politics of difference*. Princeton, NJ: Princeton University Press.

THEY SAY: It's so daunting that injustice is institutionalized and systemic. What can I—just one person—even do about it?

WE SAY: You can join a coalition of like-minded people and take action together. It's true that injustice is woven into the fabric of our institutions, underlies our policies, and tinges our interactions. But, as we discuss throughout this book, individuals occupy different types and positions of privilege, and our positionality within institutions, cultures, and contexts varies. This variation in privilege and positionality informs the power we have to take action, that is, our margins of maneuverability for intervention and action vary. This variability can be useful to coalitions—enabling the group to engage multiple strategies for revealing, rejecting, and replacing injustice. Further, engaging coalitionally in the pursuit of justice offers greater opportunities for us each to recognize injustices—particularly those injustices we do not ourselves experience—and to guard against reinscribing oppression in our activism by centering the voices, experiences, and priorities of those who are most marginalized.

One of the reasons we believe technical communication, specifically, should be committed to social justice is that injustices often live in the mundane choices that technical communicators make: How drop down menus look, whether a form is translated into another language, if captioning is included in a tutorial video, the default setting on an topic-based authoring system. We believe that, working coalitionally, the individual choices we make, the small choices about design and representation, the ways we treat our students and colleagues, and the ways we run our programs can work to redress inequities in small ways. When we join together in coalitions, these mundane choices become part of a collective that moves toward inclusion and justice as a whole. So, yes. The work that you can do matters. And your individual devotion to inclusion and social justice matters.

Further Reading

Chaves, K. (2013) *Queer migration politics: Activist rhetoric and coalitional possibilities*. Chicago, IL: Illinois University Press.

Taylor, K. (2017). *How we get free: Black feminism and the Combahee River Collective*. Chicago, IL: Haymarket Books.

THEY SAY: Social justice is unsustainable because it takes too much emotional labor and causes burnout.

WE SAY: Yes, we agree that social justice work is indeed emotionally laborious. In fact, some might liken recognizing the inequities, injustices, and oppressions that we must confront on a daily basis to opening pandora's box. Colloquially, when one begins to recognize all of the ways in which our society is unjust and oppressive, it's called being "woke." Being woke is exhausting because not only do you begin to recognize the insidious nature of white supremacist, patriarchal, normative society, you also have to consistently work to actively educate yourself and then strategize the best way forward. We argue that this, the emotionally intensive nature of social justice work, is one of the reasons that our work must be coalitional. In order to be effective, we cannot take on social justice work on our own. We cannot know all of the things, do all of the things, take on all of the tasks. Coalitions allow us to work with one another. Coalitions provide us with the opportunity to tap into to each other's strengths, and coalitions encourage us to build up each other in areas of weakness. Social justice work will never be easy, but coalitional social justice work can help to make work more manageable. Further, coalitions create a safe and protected space for individuals to share experiences, thoughts, and feelings, providing much needed emotional support for members of the coalition. In short, coalitions help to make social justice work more successful and sustainable. As hooks and Mesa-Bains assert, "We are connected" (2006, p. xiii).

Our arguments throughout this book—that we must all contribute—reflect this critique and attempt to redress it not just personally but institutionally, programmatically. We recognize that junior scholars are struggling against the dominant narratives of technical communication as they work toward social justice; and as scholars in *Presumed Incompetent* demonstrate, multiply marginalized members of our communities do the heavy lifting to support students of color. We contend that our responses to injustices, when systematic and coalitional, can lessen the burden of those who have historically been over-burdened with the work of supporting and forwarding inclusive, socially just technical communication.

Further Reading

Gutiérrez y Muhs, G., Niemann, Y. F., González, C. G., & Harris, A. P. (2012). *Presumed incompetent: The intersections of race and class for women in academia*. Logan, UT: Utah State University Press.

hooks, b., & Mesa-Bains, A. (2006). *Homegrown: Engaged cultural criticism*. New York, NY: Routledge.

THEY SAY: What's needed is for us all to show a bit more empathy. Isn't just being kind enough?

WE SAY: No. That is not enough. There is a difference between being kind and being just. If technical communication is truly a humanistic field, as it claims, then we must be genuinely concerned about how our scholarship, teaching, and practice affect others. Simply being kind does not address impact. Being kind considers only intention. Unfortunately, intentions are of little concern in regard to issues of oppression. Good intentions, kind intentions do not mitigate harm. Gorski (2007) argues that emphasizing good intentions decontextualizes systemic social oppressions and shifts focus from meaningful work that combats those oppressions. Relying on good intentions to redress inequities is short-sighted because as Kendi (2017) makes clear, hate (bad intentions, ill-will, malice) is not at the root of oppression and racism. Kendi argues that self-interest is the fundamental anchor of oppression and racism. "Hate and ignorance have not driven the history of racist ideas in America. Racist policies have driven the history of racist ideas in America" (p. 9). Clearly, it is not enough to be kind or to have more empathy. The core of the problem is systemic and foundational. Empathy only acknowledges others' suffering or pain. Empathy does nothing to address that suffering or pain. Empathy does not require critical action or movement toward redressing inequities.

As Ta-Nahisi Coates (2015) writes, "Good intention is a hall pass through history, a sleeping pill that ensures the Dream." We suspect that empathy acts similarly as a hall pass that lures dominant groups into believing they have done enough by empathizing with the plight of the oppressed. The 4Rs becomes instructive here as we think about the #metoo movement and the need not just for empathy but for action, not just for recognizing sexual harassment as a problem but for rejecting and replacing abusive behaviors. Like Coates's sleeping pill, empathetic responses alone reinforce the white supremacist and patriarchal values that maintain oppressive structures. So, no. Being kind and having empathy is not enough.

Further Reading

Coates, T. (2015). *Between the world and me*. Melbourne, VIC: Text.

Gorski, P. C. (2008). Good intentions are not enough: A decolonizing intercultural education. *Intercultural Education, 19*(6), 515–525.

Kendi, I. X. (2016). *Stamped from the beginning: The definitive history of racist ideas in America*. New York, NY: Nation Books.

THEY SAY: It's fine for you to do social justice work, as long as you don't make me do it.

WE SAY: Social justice work is not a topic choice for researchers, where some folks choose to study, for example, rhetoric of health and medicine and others decide to study intercultural communication. Rather, we consider socially just, inclusive technical communication to be foundational for *all* areas of technical communication. In other words, we agree that not everyone needs to use "social justice" as a keyword in their scholarship. Rather, we argue that if technical communication is not intentionally, coalitionally pursuing inclusion and social justice, then it is actively reinscribing oppression. Thus, it just doesn't hold that TPC scholars can "opt out" of social justice if we are to effectively take up the tasks and the foundational work of the field. One cannot engage with user advocacy without considering social justice. One cannot effectively conduct intercultural communication (and, following Davis and Williams, most communication requires intercultural understanding) without considering social justice. One cannot effectively instruct students without considering social justice. And one cannot build programs, curricula, or organizations of TPC without considering social justice.

If technical communicators choose not to consider social justice, they are working ineffectively. And unjustly. They are doing harm.

Further Reading

Jones, N. N., Moore, K. R., & Walton, R. (2016). Disrupting the past to disrupt the future: An antenarrative of technical communication. *Technical Communication Quarterly, 25*(4), 211–229.

AND THEN THEY SAY: But is social justice *really* technical communication?

WE SAY: That's the wrong question. Of course, not all social justice work is technical communication. But we think that all technical communication should be socially just or can be examined through a social justice perspective. And, more to the point, we think that technical communicators should be invested in social justice and commit to redressing inequities in the world.

In some ways, this question reflects misguided values of the field of technical communication that would separate out the ideological from the applied,
the theoretical from the practical (see Jones, Moore, & Walton, 2016). Any approach to technical communication that accounts for social (in)justice must
necessarily consider the interconnectedness among the technologies we use,
the documents we write, and the systems of oppression that they reinscribe or
begin to unravel. The choice to separate technical communication from social
justice is a willful refusal to think critically about the effects of our privilege,
positionality, and power.

Further Reading

Haas, A. M., & Eble, M. F. (Eds.). (2018). *Key theoretical frameworks: Teaching
technical communication in the twenty-first century*. Logan, UT: Utah State
University Press.
Shivers-McNair, A. (2017). Localizing communities, goals, communication,
and inclusion: A collaborative approach. *Technical Communication, 64*(2),
97–112.

THEY SAY: Coalitions should welcome everyone; they shouldn't be clique-ish or
exclude anyone.
WE SAY: The fundamental purpose of an intersectional coalition is to pursue
shared, inclusive, and socially just actions, organizations, movements,
and so on. They're not country clubs that sell membership, and they're
not families built on unconditional love and acceptance. Rather, coalitions are conditional; they rely upon a shared agreement about how we
act as a collective. Membership requires being open, listening, and contributing to that shared agreement. As such, coalitional acceptance and
rejection are enacted in different ways by different members, but coalitions support the needs of other coalition members and operate with
care. We can think of many examples where a coalition member has been
mistreated by someone who wants to be considered a coalition member.
But simply wanting to be a part of the coalition doesn't permit an individual into the coalition. Coalition members must be mindful of their
own power, positionality, and privilege, must protect those with less
power, and must amplify the work of the coalition. When a member or
potential member of a coalition fails to engage with other members this
way, the cycle of the 4Rs should be engaged—recognizing and revealing
with humility and generosity. We contend that when other coalition (or
potential coalition) members fail to engage with the 4Rs meaningfully,
humbly, and readily, they self-select out of the coalition and effectively
opt out of the coalitional work.

This discussion of offending, of failure to engage coalitionally is not based on the expectation that "good" coalition members never need an invitation to recognize. It's not that you won't mess up; it's that when you do, you reflect, you are humble, you are willing to take a beat and think. Reflect. The revealing to others comes from a coalitional mindset: A message of "that's not how we act" intends to help the offender to remain a part of the "we." If you refuse to engage coalitionally, if you immediately push back in response to "that's not how we act," then other members will lose faith in your allyship, in your sincerity, and in the coalition at large.

This requirement for mutual support does not mean that coalitions do not embrace difference—in fact, one of the defining features of coalitions is their commitment to difference. Cole (2008), citing Reagon, reminds us that coalitional work is "difficult taxing work" that "require[s] people move beyond their comfort zones to face, understand and accept difference" (p. 444). But coalition members must commit to the difficult work of listening and engaging if they want to be understood as an ally and coalition member.

Further Reading

Carbado, D. W., Crenshaw, K. W., Mays, V. M., & Tomlinson, B. (2013). Intersectionality: Mapping the movements of a theory. *Du Bois Review: Social Science Research on Race, 10*(2), 303–312.

Chávez, K. R. (2013). *Queer migration politics: Activist rhetoric and coalitional possibilities.* Champaign, IL: University of Illinois Press.

Cole, E. R. (2008). Coalitions as a model for intersectionality: From practice to theory. *Sex Roles, 59*(5–6), 443–453.

THEY SAY: Most of your examples and contexts in this book are in the U.S. What might socially just technical communication look like globally?

WE SAY: This is a good question. Whatever the national or regional context, it is important for coalitional work to be driven by the priorities of the most marginalized, those with the least power. For examples of what this can look like, some humanitarian organizations can provide a useful model (though, as discussed in Chapter 6, oppression is insidious and can operate within and through even organizations explicitly pursuing socially just goals). Specifically, many humanitarian organizations structure information flow from the bottom up, flipping traditional corporate power structures; often, too, humanitarian organizations develop their priorities and understanding of expert knowledge from local sources (Walton, Mays, & Haselkorn, 2016). These practices are particularly relevant to considering what socially just TPC may look like globally. And, as Angela Davis (2016) demonstrates, those of us invested in social justice in domestic contexts cannot simply look away from global atrocities as we focus on injustices closer to home.

Patricia Hill Collins's (2002) theories of power and Iris Marion Young's (1990) theory of oppression help us consider more directly the importance of addressing broader colonial frameworks of history, government, and politics. But we think it would be a mistake to commit to a savior-driven approach to redressing problems facing people across the world. As Walton, Agboka, Dura, Hopton, and others have demonstrated, effective international work takes immense amounts of time, resources, and heart. If efforts to build global approaches to social justice are not built from a local and decolonial framework as Agboka (2013) teaches us, we risk repeating the colonial injustices that have plagued the field. In short, we think global work is so, so important and should not be ignored. In this book, you can find some international frameworks for justice in Chapter 2 and some examples of technical communication in cross-cultural contexts in Chapter 6. But more work is need that surfaces the challenges of globally oriented technical communication.

Further Reading

Agboka, G. Y. (2013). Participatory localization: A social justice approach to navigating unenfranchised/disenfranchised cultural sites. *Technical Communication Quarterly, 22*(1), 28–49.

Chambers, R. (2014). *Rural development: Putting the last first.* New York, NY: Routledge.

Davis, A. Y. (2016). *Freedom is a constant struggle: Ferguson, Palestine, and the foundations of a movement.* Chicago, IL: Haymarket Books.

Savage, J., & Agboka, G. Y. (2015). Special Issue: Professional Communication, Social Justice, & the Global South. *connexions, 4*(1).

THEY SAY: I'd love to read and cite more work by marginalized scholars in the field, but there are just not enough Black, Indigenous, minority, transgender, scholars with disabilities, etc. in our field.

WE SAY:[1]

Keshab Acharya

Godwin Agboka

Jamal-Jared Alexander

Phill Alexander

Sonia Arellano

Sweta Baniya

Adam Banks

Samantha Blackmon

Tony Bushner

Joyce Locke Carter

Chen Chen

Geoff Clegg

Casie Cobos
Laquana Cooke
Suban Nur Cooley
Matthew Cox
Sherri Craig
Huiling Ding
Isidore Dorpenyo
Lucia Dura
Avery Edenfield
Jessica Edwards
Kimberly Fain
Michael Faris
Wilfredo Flores
Marlene Galvan
Kendall Gerdes
Laura Gonzales
Baotong Gu
Angela Haas
Kimberly Harper
Alicia Hatcher
Marcos Del Hierro
Victor Del Hierro
Alexandra Hidalgo
Allison Hitt
Elise Verzosa Hurley
Les Hutchinson
Alex Ilyasova
Cana Uluak Itchuaqiyaq
Krista Kennedy
Stephanie Kerschbaum
Loel S. Kim
Annika Konrad
Lehua Ledbetter
Emily Legg
Kendall Leon
Xiaoli Li
Temptaous McKoy
Cruz Medina
Maggie Melo
Zarah Moeggenberg
Kourtney Moore
Genevieve García de Müeller
Ryan Omizo
Sushil Oswal

Jason Palmeri
GPat Patterson
Therese Pennell
Octavio Pimentel
Patti Poblete
Keerthi Potluri
Enrique Reynoso
Flourice Richardson
Errol Rivers
Joy Robinson
Aimee Roundtree
Donnie J. Sackey
Fernando Sánchez
James Chase Sanchez
Jennifer Sano-Franchini
J. Blake Scott
Cecilia Shelton
Priya Sirohi
Huatong Sun
Jason Tham
Don Unger
Josephine Walwema
Isaac Wang
Xiaobo Wang
Travis Webster
Miriam F. Williams
David Young
Han Yu
Yunye Yu
Quan Zhou
And so on.
And so forth.

Note

1 This list is not exhaustive, but it is purposefully designed. The list was developed through a snowball approach that requested both permission and recommendations of additional scholars.

We developed the collection of scholars here to signal the multiply marginalized and underrepresented groups in our field. These groups include colleagues who are racial and ethnic minorities; colleagues who are lesbian, gay, queer, transgender, or bisexual; colleagues with disabilities and colleagues who are neurodiverse; among others. You will note, however, the omission of white women from this list, an indication that they are not underrepresented in the field, though we certainly (as members of Women in Technical Communication) acknowledge the ways women continue to face sexism in professional environments and elsewhere.

Abbreviated Further Reading

Acharya, K. R. (2017). User value and usability in technical communication: A value-proposition design model. *Communication Design Quarterly, 4*(3), 26–34.

Agboka, G. Y. (2014). Decolonial methodologies: Social justice perspectives in intercultural technical communication research. *Journal of Technical Writing and Communication, 44*(3), 297–327.

Alexander, P., Chabot, K., Cox, M., DeVoss, D. N., Gerber, B., Perryman-Clark, S., ... & Wendt, M. (2012). Teaching with technology: Remediating the teaching philosophy statement. *Computers and Composition, 29*(1), 23–38.

Arellano, S. (2016). *A maker project: Writing about material culture.* Blog Carnival 8. Digital Rhetoric Collaborative.

Banks, A. J. (2006). *Race, rhetoric, and technology: Searching for higher ground.* New York, NY: Routledge.

Barrett-Fox, J., & Clegg, G. (2018). Beyond hearts and minds: Posthumanism, *Kairos*, and technical communication in *US Army Field Manual 3-24, Counterinsurgency*. In: K. R. Moore, & D. Richards (Eds.), *Posthuman praxis in technical communication.* New York, NY: Routledge.

Blackmon, S., Kirklighter, C., & Parks, S. (2011). *Listening to our elders: Working and writing for change.* Logan, UT: Utah State University Press.

Carter, J. L. (2016). 2016 CCCC chair's address: Making, disrupting, innovating. *College Composition and Communication, 68*(2), 378.

Cobos, C., Raquel Ríos, G., Johnson Sackey, D., Sano-Franchini, J., & Haas, A. M. (2018). Interfacing Cultural Rhetorics: A History and a Call. *Rhetoric Review, 37*(2), 139–154.

Cox, M. B., & Faris, M. J. (2015). An annotated bibliography of LGBTQ rhetorics. *Present Tense, 4*(2). Retrieved from http://www.presenttensejournal.org/wp-content/uploads/2015/04/CoxandFaris.pdf

Del Hierro, M. J. (2010). Rhetorics of the Americas: 3114 BCE to 2012 CE. *Studies in American Indian Literatures, 22*(4), 85–88.

Del Hierro, V. J. (2013). *The Emcee's site of enunciation: Exploring the dialectic between authorship and readership in hip hop* (Doctoral dissertation).

Ding, H. (2009). Rhetorics of alternative media in an emerging epidemic: SARS, censorship, and extra-institutional risk communication. *Technical Communication Quarterly, 18*(4), 327–350.

Dorpenyo, I. K. (2016). *"Unblackboxing" technology through the rhetoric of technical communication: Biometric technology and Ghana's 2012 election* (Doctoral dissertation, Michigan Technological University).

Duin, A. H., Moses, J., McGrath, M., & Tham, J. (2016). Wearable computing, wearable composing: New dimensions in composition pedagogy. *Computers and Composition Online.*

Dura, L., & Singhal, A. (2009). Utilizing a positive deviance approach to reduce girls' trafficking in Indonesia: asset-based communicative acts that make a difference. *Journal of Creative Communications, 4*(1), 1–17.

Edenfield, A. C. (2017). Power and communication in worker cooperatives: An overview. *Journal of Technical Writing and Communication, 47*(3), 260–279.

Edwards, J. (2018). Race and the workplace: Toward a critically conscious pedagogy. In A. Haas & M. Eble (Eds.), *Key theoretical frameworks: Teaching technical communication in the twenty-first century.* Logan, UT: Utah State University Press.

Gonzales, L. (2018). *Sites of translation: What multilinguals can teach us about digital writing and rhetoric.* Ann Arbor, MI: University of Michigan Press.

Haas, A. M. (2012). Race, rhetoric, and technology: A case study of decolonial technical communication theory, methodology, and pedagogy. *Journal of Business and Technical Communication, 26*(3), 277–310.

Hendrickson, B., & de Mueller, G. G. (2016). Inviting students to determine for themselves what it means to write across the disciplines. *The WAC Journal, 27,* 74.

Hidalgo, A. (2012). National identity, normalization, and equilibrium: The rhetoric of breast implants in Venezuela. *Enculturation, 17.* Retrieved from http://www.en culturation.net/national-identity

Ilyasova, K. A., & Birkelo, C. (2013). Collective learning in East Africa: Building and transferring technical knowledge in livestock production. In H. Yu, & G. Savage (Eds.), *Negotiating cultural encounters: Narrating intercultural engineering and technical communication* (pp. 103–121). Hoboken, NJ: John Wiley & Sons.

Johnson, J. R., Pimentel, O., & Pimentel, C. (2008). Writing New Mexico white: A critical analysis of early representations of New Mexico in technical writing. *Journal of Business and Technical Communication, 22*(2), 211–236.

Jones, N. N. (2016). The technical communicator as advocate: Integrating a social justice approach in technical communication. *Journal of Technical Writing and Communication, 46*(3), 342–361.

Kennedy, K. (2016). Textual curation. *Computers and Composition, 40,* 175–189.

Kerschbaum, S. L. (2014, March). *Toward a new rhetoric of difference.* Conference on College Composition and Communication, National Council of Teachers of English.

Legg, E., & Sullivan, P. (2018). Storytelling as a Balancing Practice in the Study of Posthuman Praxis. In K. Moore & D. Richards (Eds.), *Posthuman praxis in technical communication* (pp. 23–45). New York, NY: Routledge.

Leon, K. (2013). La Hermandad and Chicanas organizing: The community rhetoric of the Comisión Femenil Mexicana Nacional. *Community Literacy Journal, 7*(2), 1–20.

Martini, R. H., & Webster, T. (2017). What Online Writing Spaces Afford Us in the Age of Campus Carry, "Wall-Building," and Orlando's Pulse Tragedy. In E. A. Monske, & K. L. Blair (Eds.), *Handbook of research on writing and composing in the age of MOOCs* (pp. 278–293). Hershey, PA: IGI Global.

Medina, C., & Martinez, A. Y. (2015). Contexts of lived realities in SB 1070 Arizona. *Present Tense, 4*(2). Retrieved from http://www.presenttensejournal.org/wp-content/uploads/2015/03/MedinaAndMartinez.pdf

Moeggenberg, Z. C. (2018). 14 A Queer Challenge to Repronormativity in the Digital Classroom. *Getting Personal: Teaching Personal Writing in the Digital Age, 217.*

Oswal, S. K., & Melonçon, L. (2014). Paying attention to accessibility when designing online courses in technical and professional communication. *Journal of Business and Technical Communication, 28*(3), 271–300.

Patterson, G. (2016). The unbearable weight of neutrality: Religion & LGBTQ issues in the English studies classroom. In J. Alexander & J. Rhodes (Eds.), *Sexual rhetorics: Methods, identities, publics* (pp. 134–146). New York, NY: Routledge.

Poblete, P. (2014). Battlegrounds and common grounds: First-year composition and institutional values. In *Composition Forum* (Vol. 30). Association of Teachers of Advanced Composition.

Reynoso Jr, E. (2016). *Pick Yourself Up by Your Broadband: Access, the Digital Divide, and Migrant Workers* (Doctoral dissertation, Purdue University).

Richardson, F. (2014). The eugenics agenda: Deliberative rhetoric and therapeutic discourse of hate. In M. F. Williams & O. Pimentel (Eds.), *Communicating race, ethnicity, and identity in technical communication,* (pp. 7–22). New York, NY: Routledge.

Robinson, J., Lanius, C., & Weber, R. (2018). The past, present, and future of UX empirical research. *Communication Design Quarterly, 5*(3), 10–23.

Roundtree, A. K., Giordano, S. H., Price, A., & Suarez-Almazor, M. E. (2011). Problems in transition and quality of care: perspectives of breast cancer survivors. *Supportive Care in Cancer, 19*(12), 1921–1929.

Sanchez, J. C. (2018). *Man on Fire.* Documentary.

Sano-Franchini, J., Sackey, D., & Pigg, S. (2011). Methodological dwellings: A search for feminisms in rhetoric & composition. *Present Tense, 1*(2). Retrieved from http://www.presenttensejournal.org/wp-content/uploads/2011/03/Sano-Franchini_Sackey_Pigg.pdf

Scott, J. B. (2003). *Risky rhetoric: AIDS and the cultural practices of HIV testing.* Carbondale, IL: Southern Illinois Press.

Shelton, C. D. (2014). Disrupting authority: Writing mentors and code-meshing pedagogy. *Praxis: A writing center journal.*

Sun, H. (2012). *Cross-cultural technology design: Creating culture-sensitive technology for local users.* Oxford: Oxford University Press.

Unger, D., & Sánchez, F. (2015). Locating queer rhetorics: Mapping as an inventional method. *Computers and Composition, 38,* 96–112.

Walwema, J. (2016). Tailoring information and communication design to diverse international and intercultural audiences: How culturally sensitive ICD improves online market penetration. *Technical Communication, 63*(1), 38–52.

Warren-Riley, S., & Hurley, E. V. (2017, July). Multimodal pedagogical approaches to public writing: Digital media advocacy and mundane texts. *Composition Forum, 36.* Retrieved from https://files.eric.ed.gov/fulltext/EJ1151321.pdf

Williams, M. F. (2017). *From black codes to recodification: Removing the veil from regulatory writing.* New York, NY: Routledge.

Yu, H. (2012). Intercultural competence in technical communication: A working definition and review of assessment methods. *Technical Communication Quarterly, 21*(2), 168–186.

AFTERWORD

Dr. Angela M. Haas

When Apathy Is Unacceptable and Empathy Is Not Enough: Social Justice Is the New Ethic for TPC

Despite common misperceptions about technical communication from those outside of our discipline—and a few holdouts within our discipline—technical communication scholars, professors, and practitioners no longer see ourselves as objective researchers, teachers, and transmitters of neutral technological and scientific information. Our scholarship and practice have dramatically transitioned over the past 30+ years with the work of the humanist, social, feminist, cultural, critical, intercultural, international, and global turns, and now the social justice turn. Although some have resisted calls to "position social justice inquiry and action integral to teaching, learning, and practicing ethical technical, scientific, and professional communication in the twenty-first century" (Haas & Eble, 2018, p. 9), Rebecca Walton, Kristen Moore, and Natasha Jones demonstrate that regardless of those who have yet to join us, we are in fact working in the wake of the social justice turn. And in this particular space, we are in need of a smart, useful, and useable road map for moving the discipline and our fields of practice toward intersectional, coalitional approaches to problem-solving. Thanks to the brilliance and ethical labor of three of our discipline's most prolific scholars, *Technical Communication After the Social Justice Turn: Building Coalitions for Action* provides us precisely that.

This book lays the groundwork for our discipline to better understand oppression and justice conceptually, to better develop theoretical and methodological frameworks that support social justice, and to better apply and implement these concepts and frameworks in a variety of academic, community, organizational, and industry contexts. Walton, Moore, and Jones assert that "[i]njustice IS a technical communication problem." Given that problem solving for social justice requires collective commitment and a range of diverse interventions, they equip technical communication scholars, teachers, practitioners, and community members with ways to recognize unjust practices, behaviors, and systems; understand one's own complicity in injustice; reveal injustices and oppression to others; refuse to support the behaviors and structures that oppress; replace oppressive behavior, structures, or decisions; redress oppression and inequities; and invest in and take action with coalitions. Walton, Moore, and Jones explain,

> Coalitions aid in sustainable efforts towards inclusive, activist, and socially just technical communication. Investing in coalitions allows for those with more privilege, positionality, and power…to pick up the slack as needed, with the important caveat that coalitions are built through listening and valuing difference.

Walton, Moore, and Jones provide technical and professional communication (TPC) with the best sustained and most comprehensive conversation on and shared language for discussing justice to date. Clearly, this is a must-read for technical communication scholars, teachers, practitioners, and community members interested in social justice, but I posit that this book should also be foundational to revisiting our discussions and updating our practices of TPC ethics. For example, they underscore that social justice requires intersectional advocacy and critical contemplation on our positionality in relation to intersecting spheres of power, privilege, and oppression; these strategies and tactics are also required of ethical TPC. Walton, Moore, and Jones reveal the usefulness of analyzing the relationships between Iris Marion Young's five faces of oppression—marginalization, cultural imperialism, powerlessness, violence, and exploitation—and technical communication commitments and practices. In the process, they shift the discipline "from an idle, neutral theory of power to a theory of empowerment," one that "that keeps experiences of marginalized group members in view and works from those experiences."

This ethic of empowerment offers TPC an opportunity to re-examine our current interfaces to, paradigms and codes for, citation practices in, practices of ethics writ large. In our current political and institutional contexts, how can we not consider our ethical responsibilities to respond to injustice caused and remedied by technical communication? Walton, Moore, and Jones make clear:

> If we, as scholars in technical and professional communication, are truly concerned with humans and the human experience, we cannot with clear conscious say that oppression of others is outside the scope and purview of our disciplinary domain. In fact, as a discipline that, at least in theory, has human need and human experience as a core consideration, it would

be at odds with our own conceptualizations of TPC work if we members of the field failed to address the ways that people live in, exist, and experience the world around them.

Thus, we have an ethical imperative to enact social justice, build coalitions, critique approaches to power that historically have not considered privilege and positionality, and much more.

Ultimately, Walton, Moore, and Jones offer a decolonial toolbox for not only supporting and extending intersectional social justice work but also for re-tooling ethics in TPC. Timely and timeless, the authors expand our previous discussions of social justice to also include distributive justice, procedural justice, and legal justice (retributive, restorative, transitional). Kairotic and sustainable, Walton, Moore, and Jones evidence how power and politics are always already connected to TPC. Finally, bridging theory and practice, this book provides scenarios and heuristics for enacting ethical responses to injustice that are grounded in everyday contexts. I urge scholar-teachers in the discipline and practitioners in the field to further examine how the conceptual, theoretical, and procedural frameworks provided herein might inform future conversations and treatments of ethics. Walton, Moore, and Jones call all of us to "commit to learning more about injustices from those who experience injustices." I contend that acts of injustice are also unethical acts, and thus we must also commit to learning more about ethics from those who have experienced systemic and systematic unethical behavior. Suffice it to say, *Technical Communication After the Social Justice Turn: Building Coalitions for Action* offers us a touchstone project that will prove to be useful for our scholarly discipline and professional fields in a broad range of ways for many "turns" to come.

Reference

Haas, A. M., & Eble, M. F. (2018). *Key theoretical frameworks: Teaching technical communication in the twenty-first century.* Logan: Utah State University Press.

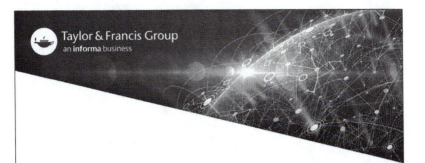

INDEX

Note: Page numbers followed by "n" denote endnotes.